ANTITERRORIST INITIATIVES

CRIMINAL JUSTICE AND PUBLIC SAFETY

Series Editor: Philip John Stead
John Jay College of Criminal Justice
The City University of New York
New York, New York

ANTITERRORIST INITIATIVES
  John B. Wolf

CRIME CONTROL: The Use and Misuse of Police Resources
  David John Farmer

FEAR OF FEAR: A Survey of Terrorist Operations and
        Controls in Open Societies
  John B. Wolf

INTERPOL: Issues in World Crime and International Criminal
        Justice
  Michael Fooner

TREATING THE CRIMINAL OFFENDER
Third Edition
  Alexander B. Smith and Louis Berlin

ANTITERRORIST INITIATIVES

John B. Wolf

PLENUM PRESS • NEW YORK AND LONDON

Library of Congress Cataloging in Publication Data

Wolf, John B.
    Antiterrorist initiatives.

    (Criminal justice and public safety)
    Bibliography: p.
    Includes index.
    1. Terrorism—Prevention. 2. Intelligence service. I. Title. II. Series.
HV6431.W596   1989   363.3'2   88-32301
ISBN 0-306-43123-8

© 1989 Plenum Press, New York
A Division of Plenum Publishing Corporation
233 Spring Street, New York, N.Y. 10013

Printed in the United States of America

To
Mary

PREFACE

Traditionally, terrorist bands operating in rural or urban areas use violence to cast themselves as a legitimate political force. Necklacing, placing an oil-soaked tire around the neck of an informer and then igniting it, and knee-capping, positioning a handgun behind the kneecap of a "tout" (a police informer) and then squeezing the trigger, are among the enforcement methods used by clandestine groups to administer "revolutionary justice." Necklacing is used by the African National Congress (A.N.C.). Knee-capping is a traditional Irish Republican Army (I.R.A.) tactic.

Governments frequently lend credibility to the terrorists' claim of legitimacy by not implementing measures intended to extirpate them. Frequently, democratic societies fear that rigid control measures pose a threat to civil liberties. Reluctant to move, a democracy is often hamstrung by terrorists bent on manipulating its values.

A media campaign, intended to mobilize public opinion against the terrorists and garner mass support for the government and its control measures, is the linchpin of any antiterrorist campaign. Centralized intelligence-gathering is another essential component. Terrorism, when it becomes a regular campaign of bombings and other atrocities, is no longer a problem for just the police and the army. The entire society is affected. For example, all groups comprising the multiethnic population of Sri Lanka and South Africa are presently exposed to the terrorist threat.

Applying the manipulative principles advocated by Lenin (Leninism), terrorists work avidly to exploit the real or imagined social grievances of a fragile society. Consequently, law and order may be the first concern for the government of a society riddled with terrorists. Once challenged by a clandestine group, a government must act against it in a timely and visible manner. Its countermeasures should include an imaginative public relations campaign geared to assure citizens that the terrorist cause has been concocted by charlatans who are about to become enmeshed in their own fabrications (lies).

Astute antiterrorist campaigns waged in the last twenty years were geared to:

- penetrate the terrorist organization to monitor its plans and moves
- deny the terrorists their essential needs (e.g., food, shelter, money, medical treatment, recruits), forcing them, therefore, to operate overtly
- identify and isolate the centers and targets of terrorist action
- identify, fix, capture, detain, and imprison the terrorist leaders

Antiterrorist commanders should be aware that a leaderless terrorist group frequently self-destructs as a consequence of internal squabbles and the paranoia endemic to life in the underground. Virtually all of the domestic groups operating in the United States in the late 1970s and early 1980s evaporated after their leaders were arrested or otherwise neutralized.

Intelligence operations provide the focus for an antiterrorist campaign. Strategic information regarding for example racial tensions or economic displacement, particularly when these insights can be translated into operational intelligence by utilizing local sources of information, is particularly valuable. Field operatives, tasked with gathering essential data, vastly simplify the work of a security force engaged in an antiterrorist campaign.

Police are the frontline in the struggle against the terrorist. Their capability to cope with political violence is usually more significant than their number. It's important that their training be theoretical as well as practical as political activists are a special breed of criminal. Membership in a clandestine organization enables them to elude conventional police operatives. This capability casts them differently from the "lone wolf" brigand.

Antiterrorists need access to individuals trained to negotiate; to talk, but not capitulate, to terrorists. Skilled communicators are another essential component of an antiterrorist force as terrorist propagandists are unrelenting in their effort to discredit the security forces.

In Northern Ireland, Irish Republican Army (I.R.A.) spokesmen continue to dwell on allegations of torture and brutality inflicted upon "political" prisoners and are still spouting tales of the widespread and wanton killings of innocent civilians by police. Public education regarding the brutality of the terrorists themselves and the dangers that engulf those who attempt to control them is another key element in any effort to counter propaganda spewed forth by terrorists.

Israel's antiterrorist initiative has demonstrated its resolve to take on the terrorist organizations at gunpoint. It is aware that the underlying maxim of all terrorist groups is to use unrelenting psychological pressure, including the seizure of hostages, to reduce the opponent's willingness to use force. Clearly perceiving the terrorist as an instrument of modern warfare, Israel reverses the basic strategy of terror and deploys it against the terrorists themselves.

South Africa, also, refuses to capitulate to terrorist demands. When three gunmen from the African National Congress (A.N.C.) seized a bank situated in a Pretoria suburb, and held about sixty people at gunpoint, a police antiterrorist squad ringed the facility. Next a senior police officer went into the bank to talk but not to negotiate with the terrorists. Their demands were never even considered. After a standoff period of several hours, the A.N.C. gunmen prepared to shoot their hostages, whereupon the law enforcement officers assaulted the bank. The shootout with the terrorists lasted about two minutes. When it was over, the police allowed people to enter the bank and photograph the bullet-riddled bodies of the gunmen. The publicity was used by the South African government to warn others who had thoughts of aggression against innocent people and the state.

To maintain its hard-line image, Israel deploys "hit teams" to stalk the leaders of Arab terrorist groups that haunt various European cities and other urban centers. These assassination squads knowingly violate the sovereignty of the nations inside whose borders they conduct their operations. The governments of the states intruded upon have no knowledge or control of the "death squads" whose mission involves the leveling of coercive power against the terrorists.[1]

Traditional power, or power derived from institutional norms and practices and from historical legal traditions of stature commensurate with that power, is commonly accepted as the only legitimate form of power to be used for social control.[2] A squad of assassins, undertaking a counterterrorist mission inside the borders of a foreign state, is without this power and its clandestine activities, amounting to intervention in the domestic affairs of another state, are contrary to international law and condemned by the General Assembly of the United Nations, which abhors indirect intervention through propaganda, subversion, and infiltration.[3]

Counterterrorist operations, conducted by the Ulster Defense Association in Northern Ireland and in the 1960s by the Secret Army Organization (O.A.S.) in Algeria, employed terror against any target, civilian, police, or military, which could be identified with their terrorist opponent or otherwise serve their purposes. Thomas Hobbes, the seventeenth-century English philosopher who wrote *Leviathan*, might regard these counterterrorists as people who perpetrate a "miserable condition of war." These groups do not attack targets at random but rather unleash their terror directly against their terrorist opponents wherever and whenever they can be fixed. Consequently, their operations may be predicated upon another notion set forth by Hobbes, which is that "where there is no common power," for example, governmental action to control terrorism, "there is no law, where there is no law, no injustice."

Conceivably, Hobbes might regard the members of the Ulster Defense Association and the European Algerians of the O.A.S. as counterterrorists who used violence against those who employed terror "to make themselves masters of other men's persons, wives, children and cattle."[4] "French Algeria or Death" therefore was an appropriate slogan for the O.A.S. to adopt.[5]

Clearly, therefore, the use of counterterror to combat terror, especially when it is directed indiscriminately against random targets, is a form of uncivilized behavior: the psychological strain on all of the people who are exposed to its use is tremendous. For some of the more fragile individuals whom it affects it is deadly. Preferably, governments will use only legally empowered antiterrorist organizations to control terrorism and develop intelligence systems which are compatible with the requirements of a free society to enhance their use.

Adoption of these measures will forestall the development of a counterterrorist organization for the purpose of self-defense, be it real, imagined, or contrived, and protect society against the counterterrorist who wields a double-edged sword, one edge cutting into the terrorist and the other edge slicing into legitimate government which forms the plinth for world order. Antiterrorism is not a game for boys. Strong men are needed to subdue maniacs. "Nice guys finish last."

My most grateful thanks are due to all those who have helped me conceive and complete this book, particularly my wife, and the many associates and students, military, police, and civilian, whose enthusiasm and needs have so often stimulated my interest. To Robert Morton, editor in chief of the *New York City Tribune*, who published my weekly column entitled "Terror Report" for the past five years, and to Professor Philip John Stead, my colleague at John Jay College of Criminal Justice in the City University of New York, who encouraged me to publish my research, I owe a particular debt of gratitude.

John B. Wolf

NOTES

1. David B. Tinnin and Dag Christensen, *The Hit Team* (Boston, Little Brown, 1976).
2. Paul M. Whisenand and R. Fred Ferguson, *The Managing of Police Organizations* (Englewood Cliffs, N.J., Prentice-Hall, 1973), pp. 205-206.
3. William L. Tung, *International Law in An Organizing World* (New York, Thomas Y. Crowell, 1968), pp. 128-133.
4. Thomas Hobbes, *Leviathan* (New York, E.P. Dutton, 1950), pp. 139-306.
5. Paul Henissart, *"Wolves in the City," The Death of French Algeria* (St. Albans, Hertfordshire, England, Paladin, 1973), pp. 223-234.

CONTENTS

                   Dimension in Warfare 21

     Attempted Assassination of the Pope 22
     Surrogate Warfare 23
         Armenian Terrorist Organizations and Operations 25
         Libyan Clandestine Operations 28
         The Croatian National Resistance........................ 30
         Suriname and the Libyans.............................. 30
         Iranian-Sponsored Terrorism 31
     Aspects of Hispanic-Contrived Terrorism in the Americas.... 35
     Notes 38

Chapter 3 • Propaganda: Activities and Analysis 41

     Elements of Propaganda................................ 42
     Analyzing Press Releases................................ 44
     Attempt to Destabilize Ecuador 45
     Guevara's "Lost" Diaries an Upset for Bolivians 48
     Use of Disinformation in India 49
     Soviet Disinformation Techniques 50
     The Panamanian Link to American Disinformation 51
     Collapse of the Public Safety Program.................... 51
     Notes 52

Chapter 4 • Antiterrorist Intelligence 55

     Bombings in Beirut 56
     Antiterrorist Legislation 57
     Controlling Terrorism in the United States 58
         Technical Means for Collecting Intelligence............... 59
         Intelligence Support Activity............................ 61
         Restrictions on Intelligence Gathering.................... 62
         Electronic Surveillance and Videotapes................... 65
     The Vice-President's Task Force on Combatting Terrorism ... 67
     Approaches to Antiterrorism.............................. 68
     Notes 69

ESSENCE AND
MANIFESTATIONS

1

THE DEADLY MASQUERADE

Is Political Assassination an Intelligence Task?

"Hit teams," performing in accord with scenarios concocted by novelists and filmmakers, stalk the earth. The man on the street is convinced that intelligence services contain groups that are tasked to assassinate the leaders of hostile governments, unfriendly clandestine agents, and terrorists. The Central Intelligence Agency (C.I.A.), according to the armchair observer, engages in this practice, employing assassins that replicate the murderous tactics used by the Soviet Committee for State Security [*Komitet Gosudarstvennoi Bezopasnosti* (K.G.B.)].

Myth—persistent, persuasive, and unrealistic—is the great enemy of truth. Reinforced by television, often regarded as the modern molder of behavioral norms and values, Americans have become isolated from the truth. Instead, they continue to link the C.I.A. to an assortment of evil schemes, in particular, political assassination.

Rumor mongers, casting the C.I.A. as a villain, are difficult to quiet as the American intelligence agency continues to be used as a model and a backdrop for contemporary spy thrillers. The mythology enveloping American intelligence has been reinforced by two films: *Three Days of the Condor* and *State of Siege*. Television viewers especially have been treated to repeat performances of these features.

In the first film, a group of freelance assassins are hired to "waste" analytical personnel. Assigned to a C.I.A. think tank, these people are about to uncover the existence of an ultrasecret control group that is used

3

by the agency to monitor its internal affairs. Featuring Robert Redford as
an intelligence analyst, *Three Days of the Condor* asks us to believe that the
company (aka the Central Intelligence Agency) can exterminate its own
employees on American soil.[1]

State of Siege had its first public performance in the United States on
April 5, 1973. The American Film Institute (A.F.I.) planned to use the film
as part of a festival inaugurating its new theater in the Kennedy Center
for the Performing Arts in Washington, D.C. This motion picture deals,
in controversial fashion, with the assassination of an employee of the
Agency for International Development (A.I.D.), an arm of the United
States Department of State. While serving as the chief American advisor
to the Uruguayan police, the A.I.D. official was suspected of having ties
with American intelligence. Consequently, he was kidnapped by the
Tupamaros, an urban terrorist group which was active in Montevideo,
and was assassinated. After a screening of the film, it was decided not to
show it at the Kennedy Center Theatre.

Continually plagued by media tales describing their wickedness,
covert operations organized by the C.I.A. are being undercut by Soviet
disinformation. For example, some leaders of the anti-Sandinista guerrillas (the Contras) want the United States government to help them
"with political pressure" but are reluctant to permit direct C.I.A. involvement because of the agency's "bad reputation in Latin America."

Hit-team sagas are also part of contemporary folklore and have become legend as a consequence of their use in the murderous war that
Israeli intelligence waged against Arab terrorist leaders in various European cities. The Yugoslavian secret police, while stalking Croatian terrorists around the world, use similar units to "waste" or "blow away" their
quarry. Contemporary novelists also concoct plots that cast presidents
and premiers as characters who are fascinated, preoccupied, and, at
times, overwhelmed by an assessment forwarded to them by an advisory
council recommending that they approve a hit of an arch-opponent of
their regime.[2]

"EXECUTIVE ACTION"

Albeit rarely, cogent assessments relative to national security issues
may, in reality, prompt a head of state to sanction an ultrasensitive operation before the opportunity to move in a specific direction is lost. The
killers of President Anwar-al-Sadat of Egypt had everything on their side:
surprise, the diversion of the planes flying overhead, the heavy weapons
needed to counter the firepower of security forces, and their target was

sitting in a reviewing stand watching a military parade. But the carefully orchestrated effort of Sadat's assassins lasted for only 76 seconds, and then it was stopped.[3] Operations of this type, consequently, cannot be sponsored by organizations that are characterized by bureaucratic infighting and blockages in key communications networks. Decisiveness is an absolute requirement.

Influenced by a situational analysis indicating that a "nefarious" political opponent can be fixed in time and place (a scheduled motorcade, a political rally), significant world leaders are popularly suspected of countenancing discreet clandestine operations—assassination, kidnapping, and bombing. Intended to improve the posture of a country vis-à-vis its competitors in world politics, chief executives supposedly opt for this type of move when alternative means are regarded as either ineffective, obtrusive, nonselective, or a combination of all three of these liabilities; at least the fictional scenario usually unfolds this way.

In the "real world," assassination (or "executive action"), which is used to liquidate a defector, a head of state, a prominent international terrorist, or some other key figure whose designs are a menace to a particular country, is useful only when it can be planned and executed in a discreet manner. Action is precluded when the identity of the group that is responsible for "contracting" with the hit teams cannot be masked. The political repercussions emanating from an investigation that fixes blame might result in the responsible government's being viewed as a pariah. The hit team itself, however, is always expendable, and in some instances, the team is dumped—that is, exterminated by its employers.

ASSASSINATIONS: SOVIET-STYLE

Using people indigenous to the area of operations as surrogates to mask their own role, the K.G.B. has been described as acting in the best tradition of American organized crime hits that are attributed to the Soviet Union's intelligence service. Its murders involve the killing of the victim and the elimination of the hired assassin. The "accidental" slaying of the United States Ambassador to Afghanistan, Adolph Dubs, in Kabul on February 14, 1979, is a classic example of how the K.G.B. charade is programmed.

On the day he was killed, the American diplomat was riding in his armored car when he noticed four men, two of whom were dressed as traffic officers, motioning him to stop. Responding to their signals, he halted his car and opened the door, whereupon he was dragged from the vehicle by his disguised assailants and taken to a room in the Hotel Kabul, where he was sequestered for four hours. During his captivity, American embassy officials requested that Afghan authorities recant their order directing a squad of armed police to assault the place where Dubs was confined.

Rejecting their pleas, the Kabuli government ordered an assault unit, directed by Soviet advisers, who were observed coordinating military formations outside the hotel, to storm the room where the ambassador was held captive. Allegedly killed with two of his abductors in the ensuing crossfire, Dubs was found dead of gunshot wounds in the head and heart, a style characteristic of a gangland killing.[4]

A subsequent forensic examination concluded that Dubs was murdered with a .22 caliber gun, which has never been produced. Weapons of this type are small, readily concealed, and are best used by assassins who are highly motivated or very callous—preferably both. This weapon is ideal for killing a victim at close range. Often the novelist, in describing an assassination with this type of handgun, mentions how the killer reacts to the stimuli of looking directly into the face of the victim and hearing his screams.

The two surviving members of the armed party that abducted Dubs were apprehended and executed by Afghan authorities, another underworld tactic intended to silence blabbers. Because of the tenuous communications link between Afghanistan and the rest of the world after the Soviet seizure of Kabul, efforts to obtain more details of the events surrounding the death of the American ambassador failed. However, the Afghan government radio described the kidnappers as enemies of the government who were anxious to "destroy the friendship between Afghanistan and the United States."[5]

In preparing the trial for the seven persons who were charged with conspiring with Mehmet Ali Agca to assassinate Pope John Paul II in May 1981, the Italian judge noticed that three Bulgarians and four Turks were suspected of involvement in this affair. Defenders of these culprits insisted that the C.I.A. recruited Agca and manufactured the Bulgarian connection to mask its involvement.[6]

The Soviet-bloc intelligence services are usually skilled at undertaking deception operations, particularly a job as heinous as the killing of the Pope. They use active measures (*aktivnyye meropriatie*) to wage covert political warfare on a global scale. Disinformation (*dezinformatsia*), a word defined in a Soviet training manual as "misleading the adversary," is used to camouflage the identity of the hit team.

Service A of the K.G.B.'s First Chief Directorate is trained to concoct these deceptive masquerades. It is a "dirty tricks" squad, believed to contain about 50 clandestine agents whose activities are financed by an annual appropriation of $50 million. Operatives who are assigned to this unit are expert document forgers and rumor mongers, skilled at manufacturing myths and legends that are contrived to smear the United States and its allies.

Stefphan Svirdlev, one of only three officers ever to defect from the Bulgarian intelligence service, said his agency had agreed to execute Soviet "wet affairs" (clandestine violent operations) in exchange for Moscow's help in developing policy and procedures for the Bulgarian Ministry of Internal Affairs, the agency responsible for managing clandestine activities unleashed.

Directed by the K.G.B., the D.S. is linked by a substantial quantity of circumstantial evidence to the plot to assassinate the Pope. It employs 700 officers and 9,000 agents, who handle approximately 18,000 informants. D.S. departments and their responsibilities include: (1) intelligence (overseas espionage), (2) counterintelligence (monitoring domestic dissidents and exiles abroad), (3) military counterintelligence (handling matters relative to military aspects of Bulgaria's neighbors—Greece, Turkey, and Yugoslavia), (4) technical support (jamming Radio Free Europe broadcasts), (5) security and vigilance (providing protective security for Bulgarian leaders), (6) information and analysis (data collection and analytical reporting), and (7) propaganda.

Vladimir Kostov, once affiliated with the committee directing radio and television broadcasting in Bulgaria, defected in Paris seven years ago. Every Bulgarian sent abroad, he said, "reports every person he meets, collects any documents from official agencies and reports on the character and the weaknesses of the people he meets."

Kostov had been the target of an assassination attempt in August 1978, while leaving the Paris Metro. Feeling a sharp pain in his back, he turned around and saw a person running away. For three days he suffered a high fever but managed to survive.

Ten days later, as he was strolling near Waterloo Bridge in London, Georgi I. Markov, another Bulgarian defector, was jabbed in his thigh by a man carrying an umbrella. Markov died two days later. His weekly anti-Communist commentaries, which were aired over Radio Free Europe, apparently had infuriated the Bulgarian government.

Kostov had his back X-rayed after reading about Markov's death. It turned out that both victims had been nicked by a pinhead-sized platinum pellet. Manufactured with four tiny holes in its surface, each pellet contained Ricin—a derivative of the castor oil plant—one ounce of which could kill 90,000 people. The most extensive research on Ricin is done in Czechoslovakia and in Hungary.

Methods and equipment for use by assassins have been perfected through the years by various governments. However, one of the most diabolical devices is the "metal ball" technique, a sophisticated K.G.B. assassination tool. When Markov was nicked in the thigh and developed a fatal "heart condition," the technology behind the metal ball was uncovered. Delivered by the man who jabbed the prominent anti-Communist Bulgarian with the umbrella, the metal ball entered the bloodstream of the dissident Markov and killed him.

During the summer of 1981, while in a suburban Virginia shopping center, Boris Korczak felt a slight sting, "something like a mosquito bite," near his kidney. At the instant he was hit, Korczak thought nothing of the "bite." Shortly thereafter, however, his temperature shot up to 106 degrees, and he became delirious. "I thought I was having a heart attack," he told the press. "One arm went numb and my heart was pounding irregularly." Doctors, however, could find no reason for Korczak's ailment. Then, just as suddenly as they had appeared, his symptoms left him. It was not until a few days later that a series of laboratory tests revealed what might have happened to him. Microscopic analysis indicated that Korczak had excreted a microscopic metal ball about one five-hundredth the size of a fingernail.

If Korczak was the target of a K.G.B.-directed murder plot, it was the first publicly known effort by a Communist-bloc intelligence service to kill a C.I.A.-connected person on American soil. A Lithuanian-Pole who had succeeded in infiltrating the K.G.B., Korczak once worked as a contact agent for the C.I.A.

The Soviet Union was also buffeted by the testimony given in an Italian courtroom by Mehmet Ali Agca, who was convicted on July 22, 1981, of shooting Pope John Paul II. Although details of Agca's testimony about an alleged plot to kill Lech Walesa, the leader of Solidarity (the independent Polish labor union), were part of the trial, the testimony was sequestered by the court. Agca revealed that he had met with Bulgarian intelligence officers in Rome to discuss the "Walesa Project." According to Italian police records, one of the persons at the meeting attended by Agca coordinated a Bulgarian spy ring in Rome, from 1978 until the fall of 1982. These plotters, who were aware that Walesa would visit Rome, obtained information of his itinerary from Italian labor leaders.

Agca's detailed knowledge of Walesa's movements in Italy amazed an Italian judge, who was investigating the possibility of a link between the person responsible for inviting Walesa to visit Rome and the D.S., the Bulgarian intelligence service. Rome police verified Agca's testimony regarding Walesa's travel plans, although his itinerary was classified as secret for security reasons.

THE PROPAGANDA COVERUP

Agca's revelations in Rome, which provided details of Communist-bloc clandestine operations designed to murder two illustrious Poles, the Pope and Walesa, jeopardized Moscow's hegemony in Poland. Consequently, the Soviets contrived a cause célèbre that was intended to induce a frenzy in Poland to counterbalance the rapprochement between Solidarity and General Wojciech Jaruzelski, the Polish Communist leader who implemented a policy of normalization.

On October 20, 1984, the Polish government announced that the body of the Reverend Jerzy Popieluszko, a pro-Solidarity priest, was recovered from a reservoir on the Vistula River, northwest of Warsaw. Popieluszko, one of Solidarity's strongest clerical supporters, attracted a large and loyal following for his sermons in which he defended the ideals of the independent labor federation.

Jozef Cardinal Glemp, leader of Poland's Roman Catholics, was alarmed by the disappearance of Popieluszko. It appeared that the priest was kidnapped near the northern Polish city of Torun on October 19, 1984. Anticipating an outbreak of violent protests, the cardinal issued an appeal for calm, saying that people should bear no revenge or hatred "because Christ took his suffering in this way."

The Polish Interior Ministry, who were handling the investigation of the Popieluszko murder, identified a suspect: a captain in charge of a Polish unit that reportedly monitored clerics. The kidnapping and murder of the priest embarrassed the Jaruzelski government and rekindled activism in urban areas. Because the government was anxious to build its credibility in the case, it permitted a pathologist, appointed by the Roman Catholic Church, to perform an autopsy on the body of the priest in the presence of a church-designated lawyer.

The Kremlin's policy of active measures succeeded in unsettling the Poles. It used the murder of the cleric to drive wedges between the faction supporting Jaruzelski's policy of normalization, Walesa's Solidarity members, and hardliners within the police and the military.

By innuendo, the Polish Communist Party's Central Committee blamed the West, an obvious attempt to counterbalance the adverse publicity the Soviet Union received as a consequence of Agca's statements in Rome. It attributed the kidnapping and murder of Popieluszko to "a few criminals, provocateurs and agents of bad causes." Jaruzelski said he would take firm actions against "antisocialist forces" that were stirring up unrest. Reacting to Soviet pressures, factions in the Polish government continued their offensive against "antisocialist forces" who were controlled by "foreign diversionary centers" that provided agitators with the technical and financial assistance needed to bolster their propaganda activities.

The Popieluszko murder was a horrendous act that shook the world. Consequently, Soviet propagandists capitalized on the assassination of Prime Minister Indira Gandhi by using the press coverage of this more recent event to divert the media from completing a detailed analysis of the slaying of the Polish priest—an investigation that might reveal K.G.B. complicity.

Reports on Radio Moscow and from the official Soviet news agency TASS said that "India's opponents abroad" and "reactionary imperialist forces" were behind the assassination of India's prime minister. The Soviet news media tried to portray the United States as a sponsor of state terrorism against any nation that is not cowed by American policies.

Moscow also published information about alleged C.I.A. involvement with Sikh separatists. A TASS dispatch charged that many of the "extremists and spies" arrested in India after the murder of the prime minister supposedly admitted that they had been trained in Pakistan under the supervision of the C.I.A. The Reagan administration strongly protested to the Soviet Union the absurd and irresponsible allegations that the United States was involved in the assassination of the Indian Prime Minister.[7]

After the killing in India, Pope John Paul II delivered an All Saints Day sermon to 7,000 people gathered in St. Peter's Square. He said he was upset by so much human bloodshed and suffering. He mentioned the killing of Mrs. Indira Gandhi and the Reverend Jerzy Popieluszko, whose tragic deaths shook the world.

THE SOVIET COMMITTEE FOR STATE SECURITY (K.G.B.)

Listing about one half million employees on its roster, the K.G.B. combines the functions of the C.I.A. and the Federal Bureau of Investigation (F.B.I.). Its dual authority makes for greater efficiency and avoids the high-level policy infighting between domestic and foreign services common in Western capitals. A unit contained within its First Chief Directorate (F.C.D.), the group responsible for foreign intelligence, is specially trained to perform political assassinations. Its designation is Department V.

All Soviet-bloc intelligence services, including the Czech S.T.B. (State Security Service) and the Cuban D.G.I. (*Direccion Generale de Inteligencia*), are regarded by intelligence professionals as the K.G.B.'s surrogates. The Armenian Secret Army for the Liberation of Armenia

(A.S.A.L.A.), a Marxist-leaning organization that claims about 140 assassinations, and an assortment of other international terrorist groups are also believed to be the K.G.B.'s pawns.

Since the end of World War II, a number of killings involving public figures who died in unexplained or suspicious circumstances have been attributed to the K.G.B. The first of these killings was the death, in 1948, of Jan Masaryk, an anti-Communist Czech cabinet minister, who, many people believed, was pushed from a window in Prague.[8]

More recently, the Soviet Union denounced an article, entitled "The Plot To Murder the Pope," written by Claire Sterling and published in the September 1982 issue of the *Reader's Digest*. In the article, Sterling claimed that the shooting by Mehmet Ali Agca appeared "to have been organized by Bulgarian intelligence agents on directions from the Soviet Union."

THE MURDER OF RICHARD S. WELCH

In their attempts to counterbalance the growing public's awareness of the K.G.B.'s involvement in international terrorism, the Soviet Union has accused the C.I.A. of being the "center of international terrorism" and of deploying spies in diplomatic posts, trade unions, and the media. Carried worldwide by TASS, Soviet propaganda tries to discredit the C.I.A. by making these allegations: that the C.I.A. uses spies and saboteurs to destabilize the internal situations in other countries and for staging coups; that the C.I.A. spends billions of dollars on payoffs, chemicals for mind-control, and military operations; and that the C.I.A.'s "sabotage" has influenced internal affairs in Iran, Chile, Nicaragua, and El Salvador.

The Soviet Union mounts a continuous propaganda effort to undermine the American intelligence service, particularly its links with foreign contacts who, for reasons of personal security, are reluctant to become publicly visible as a consequence of Senate probes and subsequent media releases. Also, the practice of masking an agent's link to an intelligence service by providing him with "embassy cover"—a pseudo-assignment as a foreign service officer—is now recognized as endangering the operative as well as the genuine staff of the diplomatic facility. Shortly after the takeover of the American embassy in Tehran, the Iranian militants, sparked by Soviet propaganda, said that the hostages were spies, and there was talk of spy trials.

Clifford P. Hackett, a former Foreign Service information officer, believes that the identity of Richard S. Welch, a C.I.A. station chief who was murdered in Athens in December 1975, was known to hundreds of persons in the Greek political and diplomatic community. "Welch's residence, where he died," was the home of a series of C.I.A. officials, he said.[9]

A group calling itself the Revolutionary Organization of November 17 took responsibility for the murder of Welch, claiming he had been killed in retaliation for "the crimes committed by the C.I.A. against our people."[10]

Senior American intelligence officials in the Reagan administration shifted intelligence gathering activities from diplomatic posts and placed them under the guise of private commercial companies. Concerned over the public disclosure of clandestine contacts between American and Iranian officials, particularly the use of a secret agent to recruit a close advisor to Ayatollah Ruhollah Khomeini, and an assortment of other security violations, the C.I.A. placed a high priority on establishing "commercial cover" for its agents and operations.[11]

THE C.I.A. AND POLITICAL ASSASSINATION

The C.I.A. was involved in the planning of an assortment of bizarre "executive actions" in the 1960s and 1970s, epitomized by the plot which targeted Fidel Castro and which would have involved organized crime (Mafia) as the triggermen. These surreptitious moves besmirched the image of the American intelligence community and eventually impeded the efforts of its agents to develop the human-based sources of information that are needed to sustain routine analytical functions.

Once it was understood in Washington that talk of executive actions was counterproductive, the United States Congress banned American clandestine operatives from using assassination for any purpose. Arguing that the limitations imposed on the C.I.A.'s covert operations left the United States with no reasonable option other than increased cooperation with anti-Communist forces abroad, some officials in the Reagan administration urged that consideration be given to improving the capability of the C.I.A. to rapidly escalate aid to anti-Communist forces. But many American leaders opposed political assassination on both moral and pragmatic grounds.

In the past, some nations have deployed hit teams in the United States. On July 22, 1980, the director general for foreign information for the Shah of Iran's Ministry of Information was assassinated by a pro-Khomeini gunman in Bethesda, Maryland—an action suggesting that the American president himself could be ambushed in retaliation for any real or trumped up American attack abroad. Once a band of killers gains access to the United States, which is not a formidable problem, they can be directed and supplied by diplomatic personnel previously positioned in the area of the target.[12]

SPECIAL OPERATIONS IN FICTION AND IN FACT

John Le Carré's novels are replete with an assortment of personalities, defectors, deceivers, and "moles," who add credence to the popular notion that intelligence organizations have a twofold objective: uncovering deception at home and creating deception abroad. "Christ had only 12 disciples," a character remarks, in *Tinker, Tailor, Soldier, Spy*, "and one of them was a double"—an agent controlled by one group but privy to the secret communications of another. In *The Looking Glass War*, another of Le Carré's characters asks, "Do you know what love is? I'll tell you: It is whatever you can still betray....There is no loyalty without betrayal."

The ethical orientation of the political assassin is suggested in *The Spy Who Came in from the Cold*, another novel by Le Carré. Further buttressing the opinion of those who regard these killers as persons who view death as merely another incident in the course of time, it seems that an assassin operates in a world in which justification of the means is selected not from emotion or even expedience, but because the killing of a matter of significance.

Once asked if he consulted with experts on intelligence matters, Le Carré said, "Those who believe they are masters of the black arts are as inept as we amateurs. I invent most of it." However, "I trust my tradecraft is credible—I've been told my books are mandatory reading for entrants into the Israeli military intelligence—but I don't know whether it's authentic."[13]

CONTROLLING SPECIAL OPERATIONS

Spy novels and motion pictures, treating themes associated with the "secret wars" which are waged by competing teams of political assassins, focus on an activity that intelligence professionals call *clandestine operations*, sometimes known as *special operations*. Persons assigned to these activities use intelligence data to achieve a certain objective; for example, to kill a head of state. They are not used to collect information for intelligence purposes, because secret agents, satellites, and an assortment of other devices are deployed for this purpose.

Special-operations units, therefore, need not be a part of the intelligence service itself. They could be organized within a group that has immediate access to the intelligence that is needed to perform a particular clandestine task and one directly supervised by the head of state responsible for sanctioning their ultrasensitive missions. American special-operations units might be placed under the jurisdiction of the National Security Council (N.S.C.), whereupon their activities could be monitored to insure compliance with presidential directives and fix accountability for their actions.

Placed under the direct control of the head of state, the intelligence services would be freed from the shenanigans associated with managing a group that the media view as rogues and thus be able to concentrate exclusively on their assigned tasks relative to the collection and processing of intelligence data. Although William Colby, the Director of the Central Intelligence Agency under Presidents Nixon and Ford, advised the media that 5 percent or less of the C.I.A. budget was devoted to covert operations, the press has continued to foster the popular notion that special operations are not the tip of the intelligence iceberg but its base.

PHILOSOPHICAL AND MORAL CONSIDERATIONS

Emphasizing that the Christian doctrine of nonviolence should not be interpreted to mean that an evil-doer should not be restrained, Saint Thomas Aquinas (1224 or 1225–1274) might applaud the decision of a government to organize a hit team and use it to remove "by death from human society...a few infected persons" who hinder the common good. Regarding the opinion that the wicked might be reformed, Saint Thomas dismissed it as "frivolous."[14]

A philosopher who provided answers to social and political questions and emphasized the sacred character of authority, Thomas Aquinas considered the head of state as the only legitimate person who could satisfy the conditions needed to sanction acts associated with a "just war," as, for example, political assassination. These conditions are a legitimate authority, a just cause, and a rightful intention.[15] Advocates of the philosopher's rationalism might also approve the use of political assassination, but only as a defensive measure and when alternative means to protect the commonwealth are not efficacious.

Moral considerations also preclude the use of assassination in densely populated urban areas. The unintentional killing of a civilian, for example, a person exiting from an alleyway into the line of fire, would negate any benefits derived from the successful completion of the mission. Additional ethical considerations would preclude the use of political assassination in a just war.

Fingerprint classification is the most reliable means of establishing the positive identification of a person. Visual identifications—photographs, physical descriptions, and profiles—are not adequate because protected persons often use a stand-in to confuse those who threaten them with harm. Consequently, the positive identification of the target would have to take place immediately before the killing, a task difficult to perform as the "infected person" must first be abducted, sequestered at a clandestine location, fingerprinted, and then killed. Kidnapping, therefore, requires intricate planning and the extensive use of supporting units and is consequently prone to detection.

Israel once sent an intelligence unit to Norway for the purpose of killing the man it held responsible for the 1972 murders of its Olympic athletes in Munich. They killed the wrong person. "Subsequently they found the right man, Ali Hassan, next door in Beirut."[16]

Regardless of these overshadowing moral considerations, some governments continue to favor the use of hit teams and train them to execute an operation in such a way as to leave doubt about the identities of the killers. Was the death an accident? Was the job performed by the underworld? Was the killing performed by an external foe of the government? If so, which one?

The unique advantage that a political assassination provides to a head of state, therefore, is the opportunity to disclaim responsibility for its impact. If the hit team succeeds, well and good. If the operation fails or boomerangs, the responsible government simply denies culpability for its results or demands that the covert practices of its intelligence service be revamped or revised.

REAGAN'S EXECUTIVE ORDER

On December 4, 1981, President Ronald Reagan issued an executive order on United States intelligence activities that contained a subsection entitled "Prohibition on Assassination," which reads as follows: "No person employed by or acting on behalf of the United States government shall engage in, or conspire to engage in, assassination."[17] Although this directive bars American intelligence from using assassination to achieve any goal, the popular press has continued to link the C.I.A. with an assortment of evil schemes.

Trying to reshape its image, the C.I.A. published *Intelligence: The Acme of Skill*, a booklet that barely mentions its covert activities. According to this publication, "intelligence has less to do with cloaks and daggers than with the painstaking, generally tedious collection of facts, analysis of facts, exercise of judgment and quick, clear evaluation."[18]

However, the revelation in the media of the material supposedly contained in a diary belonging to a deceased movie-actress has eclipsed in the mind of the public any governmental efforts to reshape the popular image of the American intelligence services. A coroner's aide told the press that discrepancies in a number of official reports caused him to believe that there was a coverup of the cause of Marilyn Monroe's death. He also said that Monroe's diary mentioned the names of President John F. Kennedy, Attorney General Robert F. Kennedy, and two high-ranking organized crime figures. An entry relative to the plot to assassinate Cuban President Fidel Castro was also alleged to have been written in the dead actress' diary.[19]

Media distribution of stories of this type, alluding to the involvement of American intelligence in dastardly deeds and the proclivity of people to confuse fictional renderings of special operations with the routine functions of the intelligence service, counterbalances the C.I.A.'s effort to sanitize its image. Consequently, it appears that the American people are destined to view intelligence professionals as "hit men for the mob" or James-Bond-007 types rather than the "unshakably moral" George Smiley type of Le Carré's novels whom they resemble more closely.

PROACTIVE ANTITERRORIST POLICY

Secret operations, which are a last resort, should pursue an existing policy and be of short duration. Protracted clandestine operations involving a democratic society are prone to failure if they are sustained over time. Some informed and trusted person will surely speak to the media prior to the completion of the covert task.

Soviet specialists who are training and equipping transnational terrorists take great pains to remain hidden. Because all their moves are covert, their involvement and control of Moscow's international network of terror are difficult to prove. William J. Casey, speaking as the director of the C.I.A., said that his agency had seen only indirect Soviet aid, mostly money and supplies, for selected individuals and groups. The Soviet presence amid a terrorist group traditionally has remained in the shadows. Casey also indicated that the Kremlin and its allies had discovered a highly cost-effective way of making the point that, in today's world, democratic states were vulnerable. The purpose of the international network of terror, according to Casey, is to destroy the self-confidence of Americans and shatter their way of life. Overseas, United States citizens and installations are regarded by terrorists as easy marks. Also, they know that targeting American human and physical resources has immense propaganda value.[20]

Sam C. Sarkesian and William L. Scully edited a book entitled *U.S. Policy and Low-Intensity Conflict*. Writing in Chapter Six, Roger Hamburg said, "Soviet theory argues that strategy is always dictated by political objectives and that conflict and coercion, though not military force *per se*, are fundamental and pervasive in international affairs."[21]

Covert Soviet ties to an international network of terror are an outgrowth of this theory. The Kremlin has identified and netted willing proxies that have helped it achieve the goals it specifies for low-intensity clandestine operations. These surrogates include Cuba, East Germany, Vietnam, North Korea, and some countries in Eastern Europe. The American development of special-force units to project power and/or to interfere in the internal affairs of other countries, using terrorists as surrogates, is practically nil.

John M. Collins, author of *Green Berets, Seals and Spetsnaz: U.S. and Soviet Special Military Operations*, in his book said:

> Virtually every U.S. macro command/control, planning and S.O.F. [Special Operations Force] posture problem derives mainly from misunderstandings. Few members of the U.S. Government and military establishment fully appreciate special operations, threats, capabilities, limitations and relationships with the rest of our security apparatus.

He also commented that "overt, covert and clandestine operations for deterrent, persuasive, coercive and war fighting purposes mix force with fraud and finesse at every level of competition." Covert operations are not anarchistic. But those who understand how to manipulate the rules are unique.[22]

It is absolutely necessary for the United States to build into its defense structure the safeguards that it needs to protect basic freedoms. Properly managed covert operations must be part of any list of necessary safeguards. Terrorists and their mentors, aware of the disparate viewpoints voiced in the Iran–Contra hearings, are often able to manipulate the democratic process to create a climate favorable to themselves.

Although confronted with a serious international terrorist threat, the United States seems reluctant to utilize covert action as a counterterrorist tool because its elected officials believe this activity is a greater threat to the legitimacy of the democratic state than a terrorist challenge itself. It is exactly this stance, however, that provides the terrorist group with the primary input into its strategic plan. Their strategy is coherent only when it is understood that terrorism is not so much a military technique as it is a political condition. Always, the strategic aim of the terrorists is not the military defeat of the forces arrayed against them, but rather the moral alienation of the masses from the existing government until such alienation has become total and irreversible.

THE CASE FOR "ACTIVE MEASURES"

President Reagan, anxious to subdue terrorists who harmed Americans, said that "swift and effective retribution could be expected." Pledges containing similar rhetoric had been previously communicated to the people of the United States. But attempts to translate these commitments into an effective and efficient antiterrorist operational policy, however, have not produced a workable system of preemptive countermeasures.

On December 9, 1984, Secretary of State George P. Shultz delivered a speech titled "The Ethics of Power" at a Yeshiva University convocation at the Waldorf-Astoria Hotel in New York City. His remarks underscored a belief that the United States should be prepared to dispatch preemptive strike forces against terrorists. Retaliatory operations, according to Shultz, should be unleashed.

Recognizing the threat posed to American national interests by the Qaddafi and the Khomeini governments and other states that sponsor terrorism, Shultz cited the Talmud as supporting the "universal law of self-defense." He quoted the Talmudic injunction, "If one comes to kill you make haste and kill him first." The preservation of all life is a central commandment of Jewish law and is the overriding principle in terms of which the quotation used by Shultz should be understood. But the Talmud also contains a cognitive duty to preserve one's own life. American criminal law, as a correlation, recognizes self-preservation as an absolute defense to a capital charge.

In his Yeshiva University speech, Shultz cited three situations in which power can be used legitimately:

> Not when it crushes the human spirit and tramples human freedom but when it can help liberate a people or support the yearning for freedom. Not when it imposes an alien will on an unwilling people, but when its aim is to bring peace or to support peaceful processes; when it prevents others from abusing their power through aggression or oppression. And not when it is applied unsparingly, without care or concern for innocent life, but when it is applied with the greatest efforts to avoid unnecessary casualties and with a conscience troubled by the pain unavoidably inflicted.

Shultz made the case for "active measures"—a program of preemptive and retaliatory actions—in his speeches. Insisting that Americans must be prepared to use force, he said that the United States should strive not to become "the Hamlet of nations, worrying endlessly over whether and how to respond."

Some Pentagon officials are alarmed about the notion of punishing terrorists and claim that "hardline rhetoric" will one day force the United States to unleash an ill-considered counterterrorist operation. One Department of Defense official noted that Shultz has made some major statements calling for retaliation against terrorists. The Secretary of State said, "Let us alone, and let us do our work quietly. . . ."You will never hear about our successes, and that's as it should be."[23]

American antiterrorist units need not and probably should not be a part of the military services. Cadres of former police officers, particularly those experienced in combating urban terrorists or unraveling drug networks, are better suited for this task. They understand the warfare in the "back alleys" and the mentality of those who wage it.

NOTES

1. "Three Days of the Condor," *Film Review Digest* ed. David M. Brownstone and Irene M. Franck (Millwood, N.Y.: A. Hudson Group Periodical, Vol. I, No. 2, Winter, 1975), pp. 191–193.
2. David B. Tinnin and Dag Christensen, *The Hit Team* (Boston: Little, Brown, 1976), pp. 2–240.
3. Phil Gailey, "Photos Show Cairo Security Breakdown Experts Say," *The New York Times*, October 13, 1981, p. 1.
4. Robert Trumbull, "Kabul's Officials Ignored U.S. Plea Not to Storm Kidnappers' Hideout," *The New York Times*, February 15, 1979, p. 1.
5. "Afghan Coverup In Yank Death," *The Star Ledger* (Newark, N.J.), February 21, 1980. p. 1.
6. "Link to Shooting of Pope Called Absurd by Soviet," *The New York Times*, August 19, 1982, p. 7.
7. "The Great Propaganda War," *U.S. News & World Report*, January 11, 1982, pp. 27–30.
8. Harry Rositzke, *The K.G.B.: The Eyes of Russia* (Garden City, N.Y.: Doubleday, 1981), pp. 63–67.
9. Clifford P. Hackett, "Covert Agents Known by One and All," *The New York Times*, April 1, 1982, p. 26.
10. Steven V. Roberts, "One Year Later, the Murder of the C.I.A.'s Chief Officer in Athens Remains a Mystery without Solid Clues," *The New York Times*, December 26, 1976, p. 8.
11. "C.I.A. Changes Spy Operations to Add Security," *The New York Times*, February 2, 1982, p. 1.
12. Thomas Powers, *The Man Who Kept the Secrets: Richard Helms and the C.I.A.* (New York: Alfred A. Knopf, 1979), pp. 147–149; Anthony Lewis, "The C.I.A.: Are Covert Operations Necessary?" *The New York Times*, December 21, 1985, p. 2.
13. Michael Wood, "Spy Fiction, Spy Fact," review of *Smiley's People* by John Le Carré (New York: Alfred A. Knopf, 1980) in *The New York Times Book Review*, January 6, 1980, p. 1; Barbara Harte and Carolyn Reilly, *Contemporary Authors Volume V–VIII* (Detroit: Gale

Research, 1969), pp. 251–253; Tony Chiu, "Behind the Best Sellers: John Le Carré," *The New York Times Book Review*, January 6, 1980, p. 30.

14. A.P. D'Entreves, *Aquinas: Selected Political Writings* (Oxford: Basil Blackwell, 1965), pp. XXVIII–XXIX.

15. Friedrich Heer, *The Intellectual History of Europe; Volume I* (Garden City, N.Y.: Doubleday, 1968), p. 219.

16. Schlomo Gazit and Michael Handel, "Insurgency Terrorism and Intelligence" in *Intelligence Requirements for the 1980's: Counterintelligence* ed. Roy Godson (Washington, D.C.: National Strategy Information Center, 1980) pp. 138–139.

17. "Text of President's Executive Order on Intelligence Activities," *The New York Times*, December 5, 1981, pp. 18–19.

18. David Shribman, "Cloak-and-Dagger Business Booming," *The New York Times*, February 18, 1982, p. 12.

19. "Coroner's Aide Suspects Coverup in Death of M.M.," *The New York Post*, August 27, 1982, p. 9.

20. Bob Woodward, *Veil: The Secret Wars of the CIA, 1981–1987* (New York: Simon & Schuster, 1987), pp. 124–406.

21. Sam C. Sarkesian and William L. Scully, *U.S. Policy and Low-Intensity Conflict: Potentials for Military Struggles in the 1980's* (New Brunswick, N.J.: Transaction Books, 1981), pp. 149–173.

22. John M. Collins, *Green Berets, Seals and Spetsnaz: U.S. and Soviet Special Military Operations* (Washington, D.C.: Pergamon-Brassey's, 1987), pp. 9–97.

23. George Dargo, "Message of Talmud," *The New York Times*, December 30, 1984, p. 12e; Robert L. Phillips, *War and Justice* (Norman: University of Oklahoma Press, 1984), pp. 3–70; Bernard Gwertzman, "Shultz Advocates U.S. Covert Action Programs to Depose Qaddafi," *The New York Times*, April 22, 1986, p. 7.

2

STATE-DIRECTED TERRORIST SQUADS

A New Dimension in Warfare

Deception is the distortion of perceived reality. Masking, which is a form of deception, can be used to hide the identity of the instigator of an action while he simultaneously resorts to innuendo to bolster a more fearsome image. A hit man, hired by organized crime to "waste" (kill) an informer, is an example of how masking is used by the underworld.[1]

In her book, *The Business of Organized Crime: A Cosa Nostra Family*, Annelise Graebner Anderson said that "violence and a reputation for its effective use are useful in extortion, criminal monopolization of an industry and labor racketeering." Organized crime, a tightly knit association of professional criminals, demands and gets complete dedication and unquestioned obedience by its members to orders, instructions, and commands from the ruling "boss." Within every American organized-crime family, a key position is held by a person who is known as the "enforcer." According to Anderson, "the role of enforcer, for example, is to arrange, when ordered to do so, the killing or maiming of members and sometimes nonmembers." Usually, the enforcer does not do the killing or maiming; instead, the executioner engaged to do the hit (murder) is responsible for pulling the trigger. Killings are done in this fashion to mask the identity of the group that placed "the contract."[2]

Mercenaries are often viewed as people who fight first for money and second for a foreign government. There are exceptions to this interpretation; for example, the Hessian conscripts who involuntarily were

21

sent to fight against General George Washington's Colonial army did not go to war to earn money.

Throughout history, a mercenary, sporting the uniform of the government he served, was easily recognized on the field of battle. His job often involved the envelopment of fortified positions and other infantry tasks that were needed to win a battle for the flag he represented. The Wild Geese, members of the Irish gentry who were defeated by the British at the Battle of the Boyne, refused to take the oath to King William and, instead, joined the armies that were engaged in combat on the European continent. Members of the French Foreign Legion and the Gurkha units in the British Army are staffed with persons who are often regarded as mercenaries.[3]

Surrogates, who are engaged by a foreign government to kill or kidnap a person, are neither mercenaries nor organized-crime hit men. These people exchange their services with an established government in return for money, weapons, supplies, and/or protection. They assume the notoriety for their actions, thereby serving to prevent anything but an inferential link being established to tie their sponsor to their exploits. Although some media accounts connected Mehmet Ali Agca to the attempt to kill Pope John Paul II, a plot thought to be inspired by Moscow, no "smoking gun" (concrete evidence) pointing to the role of the Soviet Union has been uncovered.

ATTEMPTED ASSASSINATION OF THE POPE

Despite Mehmet Ali Agca's statements that link him to Palestinian terrorists, the Rome police uncovered a pattern of connections between the man accused of shooting the Pope and an international neo-Fascist network: the National Action Party of Turkey. Information gathered by others in Western Europe indicated that Agca, though not tied ideologically to a leftist group, may have served as a hit man for the Libyans or for some other group of terrorists that were inspired by Moscow. Certainly, the Soviet Union would benefit from the death of the Pontiff because he had spoken out strongly against Soviet intervention in Poland. Additionally, Pope John Paul II represented a bulwark of hope and inspiration and faith for the Polish people; as a peacemaker, he was highly regarded by both Christians and Muslims alike.

These motivational reasons pointed to Moscow's complicity and were widely circulated by investigators who studied the case. Another Soviet objective in any plot to kill the Pope might be an effort to pit Turkish Christians, primarily the Armenians, against Turkish Muslims

for the purpose of fomenting minority discord inside Turkey and de-
stabilizing a region that was adjacent to the Soviet Union and allied with
the West.[4]

Yet, on the other hand, Agca may have been a religious fanatic who
was motivated, perhaps, by an Islamic determination to even the score
with the Armenian Christians who had unleashed repeated attacks, in
recent years, on predominantly Muslim Turkish diplomats in various
parts of the world. His brother Adnan said he was "against the Christian
world." This pose of religiosity was an excellent mask for Agca, if he was
engaged by anyone as a triggerman.

Many ultranationalist Turkish students are Islamic zealots, and
some of them expressed approval of the attack on the Pope, as when one
of them said, "the Christians have been killing Turkish diplomats and
now Agca shot the Pope. He has done a good job." Perhaps searching for
a hit man to remove a thorn in the side of Moscow, the K.G.B., after
concealing its links with the event, may have become aware of the fanaticism and prior record of Agca and recruited him.[5]

American authorities say that it is difficult to detect an international
terrorist like Agca when he tries to enter the United States. Although
details are available through Interpol about someone who is known to
have committed a violent terrorist act, officials of this international police
agency are limited to just circulating any stored identification material
they hold on these persons. Thus, it would be most difficult to fix a
person living clandestinely in the United States and using false docu-
mentation. Where do you start? How do you go about finding him?

Interpol (the full name is International Criminal Police Organization)
operates a 59-nation radio network and serves as an information-gathering and dispensing agency. It has no investigative function, and often its
role ceases after it distributes the picture and fingerprints of persons on
its fugitive list to a member country. Additionally, terrorism is a delicate
subject in Interpol work, because a terrorist in one member country may
be a hero in another. Interpol deals only with criminal offenses. Bomb
attacks, an assassination, or an attempted assassination are regarded as
criminal offenses by its staff. Yet Interpol officials cannot remain involved in anything with political ramifications. Most terrorist activity has
political aspects.[6]

SURROGATE WARFARE

On April 20, 1984, officials of the Department of State revealed that
the Reagan administration had told six Eastern European governments

that improved relations with the United States were contingent upon their willingness to cease aiding and abetting "international terrorists." Although the warning was intended to be kept secret, Soviet-bloc diplomats discussed it with reporters, and these conversations prompted Washington to provide the media with more details.

Bulgaria was criticized when information became clear about the training and sanctuary it provided for terrorists. Also, Bulgaria stood accused of aiding Agca in his attempted assassination of the Pope, and of helping finance and train Italy's Red Brigades. Czechoslovakia, East Germany, Hungary, Poland, and Romania also were rebuked.

Furthermore, East Germany, the Department of State noted, was believed to have been involved in training security personnel and providing equipment for Central American and African revolutionaries. Czechoslovakia, it added, was known to have trained and aided terrorists. It accused Communist-controlled Poland of espionage and of trying to evade American export laws. American officials also said that Hungary and Romania were the least involved in anti-American activities; nevertheless, American intelligence sources were certain that the clandestine services of these two countries were "on close terms" with the K.G.B.

Officials employed by the Defense Department and the Federal Bureau of Investigation (F.B.I.) said that East Europeans were actively involved in aiding those who were opposed to the United States. They said that Communist-bloc agents carried out illegal actions in this country, frequently in collaboration with the K.G.B.[7]

According to Secretary of State George P. Shultz, Iran, Syria, Libya, and North Korea also were involved in a planning process known by American officials as "state-directed terrorism." William Casey, onetime director of central intelligence, called government-sponsored terrorism a new weapons system that obliterates the distinction between peace and war. According to the American intelligence chief, there were 50 major terrorist groups and hundreds of "mom-and-pop shops" of terrorists available for hire. Their training bases stretched out across, and under the protection of, Iran, Libya, Syria, Southern Yemen, Bulgaria, the Soviet Union, Romania, and Cuba.[8]

The use of terrorism allows sponsoring states to act without fear of reprisal, cautions Benjamin Netanyahu, deputy chief of mission at the Israeli embassy in Washington and a director of an institute that is engaged in the study of terrorism. This research center, which is situated in Israel, is named in honor of Lieutenant Colonel Yonni Netanyahu, his brother. Field commander of an Israeli antiterrorist force, Lieutenant Colonel Netanyahu was the only Israeli commando killed in the famous 1976 rescue raid on Entebbe. The Soviets, the radical Arabs, and the

Islamic fundamentalists share one feeling: a deep hostility to the institutions and governments of the Western world.[9]

Armenian Terrorist Organizations and Operations

Since the mid-1970s, the Armenian terrorists have developed a reputation for being deadly and have murdered a score of Turkish diplomats or members of their families and over 30 non-Turks. Many people have been wounded in their attacks. In the last two weeks of July 1983 alone, Armenian terrorists killed 15 people and wounded 60 others. Among these incidents were the shooting of a Turkish diplomat in Brussels, the bombing of a Turkish airline counter at Orly International Airport outside Paris, and the seizure of the Turkish embassy compound in Lisbon.

Operationally, the Armenian Secret Army for the Liberation of Armenia (A.S.A.L.A.) is characterized as slick by analysts who monitor its activities. On January 22, 1983, one of its members sauntered into a Turkish Airlines office, on the crowded Avenue de l'Opéra in central Paris, and tossed two hand grenades. The detonations shattered windows and blasted debris to the ceiling, wrecking the office but causing no injuries. The terrorist, a gun in his hand, joined a crowd of screaming customers and employees as he fled into the street. Armed police guards managed to grab the gunman, who did not speak French. An accomplice, who was waiting outside the airlines office, eluded the police by escaping into the crowd.[10]

At Orly International Airport, also on January 22, workers found a two-pound bomb constructed of plastic explosives. John M. Macdonald, in his book *Bombers and Firesetters*, reminds us that "Composition C3 and Composition C4 are called plastic explosives because of their puttylike consistency. Their shattering power is greater than dynamite." Terrorists are able to obtain these explosives from stocks purloined from military installations. Detonated by a blasting cap, plastic explosives can be shaped to fit containers or crevices of almost any size.[11]

At Orly, the police carried the plastic device, which was uncovered by workers, outside the terminal and defused it before it could explode. A caller to a French news agency, claiming to represent the A.S.A.L.A., said that his group was responsible for the attack at the airport and the "fragging" of the airline's office.

Founded in 1975, the A.S.A.L.A. made its first killings, the assassinations within a two-day interval of the Turkish ambassadors in Vienna and in Paris, in October of that year. The January 1983 attacks on the Turkish facilities in Paris were the first strikes since the A.S.A.L.A. members seized hostages at the Ankara Airport in Turkey on August 7, 1982, killing 9 persons and wounding 63 others.

On March 9, 1983, the Turkish ambassador to Yugoslavia was ambushed by two gunmen as he sat in his car waiting for a traffic light to change at a wide intersection in Belgrade. The fleeing terrorists opened fire on bystanders, and a police officer who gave chase returned the fire. Two people were seriously wounded in the ensuing gunfight, a 24-year-old student who later died and a 58-year-old man. Ambassador Balkar died on March 11, 1983, of the wounds he received when he was bushwhacked. One of the diplomat's assassins was wounded and captured, the other escaped. The captured gunman was identified from his Lebanese passport and police said they believed the second gunman also carried a passport issued by the Beirut government.[12]

An anonymous caller to the Associated Press in Athens took responsibility for the attack on Ambassador Balkar on behalf of the Justice Commandos of the Armenian Genocide. Callers to newspapers in Paris and in Beirut also said that the Justice Commandos had carried out the assault. The A.S.A.L.A. is a Marxist-leaning organization, whereas the Justice Commandos are thought to be pro-West. The Justice Commandos say that they undertake actions only against Turkish targets, whereas the A.S.A.L.A. targets both Turkish property and groups that have commercial relations with Turkey. Some officials conclude that the two groups interface; the A.S.A.L.A. subcontracting its North American hits to the Justice Commandos.

The Armenian Revolutionary Army, another band of fanatics, claimed credit for the murder of a Turkish diplomat in Brussels on July 14, 1983. Witnesses said that a well-built man, who was wearing blue jeans and a striped shirt, walked up to a Turkish embassy attaché who was sitting in his car parked outside his home and fired through the window. He was found dead, with two bullet wounds in his head, by the time an emergency vehicle reached the scene of the attack in Brussels's embassy quarters.[13] A leader of the Armenian Social Democratic group called the Dachnak Party charged that the A.S.A.L.A. "is installed in Syria and has become an instrument of the USSR." Despite this allegation, commented an American official in Paris, there is little evidence that the Soviet Union is giving direct support to the Armenian terrorist groups.

From its first breath, the A.S.A.L.A. tried to convince Moscow to permit it to use Soviet Armenia as a staging area for its attacks against Turkey. It also became the only "national liberation movement" in the world to advocate an expansion of the Soviet state. It once declared its intention to connect Turkish Armenia "to the already liberated Yerevan regime." Yerevan is the capital of Soviet Armenia. This objective, the restoration of the traditional Armenian homeland, is emblazoned on the A.S.A.L.A.'s insignia. It features an upraised Russian assault rifle superimposed on a background depicting an Armenian state stretching across the Iron Curtain.

The Soviets are ambivalent when it comes to their dealings with the A.S.A.L.A. Fearful of the rise of Armenian nationalism inside the Soviet Union, the Soviets have granted some concessions to its Armenian population. Yerevan is a bustling commercial center, and Moscow has allocated huge sums of money for the development of Armenia. The Soviet leaders, however, are reluctant to give too much support to nationalist groups.[14]

In 1979, the Soviets hanged three Armenians who were accused of setting a bomb in the Moscow subway. A French-based Armenian terrorist group retaliated by bombing Soviet offices in Belgium and in France. Calling itself the New Armenian Resistance (N.A.R.), this group was active until October 1980, at which time it vanished when the A.S.A.L.A. was being convulsed by a power struggle.

A careful analysis of textual material distributed by the A.S.A.L.A. has revealed that the faction that won the struggle fell under the more centralized control of a group expressing itself in the hardline rhetoric of traditional Soviet agitprop (agitational propaganda or disinformation intended to inflame). The A.S.A.L.A.'s armed propaganda, which includes bombings and assassinations, was keyed, therefore, to a Soviet strategy designed to unsettle the countries participating in the North Atlantic Treaty Organization (NATO).[15]

Pro-Turkish national security experts assembled a strong circumstantial case focusing on the Soviet use of the A.S.A.L.A. to destabilize Turkey—a member of NATO and the only strong pro-Western power on the southern border of the Soviet Union. A Turkish case, tying Moscow to the A.S.A.L.A., was linked to a fatal automobile accident that took place in northern Syria in 1982. This incident revealed that the victim extricated from the wreck had studied for seven years at the University of Yerevan in Soviet Armenia. Other important leaders of the A.S.A.L.A. have also graduated from this institution. The A.S.A.L.A. has acknowledged that the victim was one of their top leaders.

On July 29, 1983, the Turkish foreign minister, in London, said at a news conference that certain countries were furnishing indirect support to the Armenian terrorists. Turkmen also mentioned that the Soviet Socialist Republic of Armenia was participating in the Armenian propaganda campaign in its broadcasts, its newspapers, and in its speeches. The A.S.A.L.A. demand that eastern Turkey become part of an enlarged Soviet Armenia was another indication that Moscow was using the Armenian terrorist organization to destabilize Turkey. The A.S.A.L.A. was often considered as *prima facie* evidence of the K.G.B.'s manipulation of international terror.[16]

Libyan Clandestine Operations

On May 8, 1984, the Reagan administration revealed some operational aspects of its effort to check state-directed terrorism in the United States by announcing that the F.B.I. had been conducting surveillance of the Libyan Mission to the United Nations in New York City. After analysis of the electronic surveillance reports, evidence emerged indicating that the former head of the Libyan Mission in New York had provided money for American black activists who supported Libya's leader, Colonel Muammar al-Qaddafi. The telephone wiretaps showed that the Libyans were encouraging support among black activist groups in the United States in order to defeat President Reagan's reelection campaign, officials said. The wiretaps also revealed that information about the Libyan diplomat's activities were obtained through surveillance started at the Libyan Mission in 1981. Shortly before the wiretaps were authorized, American authorities received information regarding a possible Libyan plan to murder Jeane R. Kirkpatrick, the chief United States delegate to the United Nations.

Information about the F.B.I. surveillance, which was disclosed in the press, upset Reagan administration officials. They said that the press release contained information that had been part of a secret F.B.I. report. The bureau had previously made the report available to the State and the Justice Departments and had asked these agencies to rigidly safeguard the information.[17]

On May 9, 1984, two Libyans were arrested in a Philadelphia suburb. A few hours before their arrest, one of the Libyans bought three .45 caliber handguns with silencers from a federal undercover agent who was operating out of an undercover van. Posing as an illegal arms dealer, the F.B.I. agent had previously sold two bulletproof vests to the Libyan.

Law-enforcement officials said they could not say what the Libyans had planned to do with the weapons or whether they were part of a terrorist group. One investigator said that they had described themselves as supporters of Colonel Qaddafi.

According to the F.B.I., a student at the University of Maryland bought the guns for $3,000 from the undercover agent. He then drove to a restaurant in Essington, a Philadelphia suburb, and met a Libyan student from the University of Pennsylvania. At the restaurant, the suitcase containing the guns was transferred to the car belonging to the student from the University. A search warrant was issued, authorizing the F.B.I.

agents to look for assassination lists and links between the students and the Libyan government.

On May 14, 1984, a Philadelphia-based United States magistrate refused to reduce the $10 million bail set for each of the Libyans, calling them a "grave danger to the community." The magistrate waived a hearing and agreed to extradition to New York to have one of the Libyans face charges of buying three pistols equipped with silencers. The court fixed a high bail, citing a sealed affidavit filed by the United States government.[18]

The Libyan threat to the internal security of the United States has continued. In November 1987, seven members of the El Rukn's, a notorious street gang, were convicted of conspiracy by a federal jury in Chicago. Described by the police as a deadly and sophisticated group, the plotters planned to blow up airplanes and government buildings as part of a terrorism-for-hire scheme. They hoped that these escapades would net them $2.5 million from Libya. According to the indictments, the El Rukn's traveled to Libya, Panama, and other locations to arrange an exchange of their services for money.

Before the trial, one of the El Rukn's gang members entered into a plea agreement and became a key prosecution witness. He described details of an elaborate code used by his associates to disguise their conversations over the telephone. This code identified Washington, D.C., possibly the Reagan administration, as the "big actor"; Muammar Qaddafi was known as the "young friend." Prosecutors identified the coordinator of the conspiracy as a person who had served time in a Texas prison on drug charges. While he was incarcerated, the inmate had made scores of telephone calls during a four-month period.

Although none of the terrorist acts that were discussed in the tape-recordings of these conversations actually occurred, federal authorities contended, however, that the contacts with the Libyans were initiated by the El Rukn's members. One of the gang members said that his group was a religious organization bent on using financing obtained from the Libyans for a mosque.

U.S. Attorney Susan Bogart was the lead prosecutor in the case. She said that "the verdict represents the product of 2½ years of very hard work and extraordinary efforts." F.B.I. agents and agents of the Bureau of Alcohol, Tobacco and Firearms spearheaded the investigation. "The agents brought down a well-organized and very dangerous group. I think it's a just and very fair verdict," she said.[19]

The El Rukn's are one of an assortment of nefarious groups that haunt North America and that are available for hire when the cause and the price are right. Among them, reportedly, a handful of Cuban exiles have an ongoing dialogue with Havana, dealing wit the D.G.I. (Cuban intelligence). Armenian terrorists, particularly the A.S.A.L.A., claimed responsibility for a spate of assassinations in Canada and in the United States in 1982. A veil of mystery still enshrouds the A.S.A.L.A.'s activities in North America. Its tactics, modus operandi, and target selection are evidence of a coordinated command structure. The K.G.B. and, inevitably, the C.I.A., have been suggested as the "heartbeat" of this group.

The Croatian National Resistance

The Croatian National Resistance (O.P.T.O.R.) was also once active in the United States and its targets were Yugoslav travel agencies and diplomatic facilities. O.P.T.O.R. sought the formation of a Croatia independent from Yugoslavia. Book bombs, manufactured with a hollowed-out center packed with an explosive charge, were a favorite weapon of the O.P.T.O.R. bomb-placers.

According to prosecutors, O.P.T.O.R. used surrogates to do its dirty work. Directing its operations from a headquarters in Chicago, O.P.T.O.R. engaged others to move dynamite and place the bombs. Maniacs who belonged to street gangs would set off a bomb in exchange for dollars.[20]

Suriname and the Libyans

Suriname, formerly Dutch Guiana, was once used as a staging area by Libyan intelligence agents tasked to direct Colonel Qaddafi's covert actions in Latin America. Facing severe economic hardships, Suriname was believed to permit the Libyans to use its rain forests and coastal areas to organize and train terrorist cadres in exchange for financial assistance. Situated on the northeast coast of South America, just north of Brazil, the country occupies a pivotal geopolitical position. In 1667, England, vying with other European powers for supremacy in the region, ceded Suriname to the Netherlands in return for the colony of New Netherland (New York).

When Lieutenant Colonel Desi Bouterse directed the government of Suriname from Paramaribo, the country's capital and principal city, after seizing power from an elected government in 1980, he immediately established close ties with Cuba. Castro's henchmen helped Bouterse consolidate his control of the former Dutch colony's population, who are predominantly Creole and bush blacks. Islam, Christianity, and Hinduism are the major religious faiths of the Surinamese people.

Latin American Muslims and representatives from Islamic groups from all over the world attended a seven-day meeting in Benghazi, Libya, in April 1983. According to American intelligence officials, the meeting was used by the Libyans to establish new contacts with terrorist networks in the Americas and elsewhere and to create channels for funneling money to clandestine groups.

Using Suriname as a base for operations and training, Qaddafi directed that death squads be positioned to wreak havoc throughout the Caribbean region and Latin America. In the 1980s, Libya made a determined effort to train assassination squads to exterminate Qaddafi's foes.[21]

Iranian-Sponsored Terrorism

As the decade of the 1980s approached, terrorism expanded at a time of growing tension between the West and the Islamic world. This friction intensified on December 7, 1979, when the nephew of Mohammad Rezi Pahlavi, the Shah of Iran, was shot to death as he walked along a quiet tree-lined street in Paris. Although some newspapers attributed this killing to agents of the Ayatollah Ruhollah Khomeini's secret police organization (S.A.V.A.M.A.), the head of Iran's Islamic revolutionary tribunal identified the killer as a member of a fundamentalist Islamic fedayee group.[22] "I take responsibility for this assassination," he declared. "The Islamic Fedayeen are continuing their activities in Europe and the United States to identify those wrongdoers and punish them for their actions. This will continue until all these dirty pawns of the decadent system have been purged."

In November 1979, members of the United States Senate were warned to take precautions against possible attacks by religious fanatics and nationalist terrorists as a consequence of information contained in a document entitled "Thoughts and Strategies of Islamic Guerrilla Warfare in the United States." This paper was distributed in Washington, D.C.

Concern in the United States was further heightened in the wake of the assassination of the nephew of the Shah and as a consequence of the statement issued by Iran that the killing in Paris by a death squad was a warning to America.

The arrests on November 16, 1979 in the Baltimore Washington International Airport of eight Iranians carrying high-powered rifles, ammunition, scopes, and a street map of Washington, with embassy buildings marked, may have prompted Senator Barry Goldwater to remark, "We are going back to an uncivilized condition in a large part of the world." "I am not ruling out," he added, "such problems in our own nation's capital and in this country. We hope and pray that it doesn't happen."23

Moscow is anxious to avoid being openly identified with the seemingly uncontrollable fanatics who use terror as an instrument of "Islamic Holy War." A few foreign affairs specialists have concluded that the Soviet Union provides the Muslim extremists with technical support and encouragement because it dreads their prowess. Swelling discontent among the Muslim population of Soviet Central Asia, fanned by the Pan-Islamic messages of Ayatollah Khomeini and the war in Afghanistan, has upset the Russians.

Fearful of the seething unrest in its Central Asian provinces, and sparked by the deaths in combat of hordes of Soviet Muslim infantrymen, Moscow has viewed Islamic terrorist fanaticism that was unleashed against American targets as a useful adjunct to its domestic and foreign policies. Its support for the terrorists was intended to compensate its Muslim people for the destruction and carnage it has caused in Afghanistan. Moscow probably hopes that this strategy will promote domestic stability and push the United States into spending more of its resources for internal security and less for the modernization of its armed services.24

Although officials have refused to comment on the details, a few years ago military bases in northern California were threatened with a terrorist attack. State officials in California, however, were tipped off that Iranian supporters of Ayatollah Khomeini might try to launch an attack on military installations. Officials at Travis Air Force Base in Fairfield and Beale Air Force Base in Marysville refused to comment on the threats. However, contingency security plans were put into effect at McClellan Air Force Base near Sacramento. In addition, Mather Air Force Base in Sacramento maintained a very high level of security because it was headquarters for the 320th Bomb Wing of the Strategic Air Command, whose pilots fly B-52 bombers and KC-135 aerial tankers.

An Iranian delegate to the United Nations warned that the United States involvement in Lebanon would lead to further retaliations. In 1983, after the attack on the United States Marines' compound in Beirut, Washington indicated that it had uncovered evidence pointing to Iranian sponsorship of the bombing.

The delegate's statement contained remarks that, although they were uttered in a largely empty assembly chamber at the United Nations in New York, put the Iranian government nonetheless in open conflict with the United States. More than 10,000 Iranian students were, at this time, enrolled in American universities. Furthermore, Iranian-sponsored hit teams were active and experienced, and were trained to fire bullets into the heads of their targets.[25]

In December 1980, the government of Bahrain, an archipelago off the coast of Saudi Arabia, uncovered a plot involving 73 members of a group known as the Islamic Front for the Liberation of Bahrain. Sixty of the terrorists were Shiites, members of the dominant Iranian Muslim sect. Equipped with radios to coordinate their operations and carrying automatic weapons, the plotters, according to the Bahrain government, had been trained in Iran. Some of the terrorists were wearing uniforms, apparently made in Iran.

Analysis of Iranian-sponsored terrorist operations in Western Europe and in the Middle East has revealed a sophisticated modus operandi. It is anticipated that their forays into North America would continue to exhibit the same level of expertise and coordination.

On September 14, 1984, Lebanese President Bashir Gemayel was assassinated in a bombing that some observers attributed to the K.G.B. Moscow's hit teams are allegedly trained in the three S's: *sanitization* (deletion of information), *sterilization* (cleaning of equipment), and *surgicalization* ("taking someone out" without leaving telltale signs). The Lebanese president may have been the victim of a Soviet "sanitization operation." A 400-pound plus explosive charge demolished his Phalange party headquarters, removing any possible shred of evidence that could be used by investigators to identify the bombers.

Terrorists in the Middle East have also used explosive-laden vehicles to unleash suicide attacks against American facilities. On April 18, 1983, a truck blew up, wrecking the United States Embassy in West Beirut. On October 23, 1983, a driver detonated another truck that was filled with explosives at the United States Marine garrison headquarters at the airport in Beirut. According to observers, a trough, about 6-feet deep and 14-feet long, was blasted into the road in front of the United States Embassy in Beirut on September 20, 1984. The hole was created when a van, packed with 385 pounds of explosives inserted between four Soviet-made GRAD rockets, exploded. The blast demolished a wall in front of the American facility and a nearby house situated on a hillside. Only the blackened engine block of the kamikaze-like vehicle remained.[26]

Secretary of Defense Caspar W. Weinberger charged at the time that the 1983 assault on the Marine Corps compound was undertaken with the "sponsorship, knowledge and authority of the Syrian government." Spokesmen for this government have denied that Damascus was tied to any of the bombings in Beirut. Although a group calling itself Islamic Holy War took responsibility for the September 20th blast in the

Lebanese capital, American officials said, however, that they did not know who was responsible for the attack.

The use of explosive-laden vehicles to destroy a target, while simultaneously sanitizing the crime scene, is a scheme that prevents investigators from fixing responsibility for the blasts—a masking that is apparently effective.

Islamic Holy War could be just a name and not even exist as an organization; just words, part of a deception operation, according to many British, French, and Israeli intelligence officials. Intelligence reports circulated in 1983 tied the group to extremists who were associated with Ayatollah Khomeini. Analysts have since debunked these assessments, concluding that the group is either a mirage or a loose collection of cells from an assortment of terrorist groups that are active in Lebanon.[27]

American intelligence agencies have consumed considerable resources in their effort to monitor and infiltrate terrorist groups. According to officials, the C.I.A. has also tried to improve the exchange of antiterrorist intelligence between the clandestine services in Western Europe, the United Kingdom, West Germany, and France. Liaison with Israeli intelligence organizations is also considered essential.[28]

Members of the United States Congress were reluctant to fault the C.I.A. for its failure to profile the Islamic Holy War group. "It may be impossible to get detailed information about a group like this," said Lee H. Hamilton, a member of the House Select Committee on Intelligence. "I don't think we know much more today than we did a year ago." Commenting further, he added, "we don't know if it's an identifiable group."

The Soviet Union's K.G.B.-managed assassinations are similar to the pattern of American organized-crime murders in that people who are indigenous to the area of operations are employed as surrogates to mask the crime, with the intended victim being killed at the same time as the hit man who was hired to do the job. Thus, the drivers of the kamikaze bomb vehicles that wrecked the American facilities in Lebanon were obliterated when their cargoes exploded. Consequently, positive identification of these drivers was necessarily prevented, since physical evidence of any sort could have been used to link them to a terrorist organization, possibly to a group aided and abetted by the Soviet Union or one of its surrogates.

The United States could have formulated and executed an appropriate response intended to neutralize the persons who were responsible for the Beirut bombings had they been identified, but they never were. Washington was wary of the machinations used by the Soviet Union to provoke the use of American armed forces against an unidentified opponent and the subsequent need to justify its moves in an international forum, the United Nations (UN).

ASPECTS OF HISPANIC-CONTRIVED TERRORISM IN THE AMERICAS

In 1983, news of the arrest of William Morales, a bombmaker and fugitive member of the Puerto Rican terrorist group F.A.L.N., by the Mexican police, shared headlines with two other reports: the assassination of an American military advisor in El Salvador by terrorist gunmen and a commitment by the United States to neutralize Fidel Castro's effort "to export revolution in the Western Hemisphere." These reports were seen to interlock as evidence of ties between domestic terrorist groups and the Communist-inspired guerrillas in Central America emerged as a consequence of Morales's presence and sinister purpose in Mexico. The fire fight that erupted as a carload of gunmen tried to free him from police custody was an indication of his connection with Mexican terrorists.[29]

One consequence of any American effort to use its military to further safeguard the Caribbean Basin from the steadily expanding partnership between Cuba and the Sandinistas would be an increase of terrorism in the United States. Cuban-directed commando squads, lurking south of the border in Mexico, might try to vent the fury of Central American violence on doorsteps in Denver, Chicago, and New York, cities that once harbored members of the F.A.L.N. or their associates.[30]

Terrorist groups operating in Central America are frequently led by cadres that are trained by the Soviet K.G.B. or the D.G.I. (Cuban Intelligence). Additionally, the Puerto Rican Socialist Party (P.S.P.), linked ideologically to the F.A.L.N., has issued statements that were applauded by Castro.[31] At one time, his agents advised the Weather Underground Organization (W.U.O.) to unleash a bombing campaign in New York at a time when American troops were engaging Communist forces in Southeast Asia. An element of the W.U.O. was involved in the botched armored-car robbery in Rockland County, New York. Led by Cuban-trained terrorists, the W.U.O. used explosives in order to garner media attention and thereby manipulate the press into printing releases that prompted Americans to focus on domestic issues rather than on Vietnam. Its bombings also helped to trigger the antiwar movement's demands that the United States extricate itself from the war in Southeast Asia and devote its energies to implementing programs of social reform.[32]

Dubbed "armed propaganda" by guerrilla theoreticians, this multimedia approach was also used by the F.A.L.N. to advertise "Independence for Puerto Rico," its primary cause.[33] The organization has claimed responsibility for 120 bombings that have killed five people and caused $3.5 million in damage in New York, Chicago, and other American cities since 1974.[34] The group is now believed to be defunct.

The arrest of Morales posed questions, particularly for the American intelligence community. Were the F.A.L.N. and the W.U.O. linked? The F.B.I. was alarmed by an F.A.L.N. communique that expressed solidarity with the radicals who were arrested in the bungled Brink's armored-car holdup.[35]

The F.B.I. and the Puerto Rican police had investigated the possibility of a link between island terrorism and mainland bombings by the F.A.L.N. The police also reviewed reports that radical students at the University of Puerto Rico were once recruited into the F.A.L.N.[36]

Some members of *Los Macheteros*, a Puerto Rican-based group, were trained in Cuba. The field operations of this group resemble guerrilla maneuvers in Central America. In 1979, its ambush of a United States Navy bus near Sebana Seca, 10 miles west of San Juan, and its bombing in 1981 of two dozen military aircraft at a Puerto Rican Airport were tactically precise.

Skeptics continue to emphasize that Communist influence on American terrorists takes place solely in the realm of ideas—political orientation. Previous investigations of the F.A.L.N., however, connected it to radicals in the Southwest and in the Mountain states.[37] These people, advocating solidarity for the Chicano, Mexican, and Puerto Rican communities in the United States, may have provided the F.A.L.N. with the dynamite used by Morales to make his bombs.[38] Preaching a Marxist-Leninist solution to the problems experienced by a quarter of a million people living in poverty along the edges of major Mexican cities, they have tried to persuade Mexican-Americans to join them in helping the Mexican Proletarian Party (P.P.M.) overthrow the government of Mexico.[39] It is known that some of Mexico's guerrillas were trained in North Korea.[40]

The F.A.L.N. achieved interlocking membership with domestic militants in the Southwest as it attempted to recruit radical Chicanos to engage in terrorism against Anglos. Also, reports circulated in a portion of the American Southwest that Chicano activists claim belongs to Mexico and to those who work the fields and not to foreign Europeans—indicated secret meetings between the F.A.L.N. and the leaders of unidentified militant groups in Texas, Colorado, and Arizona.[41] Members of these organizations could have hidden Morales when he moved into Texas. Traveling south from El Paso through the border city of Ciudad, Juarez to Chihuahua, Morales ended his trek in Cholula, a city situated near Puebla and located about 75 miles southeast of Mexico City and about 700 miles northeast of San Salvador.[42]

Tens of thousands of Central Americans, fleeing the fighting in their homelands, moved northwestward along a route extending from El Salvador through Guatemala to Guadalajara, Mexico. Contacting smugglers at the northern terminus of their escape route, some of these refugees were taken across the border into the United States for a fee of about $350 per person.[43] This refugee exodus could be used by the Cubans to mask the movement through Mexico of terrorists who are assigned the task of bombing in American cities to bolster a Cuban initiative in the Caribbean Basin.

Conservative Mexican groups demand that their country's open-door policy toward political refugees be revised and that many exiles be investigated. Some of the Chilean, Salvadorean, and Nicaraguan refugees are believed to be Communists.[44] Also, Mexican police try to prevent the illegal entry of foreigners into their country, particularly those with criminal and subversive records, who could instigate terrorist acts. The Mexican *Federales* (Federal Judicial Police) smashed the Communist League 23rd of September about a decade ago. This group was responsible for many acts of violence in Mexico City in the mid-1970s.

American law-enforcement agencies, restrained by budgetary and legal restrictions, have not been able to halt the flow into Mexico of weapons and ammunition stolen from United States military bases. For similar reasons, they have been unable to prevent drug traffickers from moving their cargoes across the border into the United States.[45]

Cooperation between law-enforcement officials in the United States and Mexico was strained by the 1987 murder of a Drug Enforcement Agency (D.E.A.) agent in Mexico, allegedly by the police, and a 1988 indictment that mentions the involvement of Mexican Army officers in a drug ring.[46] Meanwhile, the Mexican corporate executives have placed security issues uppermost on their list of concerns. These people have a life-style that is similar to the routine of the West European elite, many of whom were kidnapped by terrorists for the purpose of extorting money to finance their operations. Some of Mexico's elite have engaged the services of bodyguards. Often rude and uncouth, these people have developed a tough-guy image. Motorists in Mexico City claim they have been stopped, punched, and otherwise abused by these bodyguards, for example, for blocking a highway lane being used by an executive's motorcade. A few years ago, Mexico City's attorney general organized a three-month training course for security personnel. It included topics related to both protection and good manners, with lectures on human relations and transactional analysis supervised by a team of psychoanalysts. Defensive driving, use of communications equipment, and marksmanship are some of the other required subjects that a bodyguard must master before he receives a Certificate of Aptitude.

The indictment that mentioned the involvement of the Mexican Army officers in drug trafficking, the murder of the D.E.A. agent in Mexico, and the antics of some of the bodyguards portend an ominous situation south of the border. It is the type of situation that a terrorist propagandist, acting as a surrogate for a foreign government, relishes, ripe as it is for manipulation.

NOTES

1. J. Barton Bowyer, *Cheating: Deception in War and Magic, Games and Sports, Sex and Religion, Business and Con Games, Politics and Espionage, Art and Science* (New York: St. Martin's Press, 1982), pp. 45–64.
2. Annelise Graebner Anderson, *The Business of Organized Crime* (Stanford, Calif.: Hoover Institution Press, 1979), pp. 36, 117.
3. Anthony Mockler, *The Mercenaries* (New York: Macmillan Company, 1969), pp. 13–24.
4. R. W. Apple, "Trail of Mehmet Ali Agca: 6 Years of Neofascist Ties," *The New York Times*, May 25, 1981, p. 1; Matthew Conroy, "Terrorism Expert Calls Times Naive on Agca," *The News World*, May 26, 1981, p. 1; "Soviet Denounces Pope on Anti-Socialist Stance," *The Star Ledger* (Newark, N.J.), December 30, 1982, p. 2.
5. William Safire, "Cross in the Cross Hairs," *The New York Times*, December 16, 1982, p. 27.
6. Christopher Dobson and Ronald Payne, *Counterattack: The West's Battle against the Terrorists* (New York: Facts On File, 1982), pp. 9–10.
7. Bob Woodward, *Veil: The Secret Wars of the CIA, 1981–1987* (New York: Simon & Schuster, 1987), pp. 124–129.
8. Ibid.
9. Mort Rosenblum, "Terrorism: A Growing, Elusive International Cancer," *Asbury Park Press* (Asbury Park, N.J.), November 21, 1982, p. 44.
10. E. J. Dionne, Jr., "Armenian Terrorism: A Bitter History, Frustration and a Tangle of Motives," *The New York Times*, August 1, 1983, p. 5.
11. John M. Macdonald, *Bombers and Firesetters* (Springfield, Ill.: Charles C Thomas Publishers, 1977), p. 14.
12. "Gunmen Shoot Turkish Envoy, Slay Bystander in Yugoslavia," *The Star Ledger* (Newark, N.J.), March 10, 1983, p. 20.
13. "Turk Slain in Brussels: Armenians Claim Deed," *The New York Times*, July 15, 1983, p. 5.
14. Dionne, "Armenian Terrorism," p. 5.
15. Jacques Ellul, *Propaganda: The Formation of Men's Minds* (New York: Vintage Books), pp. 3–25.
16. "An Old Blood Feud Gets Even Uglier," *U.S. News & World Report*, August 8, 1983, p. 9.
17. Leslie Maitland Werner, "Officials Report of Libyan Inquiry," *The New York Times*, May 9, 1984, p. 28.
18. "FBI Arrests 2 Libyan Students," *The New York Times*, May 10, 1984, p. 3.
19. "$2.5M Payoff scheme," *Daily Journal* (Elizabeth, N.J.), November 25, 1987, p. 3.

20. Neal Hirschfeld, "We Are Not All Bomb-Throwers," *Sunday News Magazine* (New York, N.Y.), January 5, 1982, pp. 12–20.
21. John B. Wolf, "Suriname: Qaddafi's Latin America Training Ground," *New York City Tribune*, February 25, 1986, p. 2.
22. "Iranian Says Secret Agency Isn't Like Savak under Shah," *The New York Times*, June 1, 1981, p. 2.
23. Ernest Holsendolph, "8 Iranians with Rifles Are Seized at Baltimore Airport," *The New York Times*, November 17, 1979, p. 7; "8 Seized In Arms, Ammo Cache at Baltimore Airport," *The Star Ledger* (Newark, N.J.), November 17, 1979, p. 7.
24. Serge Schemann, "In Central Asia Age-Old Islam Meets Soviet Rule," *The New York Times*, July 10, 1985, p. 10.
25. Albert L. Weeks, "Experts See K.G.B. Hand in Embassy Bombings," *New York Tribune*, September 24, 1984, p. 1.
26. David K. Shipler, "Sharon Suggests Syria Was Tied to Slaying of Gemayel," *The New York Times*, September 30,1 1982, p. 14.
27. Joel Brinkley, "Mideast Bombers: Hard to Pin Down," *The New York Times*, December 19, 1983, p. 6.
28. Philip Taubman, "Major Questions Raised on C.I.A.'s Performance," *The New York Times*, November 3, 1983, p. 21.
29. "Terrorist Fights Return to U.S.," *The Star Ledger* (Newark, N.J.), June 1, 1983, p. 3.
30. David Binder, "Cuba Said to Aid Puerto Rico Foes," *The New York Times*, May 20, 1976, p. 11.
31. Jo Thomas, "Documents Show F.B.I. Harassed Puerto Rico Independence Groups," *The New York Times*, November 22, 1977, p. 26.
32. Nicholas M. Horrock, "F.B.I. Asserts Cuba Aided Weathermen," *The New York Times*, October 9, 1977, p. 1.
33. Regis Debray, "Revolution in the Revolution?" *Monthly Review*, July–August, 1967, pp. 47–58.
34. Robert D. McFadden, "F.A.L.N. Puerto Rican Terrorists Suspected in New Year Bombings," *The New York Times*, January 2, 1983, p. 1.
35. Robert D. McFadden, "Brink's Holdup Opens U.S. Inquiry on Links among Terrorist Groups," *The New York Times*, October 25, 1981, p. 40.
36. Clyde Haberman, "A Soviet-Type Rifle Tied to Bus Ambush," *The New York Times*, December 6, 1979, p. 23.
37. Mary Breasted "3-Year Inquiry Threads Together Evidence on F.A.L.N. Terrorism," *The New York Times*, April 17, 1977, p. 1.
38. "Judge Calls for National Inquiry into Leak in Terrorism Case," *The New York Times*, May 28, 1977, p. 20.
39. Dick Reavis, "The Smoldering Fire," *Texas Monthly*, March, 1978, pp. 80–85, 143–150.
40. Alan Riding, "Mexican Tells of Torture in Secret Prison," *The New York Times*, December 31, 1979, p. 2.
41. "Esta Lucha No Se Para—An Interview With Ricardo Romero: Chicano/Méjicano Activist from Colorado," *Breakthrough* (undated), pp. 29–36.
42. "Morales's Life on the Lam," *The New York Post*, May 30, 1983, p. 5.
43. National Committee To Restore Internal Security, *A Citizen's Inquiry on the Caribbean and Central America* (Mantoloking, N.J.: National Committee To Restore Internal Security, 1983), pp. 1–97.
44. Alan Riding, "Mexico's Refugees Fear Clampdown," *The New York Times*, November 9, 1981, p. 19.

45. "90 Powerful Grenades Vanish at Texas Fort: Wide Alert Is Ordered," *The New York Times*, August 14, 1970, p. 14; Alan Riding, "Smuggled Guns from U.S. Are Common in Mexico," *The New York Times*, January 23, 1977, p. 3.
46. Philip Shenon, "3 Linked to Army in Mexico Indicted in U.S. Drug Plot," *The New York Times*, January 16, 1988, p. 1.

3

PROPAGANDA

Activities and Analysis

Basic management concepts can be used to determine the efficacy of a terrorist group. An analyst, however, must also be familiar with propaganda-analysis models and principles of semantics. Propaganda is a systematic attempt by an individual or a group to control the attitudes of others. Semantics is the relationship between words and what those words represent. Derived from the Latin, *de propaganda fides* (for propagating the faith), propaganda is used to shape ideology. Any formidable terrorist group has a specialist responsible for propaganda production within its organization.

Four elements implicit in propaganda are: (1) the *target* of the deception, usually an audience to be hyped-up; (2) the *medium* through which the message is delivered, often a surrogate hit team that is used; (3) the *purpose*, always an effort to transform political behavior; and finally (4) the *truth*. Skilled propagandists do not lie; rather, they distort facts through apparent objectivity. An understanding of propaganda models and semantic principles enhances an analyst's ability to dissect and eventually counter a propaganda message.

When press releases are analyzed, the authors of the articles reveal themselves through the language that they use. Further, what people perceive and how they think are restricted by the language they speak. If this is true, an analyst must be free of any culture bias and have a comprehensive understanding of the region from which the propaganda is issued. Libyans and Iranians are Islamic; as a result, their values differ from the values often expressed by Westerners.[1]

ELEMENTS OF PROPAGANDA

A sophisticated terrorist organization is objective-oriented. Consequently, terrorist leaders assess the probable impact on both the target audience and their own organization before undertaking a specific operation. In the rhetoric of the Tupamaros, a guerrilla group that was active in Uruguay in the early 1970s, this process is referred to as a *"coyuntura* assessment." A dialectical approach to decision making, the coyuntura format is used by terrorists to reach a balance between the positive and negative ramifications of their actions. For example, an incipient terrorist group in need of money may decide to rob banks, thus subjecting its members to possible apprehension by the police. The alternative is the curtailment of organizational growth by financial constraints.

Conversely, an astute terrorist organization may choose to kidnap a prominent diplomat or business personality, demanding ransom to enhance its finances. In this instance, the group is willing to trade off some loss of its popular image for the opportunity to demonstrate its unswerving resolve and capability to implement its programs.[2]

Operational success for a terrorist group, however, requires media coverage. Therefore, when targeting personalities for kidnapping or assassination, terrorist planners assess the probable media impact. They anticipate that the killing of a prominent person will command front-page press coverage. However, since most dignitaries are guarded by protective-service details, the risks to terrorists who confront them are great.

Terrorists have discovered alternative means to garner page-one coverage, for example, by targeting a person of lesser repute for kidnapping and carefully manipulating the abduction over a sustained period of time. Eventually, a protracted kidnapping of almost anyone will be hyped up by the media.

In 1948, Harold Lasswell, a political scientist, developed a propaganda-analysis model that may be displayed as two units:

(A) Communication component   (B) Research area
    (Sender) Who   Control analysis
    (Messages) Says what   Content analysis
    (Medium) In what channel   Media analysis
    (Receiver) To whom   Audience analysis
    (Result) With what effect   Effect analysis[3]

Elizabeth Briant Lee of the Institute for Propaganda Analysis has developed "The Tricks of the Trade," which is a list of methods that are used by professional propagandists, including the following seven tricks:

- *Name calling*: giving an idea a bad label. It is used to make people reject and condemn the idea without examining the evidence.
- *Glittering generality*: associating something with a "virtue word." It is used to make people accept and approve the thing without examining the evidence.
- *Transfer* carries the authority, sanction, and prestige of something respected and revered over to something else in order to make the latter acceptable. It carries authority, sanction, and disapproval to cause people to reject and disapprove something the propagandist would have them reject and disapprove.
- *Testimonial* consists in having some respected or hated person say that a given idea or program or product or person is good or bad.
- *Plain folks* is the method by which a speaker attempts to convince people that he and his ideas are good because they are "of the people," the "plain folks."
- *Card stacking* involves the selection and use of facts or falsehoods, illustrations or distractions, and logical or illogical statements, in order to give the best or the worst possible cause for an idea, program, person, or product.
- *Bandwagon* has as its theme "Everybody—at least all of us—is doing it." The propagandist uses it to convince people that all members of a group to which they belong are accepting his program and that they must therefore follow the crowd and "jump on the bandwagon."[4]

A working knowledge of these propaganda models, combined with a familiarity of semantic principles, enhances an analyst's ability to dissect and counter propaganda.

Until the turn of the century, some linguists assumed that language was a neutral medium through which thought is expressed. The adage "sticks and stones may break my bones, but names will never harm me," however, is not accurate because words do indeed influence human behavior. Some linguists go one step further. They contend that what we perceive and how we think are restricted by the language we speak. When analyzing propaganda, therefore, analysts must be aware of not only the content of the message but also its context.

Additionally, analysts should look for inconsistencies or language paradoxes. Conflicts may be bold and glaring or they may be subtle and undetected. The use of disclaimers is one technique propagandists rely on to produce subtle conflicts. Disclaimers, statements which may appear either before or after a message, often disavow what was just said. One way to effectively use a disclaimer is to boast in glaring generalities, appearing to favor an action, a person, and then, later, to embed in a seemingly unimportant sentence a specific, concrete fact that contradicts the original claim.

A paradox confuses, and confusion creates uncertainty. Counterintelligence may use paradox to generate disinformation, which is a pattern of communication designed to influence a targeted audience's sense of reality.[5] Propagandists try to disinform readers, providing an incentive for prospective supporters to restructure reality in a way that justifies a terrorist's cause. Paul Watzlavick explains that "once we have arrived at a solution...our investment in this solution becomes so great that we may prefer to distort reality to fit our solution rather than sacrifice the solution."[6]

Words are powerful. They influence thought and behavior. S.I. Hayakawa's "ladder of abstraction" can help us to understand language. According to Hayakawa, words can be concrete or abstract. The more concrete a word is, the greater the number of people who agree upon its meaning. Consequently, a word can be said to be specific or factual. As we move up the ladder of abstraction, we generalize more, getting less and less specific. This movement paves the way for misinterpretations and conflict.[7]

ANALYZING PRESS RELEASES

The Ayatollah Khomeini's Iranian government once placed an advertisement in a major American newspaper. Costing about $18,000 for a single page, the advertisement included an accompanying statement in which the Iranian embassy in Washington, D.C., stated that it was running the advertisement because the Ayatollah's message had been "only briefly and selectively referred to by the media."[8] The embassy also said, "we print his message here for his intended audience, the people of the United States." The advertisement contained the 3,500 word text of a one-hour Iranian television address. It was an astute attempt to manipulate the media, since the advertisement ran on the same day that the Ayatollah ordered the release of black and female hostages.

By utilizing the methods previously described, analysts were able to interpret Khomeini's messages in this advertisement, which was entitled "Ayatollah Khomeini Defines His Stance in Respect to Embassy Occupation," and to portions of a book called *Ayatollah Khomeini's Mein Kampf*,

Islamic Government.[9] Insights derived from this examination of his philos-ophy were used to pierce the veil that enshrouded the Khomeini regime.

On June 29, 1981, American government officials said there was little information available about Iran that was not in the public domain. "We have virtually no assets in Iran," an official said.[10] But the methods described in this chapter could have reduced the confusion and distortion associated with Khomeini's remarks and Fidel Castro's manipulation of politics in Ecuador at the start of the 1980s.

ATTEMPT TO DESTABILIZE ECUADOR

On May 24, 1981, President Roldos Aquilera of Ecuador was killed in an airplane crash near his country's southern border with Peru. Although his election in April 1979 was widely viewed in Ecuador and in other countries as a victory of left-wing, populist politics, Roldos Aquilera's presidency was highlighted by his effort to make democracy work after almost a decade of military rule. His attempt to maintain the support of the poor masses, the oligarchy, and the military, while keeping friendships with a wide spectrum of countries in the Western Hemisphere, however, stamped him as a middle-of-the-road president. Consequently, his political style eventually led to feuds with his former supporters in Congress.[11]

Additionally, Roldos Aquilera wanted to maintain close ties with the Sandinista leaders in Nicaragua. This policy irritated some factions in the military and disturbed rightist elements. He sought to counterbalance the unrest by precipitating a small border war with Peru. This conflict was widely believed by diplomats to be a move to have the Organization of American States (O.A.S.) debate the issue of Ecuador's vaguely drawn boundaries.

Enhanced politically among some civilians and the military by the border war, Roldos Aquilera stepped up his diplomatic efforts to isolate his country from terrorism sponsored by the Marxist-oriented governments of Cuba and Nicaragua. His strategy was aborted when Castro gave his own political interests utmost priority.

On February 13, 1981, 31 heavily armed Cubans seeking political asylum stormed the Ecuadorian embassy in Havana and took three diplomats as hostages. The Havana government was anxious to prevent a repetition of the April 1980 incident involving 10,000 Cubans who packed themselves into the Peruvian embassy compound seeking asylum. *Granma*, the official Cuban daily newspaper, said that the takeover of the Ecuadorian embassy was an inevitable result of the protection given earlier by Peruvian diplomats to disaffected elements who forced their way past embassy guards. But the newspaper went on to say that Cuban commandos would not be used to retake the embassy until the Ecuadorian authorities asked for help.[12]

Obviously, Castro was anxious, at least publicly, to preserve his link with the Quito government. Quito and Havana had resumed diplomatic relations in 1979, after a ten-year break, when Ecuador returned to civilian rule under Roldos Aquilera. Confronted with a rash of anti-Communist activity on his island and anxious to sustain his charismatic image—a tough, cigar-smoking, military-fatigue-clad figure who is always in control—Fidel Castro viewed the seizure of the Ecuadorian embassy as a paradox.

Initially, the Havana government cordoned off the embassy building but refused to give in to the demands of the would-be emigrants, who were demanding political asylum and safe conduct out of the country. The Cubans, however, did promise to respond if criminals unleashed physical aggression against the kidnapped persons. Four days after the takeover, however, all the Ecuadorian diplomats were released. Additionally, the hostage-takers turned over their weapons to the Cuban authorities but did not surrender.[13]

Although the dangers to the foreign diplomats had been eliminated, Cuban commandos were perhaps directed not to protract the siege situation because of its probable negative impact on Castro's domestic political posture. Instead, they staged a lightning raid on the Ecuadorian embassy and seized the dissidents. The Havana government claimed that it had waited for the Quito government's agreement before moving in to end the takeover. Ecuador, however, had promised earlier to permit the dissidents, who had demanded political asylum, to stay in the embassy, under its "protection and care," if they gave up their weapons and released the ambassador and the two other hostages.

On February 21, 1981, the government of Ecuador said in an official statement that it had protested to Cuba over the seizure of its embassy by Cuban security forces. "This operation has not been authorized by the government of Ecuador, which calls on the government of Cuba to respect the lives of the persons taken from the embassy," the statement said.[14]

Recognizing the vulnerability of Roldos Aquilera to rightist elements at home, Castro could have contrived the embassy siege to short-circuit Ecuador's movement in the direction of liberal democracy by providing the rationale for a military takeover. Additional evidence that the mission seizure was a contrivance were the observations that noted a high Cuban official, reported to be Castro or his brother Raul, the Defense Minister, was present as the Cuban assault team assembled for its attack. This unit completed its mission without "firing a shot." Havana said no one was injured. Furthermore, it was revealed that most of the Cubans in the takeover group could have obtained permission to emigrate legally.

Once the exceptionally well-directed and controlled Cuban troops had stabilized the situation, it was evident that Castro used the situation to demonstrate his hard-line antiterrorist policy to both his followers at home and the international community. He also used it as a vehicle to disparage the American Central Intelligence Agency, whom leftists accused of manipulating antigovernment elements in Cuba and elsewhere in Latin America. On March 6, 1981, the Cuban government charged that Portugal's chargé d'affaires in Havana helped the C.I.A. to plan the takeover of the Ecuadorian embassy.15

Although Roldos Aquilera's government's ability to function at home was reduced as a consequence of the seizure of his country's mission in Havana, the popular masses—his power base—permitted him to govern with a semblance of authority. However, his support from this area eroded once it became evident that he intended not to use Ecuador's increasing wealth from oil exports to implement many of the promised social programs that helped to get him elected. Additionally, the liberal elite and the deprived classes were particularly outraged once it was realized that the border war with Peru threatened to drain the economy and endanger hopes for a better life for the millions of poor voters who supported the former president. Although minor in terms of casualties, the war strained relations between Peru and Ecuador and further unsettled the government of Roldos Aquilera.16

Shortly before his death, the Ecuadorian president tried to forestall further deterioration of his political position by identifying and eliminating causes that could be manipulated by terrorist elements known to be lying dormant in Ecuadorian society. Of particular concern to him were terrorist movements akin to the Colombian movement of April 19 (M–19) and Maoist terrorist groups, such as *Sendero Luminoso* (Shining Path) of Peru, a band of dynamiters. Both of these groups have been linked to Castro.

Some elements among the Colombian, Peruvian, and Ecuadorian military insist that Ecuador was being used by these terrorists as a safe haven for training their cadres in the techniques of clandestine warfare and technology and as a propaganda base. Costa Rica was once exploited by various Central American Communist organizations for similar purposes. Roldos Aquilera feared that Communist-contrived unrest in Ecuador would trigger a military takeover in his country and the installation of a military government. He knew that military rule meant stern enforcement practices that could precipitate a leftist countercoup. This scenario was often seen elsewhere in Latin America, as Communist agitators, directed by Castro, exploited those who were oblivious to his role.

GUEVARA'S "LOST" DIARIES AN UPSET FOR BOLIVIANS

Disinformation was once used to undercut the government of Bolivia. When Jorge Crespo was foreign minister of Bolivia, he said that Ernesto (Ché) Guevara's diaries "are historical documents that belong to our national patrimony. It is part of international snobbery to want them as a relic. But they were stolen and we want them back." Crespo claimed that the papers were stolen from the Bolivian military archives where they were stored after Guevara, the Cuban revolutionary theoretician, was captured and killed in October 1967. At the time, Guevara was trying to organize guerrilla operations in the mountains and jungles of Bolivia. Crespo objected to the sale of the documents by Sotheby's, a London-based auction house.

About a year after they were taken from Guevara, the diaries were stored in a shoebox in an office occupied by a Bolivian intelligence unit at the La Paz headquarters of the high command. Members of the government, including two Communist cabinet members, and military leaders were shocked when a search of their archives, prompted by the Sotheby auction announcement, uncovered the empty shoebox but no diaries.

By implicating military intelligence in the theft of the documents, Crespo bolstered the belief, held by some Bolivians, that their police and the military were disloyal. On June 30, 1984, elements of both services attempted to overthrow the government and install a conservative faction. The takeover was aborted by the government. Probably, Crespo was aware of the allegation that attributed the theft of the documents to the director of the military intelligence section. The charge, however, was not substantiated.

The attempt to overthrow the Bolivian government was investigated by a group that included the commanders of a recently formed police narcotics strike force known in Bolivia as the *Leopardos*. Trained and equipped by the United States to control Bolivia's cocaine trade, the 150 men assigned to this unit try to interdict heavily armed drug traffickers as they move their cargo through the country's hinterlands. American financing was also used to equip a special 30-man detective squad that was trained by agents of the United States Drug Enforcement Administration (D.E.A.) to pursue the big traffickers.

The image of the Leopardos and the special detective squad was tainted by their involvement in the attempted coup. Military intelligence was cast as traitorous because of its alleged link to the theft of the Guevara papers. This smear campaign set back the Reagan administration's effort to disrupt Bolivia's cocaine trade, because it was believed that personnel assigned to Bolivia's security forces could not be effective enforcers until they regained the trust and confidence of their countrymen. Meanwhile, Cuban-trained cadres organized guerrilla bands in rural areas and tried to infiltrate the tin-miners' union and various student groups.

The death of Ché Guevara in Bolivia in 1967, as he was attempting to organize a people's war, is regarded as the most serious setback that Fidel Castro had received since his forces seized Cuba. Also it was evidence that a hand-picked band of guerrillas, who were trained to evade a poorly equipped army, could not win a guerrilla struggle without the support of the local populace. In the guerrillas' area of operation, peasants helped the army, and it is widely believed that their information provided the direction for the Bolivian troops who netted Guevara—a onetime leader of the Cuban Communist regime.[17]

USE OF DISINFORMATION IN INDIA

Disinformation, concocted by the Soviet Union and its allies, is being continually manufactured and circulated. Some of it is used to thwart the activities of American intelligence agents who are trying to rebuild human sources of information at critical overseas locations. By smearing the United States, while simultaneously convincing a targeted audience to accept the lie, Soviet disinformation stymies the development of American foreign intelligence networks.

Quoting unidentified Indian intelligence officials, the *Indian Express* once said that the C.I.A. "masterminded" the moving of weapons, through clandestine channels and networks, to the Sikh terrorists who died in an Indian army assault on the Golden Temple in Amritsar, on June 6, 1984. At the time, India's Prime Minister Indira Gandhi believed that somehow the C.I.A. had interfered in India's internal affairs, even though her analysis was pure speculation. Some of her political foes, in the forthcoming national election, did not consider the notion of foreign manipulation and collusion sufficiently persuasive; regardless, the rumor spread throughout the subcontinent.

Media distribution of stories alluding to the involvement of the

C.I.A. in Indian internal affairs and the tendency of people, particularly those who watch television, to believe the tales have smeared the reputation of the American intelligence agency.[18] The effort of the agency to perform in accordance with established procedures and within the ambit of Congressional oversight goes unnoted. Television viewers often confuse fictional renderings of covert operations with the routine functions of the C.I.A.

Instead of sniping at American intelligence, Americans should ask: Who stands to benefit the most from unrest in India? For years, Mrs. Gandhi claimed that the turmoil in her country was sparked by a "foreign hand." Politically, India means less to the Soviet Union than it does to the United States. Peace in a region that is ablaze with warfare—Iraq versus Iran, and the Russians trying to subdue the Afghans—is an American objective. Perhaps Moscow's dialecticians have concluded that the continuing Indian unrest will be interpreted as a warning sign by American and Chinese leaders. However, the improved political relations between Washington and Peking have caused uneasiness in Moscow, a condition arrested only by a slowdown in Sino-American harmony.

Thus, the rage that was expressed in some Iranian circles as a consequence of Moscow's involvement in Afghanistan was counterbalanced by contrived physical evidence (weapons and documents) that linked the United States to the terrorism unleashed by the Sikhs.

SOVIET DISINFORMATION TECHNIQUES

Soviet disinformation operations are conducted in various parts of the world by the K.G.B. The local Communist party of each country and its front organizations provide the distribution apparatus for the Soviet distortions. These disinformation programs are particularly sophisticated, containing some critical passage about the Soviet Union to make them more credible to the West. Disinformation employs fraudulent documents and widely disseminates tales based on them. It also includes the clandestine planting of information by one power to the disadvantage of another power or group.

With expertise in Western paperwork-routing procedures, typefaces, and paper watermarks, the K.G.B. periodically circulates excellent forgeries of internal C.I.A. memorandums, classified United States Army manuals, and correspondence of the North Atlantic Treaty Organization (NATO). Alleging that there were C.I.A. links to the insurgency in India was once a popular theme in the K.G.B.'s disinformation campaign.[19]

THE PANAMANIAN LINK TO AMERICAN DISINFORMATION

If a senior Panamanian official is to be believed, the United States is not to be absolved from the taint associated with bogus operations. On February 3, 1988, Jose I. Blandon, once an advisor to General Manuel Noriega, Panama's military leader, said he arranged a deal involving the delivery of aid to the anti-Sandinista faction in Nicaragua in exchange for American support for international bank loans. According to Blandon, the Reagan administration tried to prove that the Sandinista government was exporting its revolution to other countries in Central America. Thus, in 1986, it devised a covert operation that involved the government of Panama as the linchpin. The Central American country's role was to arrange a shipment of East German-made arms and vehicles that would be seized in El Salvador and falsely linked to the Sandinistas. This charade was unmasked in 1986 as a consequence of Noriega's being linked by a reporter to illegal activities.

The *Pia Vesta*, the ship which was used to haul the weapons from East Germany, was seized by Panamanian officials. According to sources in the United States Congress, the cargo being moved by the vessel was arranged by a Swiss arms broker who was tied to the French foreign ministry's security service.

At one time, Noriega had directed the G-2, Panama's security service. He was the handpicked successor of Colonel Omar Torrijos, the previous Panamanian strongman who was killed in a plane crash. As director of G-2, Noriega managed a network of pilots who flew arms to the Sandinistas when they were trying to unseat the Nicaraguan government of Anastasio Somoza.[20] Obviously, Noriega was interested in cash flow; the source of his income was secondary to the balances in his financial accounts.

COLLAPSE OF THE PUBLIC SAFETY PROGRAM

In 1952, the United States began its Public Safety Program within the Agency for International Development (A.I.D.) because it realized that the task of controlling terrorism involved the whole range of police skills. In 1974, while speaking before a Congressional committee, who were holding hearings on terrorism and counterterrorism, Ernest W. Lefever said that "the civil police are the first line of defense against all challenges to established order, including acts of terrorism or plots to commit such acts."

The United States Congress terminated the Public Safety Program in 1974 because agents of the program were accused of training officers who represented "oppressive governments." Uganda, when it was governed by Idi Amin and Iran, under Shah Mohammad Reza Pahlavi, allegedly used these officers to conduct torture sessions and other brutal activities.

Prior to its termination, agents of the Public Safety Program trained more than 7,000 police officers and technicians from 73 countries in the skills needed to cope with terrorists and to perform routine police tasks, such as patrol, criminal investigation, and crowd control. A.I.D. provided equipment, mostly vehicles and communications gear, to eligible foreign police services. It did not, however, ship the electric shock wands that were designed for crowd control and the "sickening gas" that caused nausea, as was claimed by those who derided the police program.

In his remarks to the Congressional committee, Lefever said:

> From the beginning of the Public Safety effort in 1954, no advisor in any of the 49 assisted countries has been accused by the government of interfering improperly in their internal affairs and none has been declared persona non grata. No assisted government has ever requested the termination of a public safety effort in its country.[21]

Regardless of Lefever's remarks, and similar statements by other experts, the American involvement in the training of foreign police ended. Thus, the forensic and other skills needed by police to unmask deception, including those required to counter deceit, were no longer disseminated abroad.

NOTES

1. David L. Altheide and John M. Johnson, *Bureaucratic Propaganda* (Boston: Allyn & Bacon, 1980), p. 13–23.
2. Arturo C. Porzecanski, *Uruguay's Tupamaros, the Urban Guerrilla* (New York: Frederick A. Praeger, 1973), pp. 82–83.
3. Harold D. Lasswell, "The Structure and Function of Communication in Society," in *The Communication of Ideas*, ed. Lyman Bryson (New York: Harper & Row, 1948), p. 37.
4. Alfred McClung Lee and Elizabeth Briant Lee, *The Fine Art of Propaganda* (San Francisco: International Society for General Semantics, 1979), pp. 22–25.
5. Paul Watzlavick, *How Real is Real* (New York: Random House, 1976), p. 48.
6. Ibid., p. 54.
7. S.I. Hayakawa, *Language in Thought and Action* (New York: Harcourt, Brace & World, 1964), p. 179.
8. "Ayatollah Khomeini Defines His Stance in Respect to Embassy Occupation," *The New York Times*, November 18, 1979, p. 63.
9. Ayatollah Ruhollah Khomeini, *Islamic Government* (New York: Manor Books, 1979).
10. Bernard Gwertzman, "Haig Denies U.S. Role in Bombing: Aides Fear New Round of Disorders," *The New York Times*, June 30, 1981, p. 11.
11. "Ecuadorian Leader Dies in Plane Crash," *The New York Times*, May 25, 1981, p. 1.

12. "Cuba Refuses to Make Deal for Hostages," *The Star Ledger* (Newark, N.J.), February 15, 1981, p. 4.
13. "Cuba Seizes 29 Holding Embassy," *The New York Times*, February 22, 1981, p. 10.
14. "Ecuador Protests to Cuba," *The New York Times*, February 22, 1981, p. 10.
15. "Portugal Recalls Diplomat from Cuba in a Protest," *The New York Times*, March 18, 1981, p. 5.
16. Edward Schumacher, "Behind Ecuador War, Long-Smoldering Resentment," *The New York Times*, February 10, 1980, p. 2.
17. John B. Wolf, "Lost Guevara Works Implicate Disloyal Bolivian Intelligence," *New York City Tribune*, July 18, 1984, p. 2.
18. Serge Schmemann, "Soviet Press Steps up Hints of Involvement by the U.S.," *The New York Times*, November 2, 1984, p. 18 and idem, "Soviet Press Hints at a Bigger Plot," ibid., November 1, 1984, p. 23.
19. John Barron, *K.G.B.: The Secret Work of Soviet Secret Agents* (New York: E. P. Dutton, 1974), pp. 164–186.
20. Stephen Engelberg with Elaine Sciolino, "A U.S. Frame-Up of Nicaragua Charged," *The New York Times*, February 4, 1988, p. 1.
21. *Hearings Before the Subcommittee on the Near East and South Asia of the Committee on Foreign Affairs, House of Representatives* (Washington, D.C., U.S. Government Printing Office, 1974), pp. 38–42, 207–219.

4

ANTITERRORIST INTELLIGENCE

Intelligence operations were a key component of the Reagan administration's antiterrorist policy and were upgraded by William F. Casey, who served as director of the Central Intelligence Agency (C.I.A.) from January 28, 1981, to January 29, 1987.[1]

On October 23, 1983, the headquarters of the United States Marine contingent in Beirut, Lebanon, was demolished when explosives packing the power of 12,000 pounds of TNT detonated. The charge was concealed in the back of a Mercedes truck that had managed to enter the compound. This explosion emphasized that technical surveillance (satellite imagery), upon which the C.I.A. relies for a considerable amount of its information, must be supplemented with data gleaned from human sources of information when monitoring terrorists.[2]

A severe shortage of qualified agents plagued the C.I.A. and the other American intelligence agencies when Casey was appointed director. Thus, it was difficult for these organizations to make an accurate and expeditious analysis of the information being funneled to them. Data are usually evaluated by assigning others to gather details about the same matter. This was a slow and ponderous process to use when people to do this work were in such short supply. As a result, much of the information the United States received on terrorists went out to the field undigested. "Too much is almost worse than none at all," said a Pentagon official. "Guys out in the field (users) don't have the time or the assets to sift through all that stuff." Analysts, who are typically housed in a remote facility, screen and verify the data when enough is available for them to assess for accuracy and reliability. Those who manage the collection and analytical processes that are keyed to the activities of terrorists have to wade through an extraordinary amount of fragmentary information, some of it lies, or exaggerations, or distortions.[3]

BOMBINGS IN BEIRUT

After the bombing of the United States Marines' complex in Beirut, the American intelligence agencies were strengthened and streamlined. The Department of Defense (D.O.D.) formed three new antiterrorist organizations. The United States Navy's Antiterrorist Indication and Warning Alert Center, which is one of these new groups, was formed on December 19, 1984, and assigned the mission of gathering antiterrorist information from domestic and foreign sources and distributing a finished product. Often, its report is a specially tailored terrorist-threat assessment, released to designated U.S. Navy and Marine commanders.

Charged with the sifting out of information that is not immediately useful to operating units, the Alert Center was established as a consequence of the sharp criticism that was directed against the U.S. Navy by a Pentagon review panel that set up after the bombing of the marines' compound in Beirut.[4] This commission revealed that the marine commanders in Lebanon received volumes of intelligence information, but none specific enough to have prevented the attack. Also, it mentioned that some intelligence reports on the bombing in April 1983 of the American embassy in Beirut contained some information that would have been useful to the marines. These reports, however, were never sent to them.[5]

The reviewers said its most important message was that terrorism had become tantamount to an act of war; a conflict in which the United States military was ill-equipped to engage. Among the commission's other recommendations was a suggestion that "the Secretary of Defense direct the development of doctrine, planning, organization, force structure, education and training necessary to defend against and counter terrorism." Headed by Admiral Robert L. J. Long, retired, the commission also noted that the Defense Department's official definition of terrorism, used by officers for guidance while combating it, did not recognize that terrorism could be sponsored by a government.

President Reagan said, " 'I wholeheartedly agree' with the Long Commission's finding that the military is not adequately equipped to fight state-sponsored terrorists." He said that "the United States needed to 'systematically redevelop our approach to the problem.' "[6]

After the bombing in Beirut, officers involved with training units at Camp LeJeune, North Carolina, the base where all marines sent to the Middle East were housed, said that no special emphasis was given to counterterrorism. Colonel Robert B. Johnston, Commander of the Eighth Marine Regiment, the parent organization for four of the five units sent to Lebanon, remarked, "People have this notion that there's this magic package of counterterrorism training that would have prevented that attack." But really it's just common sense. "Only about 5 percent" of the training Marines received before going to Beirut is keyed to their specific mission. The rest is general training.[7]

Viewing Middle East terrorism as a new dimension in warfare, the Long Commission recommended an active antiterrorist policy. It believed that a reactive policy surrendered the initiative to the terrorists. In its concluding remarks, the commission suggested that the Defense Department recognize the importance of state-sponsored terrorism and take appropriate measures to deal with it.

Upon receipt of these recommendations, the Joint Chiefs of Staff urged all the services to find military solutions to terrorist attacks. Some military analysts suggested that the Pentagon upgrade the Green Berets, an outfit trained for countersubversion operations. The same people also emphasized that successful antiterrorist operations should not be passive; rather, a specialized force would have to take the offensive against the terrorists.

An offensive action against terrorists by special-force-type units could alter the American political posture in a country, changing it from a peace-keeping to a punitive military role. However, if terrorism is to be defeated, it must be done by specialists using innovative tactics. If this is to be accomplished, the Pentagon must view terrorism as a form of warfare that requires the development of new response patterns and the abandonment of some of its traditional methods.[8]

ANTITERRORIST LEGISLATION

On April 26, 1984, President Reagan proposed a set of additional measures to combat state-sponsored terrorism. He sent to the United States Congress four bills intended to help detect and prosecute people involved in international terrorism. This package authorized rewards of up to $500,000 for information on acts of terrorism in the United States or abroad, broadened laws against kidnapping, and strengthened laws against aircraft hijacking and sabotage in accordance with existing international agreements. Other provisions of this package included prison terms of up to 10 years and large fines and forfeitures for people who provide training, support, and similar assistance to nations or groups found, by the Secretary of State, to be involved in terrorism. Also, the bill specified that the validity of the Secretary of State's designation of a foreign nation or group as engaged in "acts or likely acts of international terrorism" harmful to the United States could not be questioned by the courts or raised as a defense in a prosecution.

In a written statement released by the White House, President Reagan said that the legislation was aimed at the provision of assistance to countries that support terrorism and use it as a foreign-policy tool. According to the statement, state-sponsored terrorism was the cause of "the great majority of terrorist murders and assassinations."

Donald Rumsfeld, President Reagan's special Middle East envoy, resigned his post on May 18, 1984, to return to private business. In an exchange of letters released by the White House, Rumsfeld wrote the President:

> The conflicts in the area (Middle East) are deep-seated. While a continuation of our steady efforts is vital, you have rightly identified the growth of state-sponsored terrorism and the use of surrogates to mask accountability as profound threats to hope for progress in the area. A broad public understanding of the nature and magnitude of these threats is necessary.[9]

CONTROLLING TERRORISM IN THE UNITED STATES

The upsurge in terrorism abroad prompted those responsible for controlling terrorism within the United States to upgrade their respective agencies' antiterrorist capabilities. F.B.I. Director William H. Webster, while testifying before a congressional committee on behalf of his agency's budget request, said that law-enforcement computers monitored the 85 to 95 people the Secret Service regards as "most dangerous" to the President. Secret Service Director John R. Simpson told Webster that the computer program enabled his agency to know the whereabouts of those individuals.[10]

The F.B.I. computer, known as the National Crime Information Center (N.C.I.C.), is the heart of one of the largest and most elaborate communications systems in the world. It links 64,000 federal, state, and local justice agencies. Once limited to holding information about people who had been officially accused of a crime, the computer now holds in addition the names of individuals who pose a threat to the President of the United States. For example, when a police officer, anywhere in the United States stops a person whose name is on the Secret Service list and asks the N.C.I.C. for information about the individual, the Secret

Service is informed immediately of that person's whereabouts and the police officer is advised that the person is considered dangerous by the Secret Service.

Criteria used by the Secret Service to assess "dangerousness" include the "facts of the action" that brought the individual to the agency's attention, his or her potential for or capability of carrying out any threat, a background investigation that includes criminal and mental inquiries, and an interview, in most cases.

Jerry S. Parr, an assistant director of the Secret Service, said that the computer system is not subject to abuse and that any such abuse, were it even to be attempted, would be readily apparent. However, a professor affiliated with Pace University's Law School in New York City maintained that the relevant law and judicial systems allow the F.B.I. to disseminate only factual information, such as details about a person's arrests and convictions.[11]

Restrictions placed on law-enforcement and intelligence agencies after the Watergate incident and the subsequent probe of the F.B.I. and the C.I.A. by the United States Congress impeded the American antiterrorist effort at home and abroad. Also, the Iran-Contra affair generated a hue and cry for further congressional oversight of the clandestine services. Covert methods, used primarily to identify links between terrorist movements and foreign organizations, were the primary target of attack.

Technical Means for Collecting Intelligence

The leakage of highly sensitive information, in part related to the investigations of the intelligence services by congressional committees, made it extremely difficult for American agents, who were operating in foreign areas, to develop meaningful contacts with persons who believe their identities may one day be revealed to the public. Although human intelligence (humint) is needed to gain access to motives, intentions, thoughts, and plans, American privacy legislation has caused the C.I.A. to rely inordinately on technical means of collection.[12] Thus, in January 1979, members of the United States Congress should not have been surprised when the House of Representatives Permanent Select Committee on Intelligence reported that the C.I.A. had produced no assessments, utilizing sources who were opposed to the Shah of Iran, for two years, ending in November 1977, and produced none in the first quarter of 1978.[13]

Emphasizing earth–satellite photography as the vital element in its ongoing program of modern intelligence research and analysis, the C.I.A. now has earth-orbiting vehicles that are capable of transmitting back to the ground the same high level of photographic imagery that the U-2 reconnaissance aircraft had provided of Cuba, earlier in the late 1950s. This extraterrestrial surveillance operation has used cameras capable of taking photographs at altitudes higher than 100 miles and accurate enough to record objects the size of a suitcase or even as small as a grenade in a person's hand. Satellite enthusiasts currently boast of orbiting spacecraft whose equipment can read auto license plate numbers in Red Square or pick out the warm outline of footprints left by a terrorist band in the snows of the Pyrenees. Skeptics inside and outside the intelligence community, however, point to an instance, a few years ago, when American intelligence officials could not say for certain (based on satellite information) whether an explosion over the South Atlantic was an atomic detonation or not.

Although widely used by both the United States and the Soviet Union, photographic satellite surveillance has limited capabilities. On the one hand, satellites are very sensitive to weather changes; foul weather and erratic lighting conditions during the winter months can affect their functioning. In addition, since satellite routes are predictable, target countries can halt transmission, feed the satellites deceptive data, or cease their clandestine outdoor activities whenever the crafts are due overhead. Oftentimes, jammers and other deceptive devices are used to distort the signals that are picked up by "ferrets"—the radar- and radio-signal intercept satellites.

Electronic interception satellites, however, are difficult to confuse. The terrorists who seized the *Achille Lauro*, a cruise ship which was sailing in the Eastern Mediterranean, used radios to coordinate their moves. A satellite, properly positioned, could have monitored their transmissions.

The United Kingdom has spent about $750 million to build, loft, and position "Zircon," a signals intelligence satellite that serves as an electronic listening post. It is capable of intercepting radio traffic and other electronic communications from the Soviet Union, Eastern Europe, and the Middle East. For almost two decades, the British have used aerial surveillance as an antiterrorist control measure. Royal Air Force (R.A.F.) photoreconnaissance aircraft, operating from a field in England, supplement the British Army's surveillance effort in Northern Ireland by providing analysts with aerial pictures of the region on a monthly basis. Special photographs, in ordinary color, "false" color, and infrared, are supplied upon request. Infrared photography penetrates cloud cover and operates as well at night as during the day. On a cold night, the warm spots that are left by a person crossing a field stand out as clearly as a bonfire. The film, taken during R.A.F. overflights, is sent to the Joint

Air Reconnaissance Center at an airfield in England for processing and then passed on to the security forces.

American antiterrorist operations also use intelligence gleaned from satellites. The most detailed evidence fed to the United States about Sandinista airfield and military encampments in Nicaragua came from photographs snapped by satellites and reconnaissance planes. Furthermore, American satellites in orbit over the Falkland Islands provided Washington with information about Argentina's military dispositions. These data were passed along to the British.

Approximately forty American military satellites are presently in orbit. However, details of their performance and the information they collect are top secret. Since some of these vehicles are in a north-south polar orbit, this track permits them to pass over each part of the globe every few hours.

Antiterrorist planners have learned to shield their operations from an adversary's reconnaissance satellites. Just prior to the launching of the helicopters that were used in the abortive attempt to rescue the American hostages in Teheran, the United States aircraft carrier U.S.S. *Nimitz* suddenly made a turn and sailed away at top speed to elude detection by Soviet electronic tracking vehicles. During the war in Vietnam, an American assault force, which was training at Eglin Air Force Base in Florida for an operation intended to free prisoners of war, who were being held in a compound near Hanoi, each morning constructed a full-sized wood and canvas replica of the prison camp and each night took it down to prevent Soviet satellites from monitoring their exercise.[14]

Intelligence Support Activity

Intelligence Support Activity (I.S.A.) supplements information obtained from satellite overflights. A far-ranging intelligence organization, I.S.A. has a network of data collectors located in Morocco, Nigeria, Somalia, Sudan, and in 10 Latin American nations. In El Salvador, its operatives gathered information that was used to counter a Communist takeover attempt. I.S.A. personnel also participated in the planning of a 1981 raid into Laos, the objective of which was to discover Americans who were thought to be missing in action since the Vietnam War.

Formed shortly after the aborted 1980 attempt by the United States to rescue hostages from the American embassy in Tehran, I.S.A. had about 50 operatives at its inception. By 1985, the group had expanded to 283. An unnamed special operations officer has said that "the units still exist, but their morale and our ability to use them are in shambles."

According to a media account, former Secretary of Defense Caspar W. Weinberger once ordered the United States Army's secret intelligence unit disbanded. Managing to survive, the I.S.A. was used to collect information on terrorists in Lebanon, among other activities.[15]

John Prados, author of the *President's Secret Wars: CIA and Pentagon Covert Operations since World War II*, writes:

> Though some reports maintain the I.S.A. has functioned as an organization conducting its own operations, other observers believe the unit can be more nearly described as a computerized data-bank managing covert action personnel and logistics resources.[16]

The use of an I.S.A. network in Iran could have facilitated an American effort to organize and unleash an attack from within the country itself. I.S.A. operatives would have been slipped into Tehran and assembled at a point near the embassy for an attack. Thus, the disjointed and tenuous plan involving the assembly of troops and equipment at a landing zone in the Iranian desert would have been shelved.

Restrictions on Intelligence Gathering

Antiterrorist intelligence gathering is a task vital to the attainment of the national mission of the United States. Some members of the Senate, however, have restrained the ability of the American clandestine services to covertly gather information. They advocate that restrictions be placed on the activities of individual law-enforcement officers and intelligence agents who are assigned to field collection. Consequently, in 1978, William H. Webster, then director of the F.B.I., said that his agency had 42 informers on domestic intelligence and terrorism matters. At one time the bureau used approximately 1,300 informers in its single protracted investigation of the Socialist Workers Party.[17]

Additionally, vital intelligence tools needed to gather data to control terrorism and espionage, such as audio surveillance and mail covers, little used since Watergate, have not been relied on. Therefore, information pertaining to some terrorist activities is simply not available. For example, police had little or no access to reliable information about the F.A.L.N. From the group's precise and well-planned movements, intelligence sources inferred that this Puerto Rican liberation organization was highly intelligent, deeply dedicated, and virtually invisible.

Continuing sharp criticism of the domestic intelligence services by United States Congressmen and others focuses mostly on their use of the vital tools needed to conduct protracted operations. These processes and methods are intended to identify links between domestic terrorist movements and foreign governments. The F.B.I. has transferred responsibility for these functions from its intelligence division to its general investigations branch, where they are currently handled like all other criminal cases.[18]

Essentially, individuals who are charged with antiterrorist information-gathering assignments are obligated to develop those human sources of information who can provide accurate, reliable, and pertinent data on a continuing basis and in crisis situations of an emergency nature. Although these "sources" are frequently varied, consisting of persons in key positions and others adjudged to be performing innocuous tasks, the development of confidence and trust between the agent and his contacts is prerequisite for any meaningful flow of information. But foreign sources are finding it most difficult to adjust to revelations in the media of contacts between American agents and their overseas informants, making it difficult, at this time, for these agents to develop meaningful contacts with people who feel that their identities may one day become public information.[19]

A 1974 congressional report noted that the critical weakness in intelligence collection on Iran had been the lack of widespread contact with Iranians of various persuasions.[20] Consequently, once the United States was confronted with the crisis in Iran, the country suddenly discovered how little it knew about the identities, whereabouts, and organizational tactics of the opposing forces. Thus, the inadequacy of field sources of information narrowed American choices during the Iranian situation, forcing the Carter administration to adopt a policy of voicing support for the Shah, but doing little more than watching, waiting, and hoping.

Lacking the implementation of a meaningful program of domestic and foreign antiterrorist information gathering, the options of the executive branch of government in formulating a strategy to release the American hostages in Tehran were once again limited, as they were during the previous year when the Shah was overthrown. Until American intelligence operatives are able to gain access to vital human sources of intelligence, which tend to gravitate to a strong nation that has its national mission in clear focus and is able to guarantee their anonymity, the proactive antiterrorist capability of the United States must be regarded as marginal.

Inherent in the American democratic process, therefore, are factors that impede the flow of the intelligence required by decision makers to shape a comprehensive antiterrorist response to check terrorism in its incipient stage. These constitutionally derived legal constraints, although not immutable, are altered with caution and are apt to prevail in the United States regardless of the realization, in all branches of the American federal and state governments, that the initial decisions and reactions of a government to a terrorist threat are crucial. Policies and procedures instituted at the onset of a campaign against terror are dependent on intelligence for alacrity and comprehensiveness. Intelligence is used to define the issues at stake, shape the character of the response, and provide the legitimate basis for any termination of the threat.

Inevitably, this paradox of acting within constitutional limitations, while simultaneously ensuring the survival of the state, is perceived by the intelligence community as quixotic. For example, F.B.I. officials once believed that their agency had been too severely restricted in intelligence investigations following the public disclosures in 1976 of allegations that their agents burglarized the homes of militant political figures, leftist suspects, and antiwar radicals. Covert collection methods, including the use of informants and audio surveillance, are closely regulated. Consequently, domestic antiterrorist intelligence activities conducted by the F.B.I. were greatly reduced as a result of the agency's effort to adhere to investigative guidelines.[21]

On November 7, 1983, a time bomb exploded in the Capitol Building in Washington, D.C. Meeting with reporters at F.B.I. headquarters a few days after the blast, Director Webster said that the device detonated in the Capitol had a dual-firing mechanism similar to systems used in other bombs that had exploded in the United States since 1981. Commenting on his agency's investigative activities, Webster said that "the FBI was still trying to decide whether 'it's the same people doing the same thing, or different people getting explosives from the same source, or a teacher teaching a number of people how to do it.' "

On March 14, 1984, Webster, in open testimony before the Senate Judiciary Committee's Subcommittee on Security and Terrorism, said the F.B.I. was hoping to pinpoint a suspect in the bombing of the Capitol. He did not discount the possibility that those involved in the blast were linked with other terrorist groups through the use of the same "safehouse" network and other support systems.[22] As part of his testimony, Webster mentioned that the F.B.I.'s antiterrorist capability was enhanced by Attorney General William French Smith's revision of the Domestic Security Guidelines that were promulgated by Attorney General Edward H. Levi during the Ford administration. Guided by the so-called Smith revision of the Domestic Security Guidelines, Webster told the subcommittee that the F.B.I. was reading and monitoring publications of suspected terrorists, violent, and subversive groups and maintaining a library-type reference system. He said the privacy act precludes the bureau from taking that information and placing it in the file of an individual person who might be a member of such an organization.

The F.B.I.'s antiterrorist investigations are currently conducted in accord with "Criminal Intelligence Investigations," a section of "Guidelines on General Crimes, Racketeering Enterprise and Domestic Security/ Terrorism Investigations." Issued on March 7, 1983, by Attorney General

Smith, these guidelines make it somewhat easier for federal agents to investigate groups that try to achieve political or social change through the use of violence. Although not intended to erode protections for lawful, peaceful political dissent, these rules were the first comprehensive revision of the Levi investigative guidelines.

In addition to maintaining a proactive program designed to learn about acts of terror before they happen, the F.B.I. also collects and analyzes field information gathered by specially trained agents situated throughout the United States. This effort has enhanced the bureau's antiterrorist capabilities. In terms of domestic groups, the F.B.I. relies on leads from informants.[23]

Electronic Surveillance and Videotapes

During the Reagan administration, court-ordered electronic surveillance (wiretaps) that were operated by federal authorities increased. Figures contained in the annual *Report on Applications for Orders Authorizing or Approving the Interception of Wire or Oral Communications* show that there were 130 federal taps sanctioned by court orders in 1982 compared with 108 in 1981. This report is prepared by the administrative office of the federal court system in Washington, D.C.

In the four years of the Carter administration (1977 to 1981), the report listed 77, 81, 67, and 79 taps, respectively. In the two full years of the Ford administration, 1975 and 1976, there were 108 and 137 taps. The numbers for the Nixon years reached a peak in 1971 when 285 taps were approved. The report also adds that the cost of federal wiretapping has increased by about 50 percent since 1982 and now averages about $34,000 per tap.[24]

The United States Attorney in Manhattan, according to the report, authorized two federal wiretap operations in 1982 that were "related to a murder investigation," but not otherwise identified. These investigations involved 50 agents over a period of 169 days and cost a total of $2,007,935. Wiretapping expenses included tape decks, telephone connections, the rental of office space as "fronts" (interception points), and manpower.

Reportedly, the F.B.I. used scores of expensive Swiss-made Nagra tape decks to record the interceptions. These devices are regarded by experts as the "Rolls-Royce of reel-to-reel electronics." Additional and unreported costs were incurred in electronically enhancing some of the conversations to improve their audibility when they are played before a jury.[25]

Of the average of 1,082 intercepted conversations per tap, the report said that only 19 percent "produced incriminating evidence." But it said

1,725 federal and state suspects were charged with criminal acts in 1982 as a result of wiretaps; 453 of them were convicted.

In 1982, twenty-one states reported the use of wiretaps during the course of criminal investigations: Arizona, Colorado, Connecticut, Delaware, Florida, Georgia, Maryland, Massachusetts, Minnesota, Nebraska, New Hampshire, New Mexico, New Jersey, New York, Oregon, Pennsylvania, Rhode Island, Texas, Utah, Virginia, and Wisconsin. An additional 7 of the 28 nonfederal jurisdictions with local wiretapping statutes made no use of them in 1982: the District of Columbia, Hawaii, Idaho, Kansas, Louisiana, Nevada, and South Dakota.

Some states have imposed most strict limitations on the use of wiretaps; Connecticut, for example, allows no more than 34 judicial orders authorizing such surveillance in any calendar year. It also limits surreptitious entry by the police to install electronic devices to cases in which "no reasonable alternative exists."

In 1982, state prosecutors in the states that permit the use of wiretapping authorized 448 electronic surveillances of this type. This is a decrease from the years 1980 and 1981, when the number was 483. New Jersey alone accounted for 30 percent of the state-installed wiretaps in 1982.

Under the provisions of Title III of the Omnibus Crime Control and Safe Streets Act of 1968, authorizing the use of court-approved wiretaps, federal and state prosecutors who request "wires," and the judges who authorize them, have reporting obligations: numbers of taps and related details must be furnished to the Administrative Office of the United States Courts for inclusion in its annual report.[26]

The F.B.I. also has used videotapes in its investigations of terrorist groups. Winning court permission to use video surveillance in two apartments frequented by four reputed members of the Puerto Rican nationalist group F.A.L.N., the F.B.I. installed two concealed cameras that "rolled" more than 130 hours of tape over six months. Demonstrating "probable cause" to believe that crimes were being planned, the agency based its argument on information from a convicted member of the F.A.L.N. who became an informer.

The federal prosecutors said that their electronic "eyes" recorded bombmaking, weapons stockpiling, the assembly of detonating caps, disguise materials, and false identifications. Edward D. Hegarty, head of the F.B.I.'s Chicago office, said that cameras portray the crime "as it's taking place. That's the beauty of television. It's a far more effective tool than audio."[27]

As the United States rebuilt its military forces during the years of the Reagan administration, the F.B.I. was geared to protect the country from foreign-directed terrorist groups who might attempt to operate within its borders. Director Webster, however, has declined to say whether or not the blast in the Capitol and the bombings of other buildings resulted from foreign backing of groups operating in the United States.

THE VICE-PRESIDENT'S TASK FORCE
ON COMBATTING TERRORISM

George Bush once chaired the Vice-President's Task Force on Combatting Terrorism, a group that emphasized the role of intelligence in controlling terrorism. This task force recommended the establishment of a Consolidated Intelligence Center on Terrorism to collect and analyze information from all agencies engaged in antiterrorist operations. The American effort to control terrorists was viewed as being somewhat disjointed; various federal entities were maintaining their own analysts to transform collected information into intelligence.

Bush's task force, anxious to upgrade the posture of the United States vis-à-vis the terrorists, stated in a report that:

> The addition of such a central facility would improve our capability to under-
> stand and anticipate future terrorist threats, support national crisis manage-
> ment and provide a common data base readily accessible to individual
> agencies. Potentially, this center could be the focus for developing a cadre of
> interagency intelligence analysts specializing in the subject of terrorism.

The formation of a Joint Committee on Intelligence is another recommendation forthcoming from Bush's task force. It said, "Procedures that the Executive Branch must follow to keep the Select Committees informed of intelligence need streamlining." Other recommendations include the establishment of incentives (rewards, immunity from prosecution, U.S. citizenship) for persons who furnish information about the identity or location of terrorists and the closure of loopholes in the Freedom of Information Act.

The *Public Report of the Vice President's Task Force on Combatting Terrorism,* largely overlooked by the media, was published in 1986. Concise and incisive, the report stressed the significance of collecting tactical police intelligence. This information is useful when tracking domestic terrorists and hit teams that are being managed by foreign sources.[28]

Fettered both politically and economically, most American police departments are unable to construct the top-level operational intelligence networks that are required to keep records on extremist groups. Yet these same intelligence networks would be an effective counter to terrorism, in particular, when they contain components that permit the rapid acquisition, analysis, and dissemination of current data.[29]

It is absolutely necessary for a free society to build into its structure the safeguards that it needs to protect basic freedoms. It has been judgmental, however, whether intelligence systems should be included in or omitted from any list of necessary safeguards.

After the second world war, fearful of the designs of the Soviet Union, Congress authorized the creation of the C.I.A. But Congress was also concerned about the designs of the agency itself and specifically provided, in the National Security Act of 1947, that the C.I.A. "shall have no police subpoena, law enforcement, or internal security functions."

APPROACHES TO ANTITERRORISM

The report issued by the Bush task force was timely. An effective American antiterrorist effort necessitated that there be an overlap between the domestic jurisdiction of the F.B.I. and the foreign intelligence function of the C.I.A. Without detailed and specific information on terrorist groups in the United States, it was impossible for C.I.A. agents abroad to be alerted to the foreign travel of hit teams and other terrorists and to identify their international contacts.

However, the statutory definition of C.I.A. authority charged the Director of Central Intelligence with the responsibility for "protecting intelligence sources and methods from unauthorized disclosure." It also forbade the C.I.A. to exercise law enforcement and police powers and to perform an "internal security function." Consequently, only the foreign aspects of domestic terrorism were clearly within the C.I.A.'s jurisdiction. The F.B.I., operating under strict guidelines, had exclusive jurisdiction over domestic counterintelligence activity undertaken to prevent foreign espionage penetrations and leaks of classified information.

Guidelines that are used to curtail terrorism in the United States have worldwide applications. Citing improved intelligence as one of the reasons for a decline in domestic terrorist incidents, Webster believes the American antiterrorist principles can be applied on the international scale. Figures released by the F.B.I. in 1985 listed seven terrorist incidents for the country during the previous year. The prevention of 23 such incidents also was revealed. One hundred acts of domestic terrorism occurred in the United States in 1978, thirteen in 1984.

Webster claims various covert intelligence-gathering techniques have contributed to the F.B.I.'s crusade against terror. These clandestine methods include the active use of informants, undercover agents, and court-ordered electronic surveillance.

Charles Allen, the C.I.A.'s antiterrorism head, has mentioned that his agency and others that are engaged in intelligence operations had doubled their analytical and operational resources since 1984. The C.I.A. was working actively, he said, "to penetrate terrorist networks, mount operations to sow seeds of suspicion among the cadres and among the leaders and identify new technical capabilities." Allen also mentioned that terrorist incidents overseas had increased, almost 800 recorded incidents in 1984 as against 500 in the early 1980s. "Softer, less protected targets," he said, "were being hit by the terrorists, for example, businesses, hotels and restaurants."

Allen, then Attorney General Edwin Meese III, and a number of other government officials cited the American air raid in Libya as a deterrent to terrorists. According to Allen, state-supported terrorism, the variety backed by the Communist bloc and its supporters, decreased after American warplanes hit Qaddafi's state. Praising President Reagan for the Libyan raid, Meese said, "When someone commits an impermissible act, you swat him."

Allen believes that the sharing of intelligence with allies had increased the C.I.A.'s ability to track terrorist operations, disrupt their financial network and supply lines, and preempt terrorist attacks. An information exchange among allies was a key ingredient of any antiterrorist campaign.[30] Thus, an upgraded American antiterrorist intelligence system will further enhance this effort.

NOTES

1. Bob Woodward, *Veil: The Secret Wars of the CIA 1981–1987* (New York: Simon & Schuster, 1987), pp. 35–507.
2. "Marines Sketch of Beirut Bombings," *The New York Times*, October 22, 1983, p. 8.
3. Philip Taubman, "Major Questions Raised on C.I.A.'s Performance," *The New York Times*, November 3, 1983, p. 21.
4. Joel Brinkley, "Report Disputes Marine on Attack," *The New York Times*, December 22, 1983, p. 1.
5. Francis X. Clines, "Weakened Intelligence-Gathering Cited by President in Beirut Blast," *The New York Times*, September 27, 1984, p. 1.
6. B. Drummond Ayres, Jr., "Pentagon Acts on Report about Marine Bombing," *The New York Times*, February 9, 1984, p. 14.
7. Joel Brinkley, "U.S. Called Ill-Equipped to Fight 'On The Cheap' War by Terrorists," *The New York Times*, December 29, 1983, p. 1.
8. Bill Keller, "Conflict in Pentagon Is Seen Harming Commandos' Unity," *The New York Times*, January 6, 1986, p. 1.
9. "Mideast Envoy Resigns," *The Star Ledger* (Newark, N.J.), May 19, 1984, p. 1.
10. "Why the F.B.I. Uses Undercover Agents," *U.S. News & World Report*, August 16, 1982, p. 51.
11. David Burnham, "Secret Service May Get to Use F.B.I. Computer," *The New York Times*, December 25, 1982, p. 1.

12. Stansfield Turner, *Secrecy and Democracy: The CIA in Transition* (Boston: Houghton Mifflin, 1985), pp. 280–285.
13. "Carter Critical of CIA in Iran," *The Home News* (New Brunswick, N.J.), November 24, 1978, p. 3.
14. "Judging Spies and Eyes," *Time*, March 22, 1981, p. 22; "The Motto Is: Think Big, Think Dirty," ibid., February 6, 1978, p. 12; John Noble Wilford, "Eyes In the Sky: Satellites, Uses Growing with Capabilities," *The New York Times*, March 29, 1983, p. C3.
15. "The Secret Army," *Time*, August 31, 1987, pp. 12–14.
16. John Prados, *President's Secret Wars: CIA and Pentagon Covert Operations since World War II* (New York: William Morrow, 1986), p. 376.
17. Nicholas M. Horrock, "Senate Panel Offers Legislation to Curb Intelligence Agents," *The New York Times*, February 10, 1978, p. 1.
18. John M. Crewdson, "FBI Chief Curbs Intelligence Arm in Command Shift," *The New York Times*, August 12, 1976, p. 1 and idem, "F.B.I. To Transfer Socialist Inquiry," ibid, August 17, 1976, p. 15.
19. "C.I.A. Seeks Jail Terms for Disclosure of Agents," *The New York Times*, June 25, 1980, p. 16.
20. Bernard Gwertzman, "House Blames Intelligence Agencies and Policy Makers over Iran," *The New York Times*, January 25, 1979, p. 15.
21. "F.B.I. Domestic Intelligence Found Curbed," *The New York Times*, November 10, 1977, p. 4.
22. Leslie Maitland Werner, "U.S. Undercover Techniques Spur a Debate on Curbs," *The New York Times*, May 27, 1984, p. 40.
23. Leslie Maitland Werner, "U.S. Officials Cite Key Successes in War against Organized Crime," *The New York Times*, November 7, 1983, p. 1.
24. Ben A. Franklin, "Report Says Federal Wiretaps Rose 23% in 82," *The New York Times*, May 1, 1983, p. 21.
25. Ben A. Franklin, "Wiretapping Cost a Record in Trial," *The New York Times*, April 2, 1983, p. 5.
26. "Wiretapping Up," *The New York Times*, May 31, 1983, p. 18; David Burnham, "Panel Cites U.S. Compliance with Law Limiting Wiretaps," *The New York Times*, October 19, 1984, p. B5.
27. "Videotapes of Bomb-Making Pose Judicial Puzzle," *The New York Times*, January 28, 1984, p. 22.
28. John B. Wolf, "Task Force Urges a Central Agency to Fight Terror," *New York City Tribune*, June 17, 1986, p. 2.
29. Richard E. Morgan, *Domestic Intelligence: Monitoring Dissent in America* (Austin: University of Texas Press, 1980), pp. 88–103.
30. Elaine Sciolino, "FBI Chief Hails Gains on Terror," *The New York Times*, August 12, 1986, p. 20.

5

ANTITERRORIST MILITARY UNITS
Organization and Operations

Democratic societies that advocate the use of minimum force to control terrorism and other forms of criminality deploy their regular military units only after the police and the national guard are unable to check an outbreak of violence.

It took a series of hijackings of American aircraft and an assortment of other outrageous acts by Middle East gunmen to push the United States and its allies into a review of their antiterrorist policies and procedures. This analysis was undertaken to determine if additional methods could be devised to enhance the capability of special military units.

Various West European governments have used elite military units to counter terrorists. On December 2, 1975, a 30-man antiterrorist force of the Dutch Marine Corps surrounded a train that had been seized by five armed extremists who were holding 50 hostages at gunpoint. After a siege of 16 days, the terrorists surrendered to the marines.

In 1973, the Italians deployed a specially trained paramilitary police squad to raid an apartment that was being used by a group who were planning to use a shoulder-fired surface-to-air missile (SAM) to shoot down an Israeli airliner. The attack was to have taken place as the passenger jet used Rome's Flumecino Airport for a scheduled arrival or departure.

Great Britain also used its Special Air Services Regiment (S.A.S.) to check terrorists, in particular, gunmen from the Irish Republican Army (I.R.A.) when they operated in rural areas of Northern Ireland. On May 6, 1980, a crack S.A.S. unit stormed the besieged Iranian embassy in London after two hostages were killed. The S.A.S. squad rescued 14 hostages but their maneuver precipitated a gunfight that produced a flaming combat zone.

France, too, has used specially trained personnel, organized in squad-sized units (9 to 12 people), to combat small groups of terrorists. The *Groupe d'Intervention de la Gendarmerie National* (G.I.G.N.) is in the forefront of the French antiterrorist effort. In March 1980, one of its units was airlifted to Martinique, an overseas department of France, where they were used to suppress a strike by a pro-independence group that allegedly received financial and political support from Cuba. In April 1988, a G.I.G.N. detail was airlifted from Paris to New Caledonia to battle a dangerous terrorist uprising.

French antiterrorists have trained other specialized units, including the Saudi Arabian assault teams that retook the Grand Mosque in Mecca on December 3, 1979. Because the Saudi Minister of Internal Affairs and the head of French counterintelligence maintained a close relationship, the French were asked to help the Saudis oust several hundred ultraconservative Muslims from the Islamic shrine.

Israel's General Intelligence and Reconnaissance Unit Number 269 lists the 1972 rescue of 90 hostages aboard a Sabena airliner at Lod Airport and the spectacular rescue operation at Entebbe, Uganda, on July 4, 1976, among its accomplishments. This unit is skilled in the art of hostage rescue.

Geared to function as a police commando unit, West Germany's Border Group 9 is organized into squads of 30 persons and a few smaller specialized teams, including specialists in explosives, weaponry, and other essential skills, and is also experienced in hostage-rescue operations. Formed in 1972 after Arab terrorists attacked and murdered members of the Israeli team at the Olympic Games being held in Munich, Border Group 9 rescued 86 hostages aboard a hijacked Lufthansa jetliner in a daring and perfectly executed surprise attack at Somalia's Mogadishu Airport on October 18, 1977.[1]

THE AMERICAN DELTA FORCE

The successful West German and Israeli rescue of hostages from hijacked aircraft prompted the United States to form a small antiterrorist force. The purpose of this group was to conduct surgical strikes intended to overwhelm those who perpetrated terroristic crimes against Americans abroad. In March 1978, President Jimmy Carter announced the decision to form this force. Volunteers from all branches of the American armed forces are members of the force, but its core is a cadre of personnel from the U.S. Army's Special Forces.

Colonel Charles A. Beckwith, now retired from the U.S. Army, organized and initially commanded the American antiterrorist unit. Dubbed the "Delta Unit," it was in the Mediterranean region in 1985 when an episode involving the hijacking of a TWA jet unfolded. Five years earlier, Beckwith's command served only as the nucleus of the multi-services raiding party that was formed to free the American hostages held in Iran.

On April 24, 1980, Operation Eagle Claw was unleashed. This maneuver called for a daring commando raid with the Delta Force to rescue 53 hostages in Tehran. The mission was aborted in an Iranian desert after eight American servicemen were killed when an RH-53 helicopter collided with a C-130 transport. Ninety members of the Pentagon's antiterrorist unit and a supporting group of Air Force crewmen were ordered to withdraw from their desert staging area after the air crash.[2] For the world's most technologically sophisticated nation, the failure of this rescue effort was particularly painful: three of the eight helicopters assigned to the mission developed electrical or hydraulic malfunctions that rendered them useless.

Details of the ill-fated American rescue venture were broadcast by the media. The news encouraged thousands of Iranians to rush into the streets of Tehran and gloat over the American failure. TASS, the Soviet news agency, accused President Carter of an abortive provocation that could have caused mass bloodshed and the death of the hostages.[3]

Since the attempt to rescue the hostages in Tehran, the Delta Unit has been positioned for an attack in a few instances. Supported by helicopter gunships, it was the core of a joint task force that was formed for the invasion of Grenada.

MANAGING THE DELTA FORCE

Communications and control shortcomings continue to vex the American antiterrorists. During the Grenada expedition, one "operator," as the members of Delta call themselves, allegedly used his A.T.&T. credit card to telephone a request for close air support. The call was made to a telephone number in the United States. This incident, which was evidence of the personal initiative and skills of the personnel assigned to the Delta Force, only highlighted the technological weakness in the unit's coordination systems. The Iranian debacle and to a lesser degree the invasion of Grenada underscored the complexity of organizing and executing hostage expeditions in an age of technological sophistication, in particular when the terrorists are apt to have advance information of a pending strike against them.[4]

Robert E. Osgood, author of *Limited War Revisited*, mentioned in his book that the hazards associated with American participation in small wars will become more formidable in the future. He cited the acquisition by small nations of modern weapons as one of the factors to be considered by the Pentagon's planners as they draft a scenario for a hostage-recovery operation or some other foreign expedition involving the deployment of American force.

NORINCO (China North Industries Corporation) handles armament exports for Peking. Its slogan, "affordable innovations for today," was emblazoned on its slick full-page advertisement for small arms once published by *Jane's Defense Weekly*. Established in the early 1980s, NORINCO's operations are directed by China's leaders. Quantities of the company's basic infantry weapons and artillery pieces have been sold to various Asian, African, and Latin American countries. Afghan and Cambodian freedom fighters also used NORINCO's guns. It was alleged that Iran had contracted with the Chinese weapons exporter for T-59 tanks, antitank guns, and rocket launchers. The company's weapons are used by insurgents and small armies around the world because they are light, durable, transportable, and easy to handle.

Osgood suggested that an elite antiterrorist unit, such as the Delta Force, might not have a clear technological advantage over a group of terrorists who are armed with weapons obtained from NORINCO or perhaps stolen from an American shipment that was intended for anti-Communist guerrillas. This consideration should not be minimized, especially when a decision has been reached to dispatch an American military unit to protect United States citizens and property ashore or afloat in a foreign territory.[5]

Although the current American antiterrorist policy emphasizes deterrence, military units should nonetheless be positioned to smash terrorists in Beirut or elsewhere, in the first critical hours of a hijacking, bombing, or some other horrendous event. Before this task can be accomplished, however, the supersecret Delta commando force would have to be airlifted from Fort Bragg, North Carolina, to a safe assembly area with access to the scene of a terrorist incident. Antiterrorist units could be more useful if they were pre-positioned in protected areas near a nexus of intense anti-American terrorist activity, for example, in Cyprus, which is accessible to Lebanon.

SOUND INTELLIGENCE NEEDED FOR RAIDS

Antiterrorist strike-force commanders must rely on detailed intelligence information and a sophisticated analytical process to ensure the success of their operations. William Stevenson, author of *90 Minutes at Entebbe*, the story of the spectacular Israeli strike against terrorists who were holding hostages at an airport in Uganda, described in his book how the Israelis used intelligence services to support their African strike force. According to Stevenson, a former British intelligence operative, the Israelis dispatched 50 of their agents to Kenya three days before the raid. They were used to monitor the traffic at the airport in Nairobi, because the antiterrorist force needed to refuel their C-130 Hercules aircraft at this facility on their way back to Israel. Also, the raiders were provided with information obtained from African informants who were hired by their Central Institute for Information and Espionage. The Africans reported on Entebbe's defenses and environment, while British intelligence in Kenya was tasked to provide other critical details. All this information was used as input into the Israeli planning process that was established to assess the prospects of success at Entebbe.

Israeli intelligence also used: (1) "invisibles," knowledgeable observers on the scene who were consulted about specific details without being aware that they were being exploited for this purpose; (2) "buy money," which was available in large sums at an El Al Airline office in Nairobi; (3) hypnotists who were skilled in the debriefing required to obtain information from released hostages about the psychological atmosphere among Ugandans and the terrorists at Entebbe; (4) analysts to integrate personality assessments of President Idi Amin, the Ugandan dictator, into his psychological profile, which was updated daily; (5) a full-scale model of the hostages' "prison" and scale models of the airport at Entebbe; and (6) a replica of the tarmac and structures as derived from blueprints used by an Israeli construction company that built sections of the Ugandan airfield. (Israel once had had good relations with President Amin.) The replica was modified daily by intelligence gleaned from freed hostages and from photographs taken by Israeli reconnaissance jets and American satellites.[6]

Also grounded in sound intelligence, the effort to free the American hostages being held in Iran was linked to a plan derived in part from blueprints of the embassy buildings and refined with information obtained from reconnaissance satellite observations and electronic intercepts. Additionally, the placement of the American embassy's electric and telephone lines had been pinpointed, and individual raiders from the American Delta Force were assigned the responsibility for cutting these lines.

Some individuals who were knowledgeable about details of the raid did not believe it was possible for American intelligence agents to penetrate the student militants who had direct control of the 50 hostages inside the embassy compound in Tehran. Consequently, they insisted that the lack of information about this group pointed to the possibility of a bungled operation, once the raiders entered the Iranian capital.

Admiral Stansfield Turner, Director of Central Intelligence during the administration of President Carter, in his book *Secrecy and Democracy: The CIA in Transition* said, "What compounded our failure to collect enough information about the dissidents and to appreciate the combined appeal of Islamic fundamentalism and Khomeini's personal charisma was that some of the CIA's key analysts were hung up on the durability of the Shah."[7]

Entebbe succeeded because the Israelis fully exploited their knowledge of the dispositions and the location of the hostages. In some ways, the American raid into Iran was more difficult because it involved operations in three elements—sea, air, and land, rather than only land and air. However, one of the lessons derived from both of these operations was the need to devote an enormous amount of time and effort to the preparations required to undertake a long-range hostage-relief expedition.

AMERICAN ACTIVITIES IN THE MIDDLE EAST

American antiterrorist operations in the Middle East have been short-circuited by a dearth of current information gleaned from the bazaars, campuses, and the streets where the life of a nation, such as Lebanon and Iran, takes place. The C.I.A. lacks the requisite number of agents on the ground to piece together a comprehensive picture of the psychosocial and religious inputs that shape contemporary life in Beirut, Tehran, and other Middle Eastern cities. Additionally, some officials insist that it often takes years to train agents to work in the Arab world because of the language and cultural factors. It takes still more time to deploy them and provide them with cover. Without intelligence gleaned from human sources, the American antiterrorist units will continue to lack the data they need to pinpoint their preemptive and retaliatory strikes against terrorist bases and training camps.

Positioning Strike Forces

Almost every recent terrorist episode involving the seizure of Americans aboard ships and planes has triggered suggestions that the United States should station its antiterrorist military units at overseas bases. As previously mentioned, pre-positioning a Delta Force unit in the Middle East would certainly expedite their deployment and assistance to another government in defusing a situation.

If they were emplaced in a foreign country, however, antiterrorist units might be fixed in their barracks by terrorists. Would the Delta Force be permitted to protect itself on foreign soil if it was attacked? In the aftermath of an incident that was intentionally designed to embarrass the American unit, would somebody in West Germany or Britain scream, "Why was it here?" If so, within hours, the Delta unit would have to be withdrawn to its homebase in North Carolina.

The southern part of the United States is thousands of miles from terrorist-operating areas in the Middle East and Latin America. But it is not that far! Preplanning and close coordination with the Air Force's military airlift units could reduce the time needed by an American antiterrorist unit to deploy on a foreign shore.[8]

Preparing for a Raid

For its Entebbe operation, Israel loaded a strike force of paratroopers and special infantry units onto three Lockheed C-130 "Hercules" transports. Doctors, communications units, two complete field medical hospitals, and forensic investigators also were placed on the aircraft. A full-dress rehearsal of the operation was conducted in Israel the night before the transports landed at Entebbe. The actual rescue of the hostages at the Uganda airport took 53 minutes, two minutes less than the practical exercise conducted the night before.

Rehearsals of American antiterrorist troops on foreign soil could be compromised. Transports landing in pitch darkness at a foreign airport, particularly if their arrival was anticipated, would be "sitting ducks" for terrorists.

Problems associated with operations similar to the Entebbe raid, however, differ markedly from those associated with urban antiterrorist operations. Long-range hostage-relief expeditions often involve at least two and possibly three of the military services, whereas controlling urban terrorism is essentially a police function.

Recently, Delta Force has been retailored to enable it to circumvent its ever becoming bemired once again in anything resembling the disaster in the Iranian desert. The command structure of the force has been streamlined, allowing its subunits to bypass the inflexible chain of command that caused the short circuit in the Iranian operation.[9]

The Delta Team's Exploits

Since 1982, Delta teams have been secretly deployed for the purpose of bolstering American overseas facilities that are menaced by terrorists. The Delta teams are deft and trained to be surgical. They have checked several incipient terrorist moves in Third World countries. The Delta Force and some of the countries in which it has operated are sensitive to disclosures in the media about these activities. Geared for deep-cover operations, Delta Force activities could be adversely affected by publicity.

When General James Dozier was kidnapped by the Red Brigades in 1982, American antiterrorists served as advisers to the Italian police who freed him from his place of confinement. Two years later, a Delta Unit was sent to Oman to stand-by in an area close to Iran. At the time, hijackers held a Kuwaiti airliner carrying American passengers at Tehran Airport. The hostages were eventually released by the hijackers, negating the need for military force.

Currently, the Delta Force has a mixed record: some spectacular successes and a few failures. Nonetheless, efforts to upgrade this organization are continuous.

UPGRADING THE AMERICAN ANTITERRORISTS

A review of management information, although sketchy, revealed that more than $100 million was spent to develop an American clandestine antiterrorist capability in 1983. In the 1984 fiscal year, Congress approved $500 million for this program, earmarking the money for the procurement of night-vision devices, special weapons, and communications gear. Funds were also allocated to update and revise training programs, field maneuvers, and to gear instructions to deal with the threat. Much of the training continues to be keyed to special operations for the purpose of upgrading the skills of Army Rangers and Special Forces and Navy Sea Air Land Teams (SEALS).

Antiterrorist specialists, faulting the United States, have claimed that the Americans are reluctant to gear their units to confront terrorists. By making unrealistic estimates of the terrorists themselves, the Armed Forces, they claim, have yet to draft policies and adjust training procedures to reflect the impact of terrorism on their tactics and strategy.

Terrorist attacks, for example a kidnapping or an assassination at curbside, are fast moving. The commencement and termination of these tactics telescope. Furthermore, the legal limitations imposed on the American intelligence services prevent them from substantially improving the quality of their antiterrorist information. It is most difficult for these agencies to develop human sources of information inside the movements that are responsible for the acts of terror. Lacking this capability, it is almost impossible for the C.I.A. or any other intelligence agency to warn anyone about a forthcoming attack against Americans.[10]

Meanwhile, the buildup of the United States antiterrorist force continues. According to the February 1985 issue of *Jane's Defense Weekly*, this organization will receive six nuclear-powered submarines for use on special missions in the coming years. The submarines, which are converted Polaris missile carriers, will be used for "black" (top secret) operations. Modified at the Puget Sound Naval Shipyard in Washington, the first "boats" were ready for use by the special forces in October 1985.

The United States Navy was detailed to form a seventh SEAL Team in 1985 and advised to train it for special operations. Also, the Joint Chiefs of Staff have tried to eliminate the fragmented tactical intelligence system used by American special operations units.

A bill intended to streamline the Pentagon's monolithic organizational structure has given additional authority to field commanders who are responsible for directing unified and specified commands. Derived from a two-year staff study, the legislation is known as the Defense Department Restructuring Measure. Its purpose is to enhance the efficiency of combined field operations and reduce the confusion that is characteristic of American tactical maneuvers involving different service groups. Organizational shortcomings, according to the study, were the root of the failed rescue of American hostages in Iran in 1979, and gaps in the communications interface used to coordinate and control air, land, and sea operations created the confusion that enveloped the 1983 invasion of Grenada.[11]

The Pentagon, confronted with an abysmal performance by the armed services in hostage-rescue operations, purchased equipment that would allow the services to develop more effective tactics. It considered moving forward with a $20 billion program to develop the Osprey, a new type of "tilt-rotor" aircraft for use mostly by U.S. Marines. Using engines affixed to its wings, the Osprey combines the capability of a helicopter and a fixed-wing propeller-driven aircraft. These capabilities would permit the marines to move more troops into a landing zone faster. Replacing the CH-46 helicopter, a workhorse from the Vietnam years, the

Osprey would enhance the antiterrorist capability of the American armed forces.[12]

Success in the Persian Gulf

The remedial measures undertaken to improve the strike capability of the American antiterrorist forces were wise and have proven to be prudent. In 1987, American human and technological resources deployed to the Persian Gulf neutralized an Iranian mine-laying venture, vindicating the record of the antiterrorist units organized by the United States.

While visiting the U.S. Navy ships in the Persian Gulf, former Defense Secretary Caspar W. Weinberger talked to Marine Corps pilots aboard the U.S.S. *Guadalcanal*, a helicopter carrier. His conversation with a young captain underscored the advanced state of American weapons. The officer showed the secretary his pilot's helmet, a headpiece wired so that the guns of his helicopter followed the movements of his head, "which is good when you're trying to sneak up on ships," the marine said.

According to Weinberger, the American helicopters that shot at an Iranian mine-laying ship shortly before midnight on September 21, 1987, were from the U.S. Army. He would not confirm that the craft had come from Task Force 160, an outfit based at Fort Campbell, Kentucky, and capable of operating behind enemy lines.

Concerned about the possible Iranian capability to unleash guerrilla warfare at sea, the Chairman of the Joint Chiefs of Staff, Admiral William J. Crowe, Jr., requested aerial support from the army in the Persian Gulf. Naval aviators are trained to use helicopters for minesweeping, antisubmarine operations, and transport. They are not qualified to use a gunship to attack an Iranian speedboat bent on destroying an American warship.

The U.S. Marine Corps has Harriers, which are planes that are capable of taking off and landing in the space used by a helicopter. But General P. X. Kelley, who retired as Commandant of the Marine Corps in 1987, believed that the logistic effort needed to sustain Harrier operations in the Gulf precluded the use of these planes. Consequently, Crowe turned to the army for gunship support.

Formally organized in October 1984, Task Force 160, which participated in the landings on Grenada, is believed to contain about 900 men and 75 helicopters of at least three types. According to a press report, the unit has spent the last six years trying to perfect the equipment and tactics needed to perform one of the most difficult jobs in all aviation — flying a helicopter in the dead of night, at top speed, at treetop level.[13]

American Moves in the Eastern Mediterranean

Another noteworthy American antiterrorist move was executed during the summer of 1984. This time it was an airborne military interception mission that unfolded over the Eastern portion of the Mediterranean Sea. Carrier-based jets forced a civilian Egyptian airliner to land at a NATO base in Sicily. Four Palestinians, responsible for the hijacking of the Italian cruise ship *Achille Lauro*, were aboard the plane. The terrorists were seized at the airfield and handed over to the Italians for prosecution.

Some military analysts attributed the American success in this affair to SIGINT (signals intelligence). Intercepted radio conversations between the hijackers of the cruise liner and an associate were monitored by Americans using SIGINT equipment. Senate bill S.2525 (National Intelligence Reorganization and Reform Act of 1978) defines SIGINT as information obtained from communications intelligence (COMINT), electronic intelligence (ELINT), foreign telemetry, beaconry, and associated signals, and nonimagery infrared and coherent light signals.

The United States has conducted an active program of SIGINT operations in the Mediterranean region. American SIGINT systems, for example, monitored the moves of the Libyan leader, Colonel Muammar al-Qaddafi. The Reagan administration regarded Libya as a major base for terrorism in the world and severed all ties with the country in 1987.

Israeli electronic "snoopers" have also conveyed essential elements of information (E.E.I.) to the United States as a group of Palestinians prepared to depart from a Cairo airport aboard an Egyptian airliner. The E.E.I.s that were provided included the departure time of the passenger jet and the registration number painted on its tail. Without this information, American naval aviators could not have screened air traffic over the Eastern Mediterranean as they searched for the jet with the correct tail marking. Since this incident, the Egyptians have moved to control their transmissions. The revelation of the link between Israeli SIGINT and the American interception of their aircraft alerted the Egyptians to the efficacy of electronic intelligence gathering.[14]

ISRAEL'S ANTITERRORIST STRATEGY

Israel's hit teams and its long-range penetration group, acting in concert, are used to bolster the international prestige of the Jewish state. In the Levant, Israel's conventional military forces continue to frustrate the planning staffs of the various terrorist groups who are anxious to establish an independent Palestinian state.

During the summer of 1987, terrorists based in Lebanon fired a Katyusha rocket into northern Israel. Normally issued to Soviet military units, the Russians have also distributed this weapon to their surrogates. Shortly after the rocket landed, Israeli helicopter gunships raided a building in a terrorist camp situated northwest of Tibnin, a hamlet in south Lebanon. A spokesman for the Israeli Defense Forces (I.D.F.) said that the aerial assault was unconnected to the Katyusha firing. It was, however, the 20th I.D.F.-sponsored air raid into Lebanon in 1987. Commenting on the raid, the spokesperson said that the targeted building was a headquarters used by Hezbollah to direct attacks against the Israeli army. Hezbollah is an extremist Iranian-sponsored Shiite terrorist organization that is active in Lebanon.

Traditionally, Israel uses force to counter terrorists who are being used as the cutting edge of a drive to discredit, embarrass, and immobilize a state engaged in a protracted war with an array of clandestine organizations. Israel has always been ready to take on the terrorist organizations at gunpoint. As it recognizes that the underlying maximum of all terrorist operations is that the psychological impact of terror in each case is to lessen the opponent's ability to use force, Israel clearly perceives the terrorist as an instrument of modern warfare. Its antiterrorist policy, therefore, is designed for the contemporary scene. By tracking these criminals around the world and retaliating against their installations in the Middle East, Israel intimidates them by reversing the strategy of terror and using it against them. Acting in conformity with this policy, the I.D.F. has stormed aircraft, apartments, a high school at Maalot, Israel, and undertook the spectacular raid at Entebbe. All these terrorist incidents were intended to make Israel appear powerless in the world arena, but the I.D.F. has aborted this strategy.

Israel's antiterrorist moves are not isolated reactions to specific acts of terror, such as the flight of the Katyusha rocket into the Jewish state. Instead, they are part of a strategic policy of continuous warfare against the terrorist organizations that threaten it. Still, the Israelis, in particular those who are in settlements near the Lebanese border, live with a cycle of terror and counterterror that the I.D.F. has been unable to check. Israel's attempt to frustrate the terrorists and force them to turn inward upon themselves and begin an internecine war resulting in eventual self-destruction has had only marginal success.

Israel's combat with the Palestinian terror organizations is likely to continue for the foreseeable future. These groups have tried to redeem their traditional lands inside Israel through the use of diplomacy, conventional war, and Maoist-style guerrilla war. It seems that the Palestinians, and especially those who constitute the terrorist organizations, have now shifted to the tactics of terror once they became aware that these other methods were futile.

Leon Trotsky, Lenin's contemporary and erstwhile associate when the Bolsheviks seized power in Russia, defined the tactics of terror as measures that "kill individuals and intimidate thousands." Today the Israelis and their supporters everywhere are the targets of Middle East terrorist organizations. Arab radicals view these terror organizations as components of their own national liberation movement. They view the origin and operations of the terrorists as a natural outgrowth of their struggle for independence, a drive which has been marked by abysmal failure.[15]

SOVIET SPETSNAZ: ORGANIZATION AND OPERATIONS

The antiterrorist military units of the free world must also be alert to the activities of Spetsnaz (*voyska spetsial'nogo naznacheniya* or special designations). These Soviet commando-type units are charged by the Central Committees of the Communist Party (C.C.C.P.) with missions too sensitive for the regular military. The neutralization of nuclear weapons sites controlled by NATO units is a Spetsnaz assignment, particularly any effort to neutralize the retaliatory capability of the U.S. Pershing II and Lance missile emplacements in West Germany and the cruise missiles that are situated in Italy, the United Kingdom, and West Germany.

Spetsnaz forces have been used for sensitive strategic missions during the Cold War. In 1968, they conducted an airborne drop on the Prague, Czechoslovakia, airport, securing access routes to the facility until they were relieved by regular Red Army units. Spetsnaz airborne units repeated this scenario in Afghanistan in 1979, spearheading the seizure of Kabul from a drop zone in Bagram airfield north of the Afghan capital.

In wartime, the Russians have the capability to field 41 Spetsnaz companies, one attached to each Soviet army. Additionally, 16 Spetsnaz brigades have been organized to operate with an army group and four naval brigades of these special-forces-type units have been formed, with one attached to each Soviet fleet. Wearing Western uniforms and speaking Western languages, East German, Polish, and other Warsaw Pact special-purpose forces would, in the event of war, unleash havoc against NATO countries.

Soviet strategic doctrine emphasizes the conduct of operations in the rear of the enemy to support frontal assaults. These planners know that the destruction or neutralization of NATO governments requires the use of "active measures" (*aktivnyye meropriyatya*) by Spetsnaz forces. The measures include assassinations of leaders, kidnappings, bombings, and other terrorist activity in the enemy's homeland.

The mission of Spetsnaz units, a key element of which is the use of active measures, is characteristic of the type of aggressive Soviet security operations that have occurred since the heyday of the Bolsheviks. After World War II, the chief of the Russian Partisans, General Paul Anatolevich Sudoplatov, was ordered to remake his operations into active measures (sabotage, assassination, and terrorism). Since the beginning of the Cold War, the Western intelligence community has reviewed an assortment of studies of Soviet-sponsored assassinations, kidnappings, and chicanery intended to enhance Moscow's political objectives. The ties between Spetsnaz units and foreign terrorists who were trained by the Soviet Intelligence Services, however, are difficult to define.

Recently, the strategy responsible for the use of Spetsnaz forces and other active measures was dissected. Analysis revealed that these measures are used to a greater or lesser degree depending on the significance of the target country and Moscow's estimate of the situation. Consequently, when the Russians openly used regular military forces to invade a country, they already had their Spetsnaz assets in place.

American nuclear facilities could be vulnerable to penetration and destruction by Spetsnaz units pre-positioned in the United States prior to the outbreak of hostilities. Nuclear security measures, according to Representative John D. Dingell of Michigan, are deficient. To improve security at nuclear installations in the United States, mock raids are conducted by commando teams. At Lawrence Livermore Laboratory in California, there has been an increased emphasis on security for several years. Also, training exercises at nuclear sites have improved in realism and in frequency. Additional safeguards have been recommended by congressional investigators. They have suggested the stationing of standing military units at some of these sites with the offensive capability to deter and fight off attacks.

There are indications that Spetsnaz units once penetrated United States borders with landings on remote Saint Lawrence Island in the Bering Sea. Eskimo scouts attached to the Alaska National Guard declassified some of their intelligence files in February 1988. The media were permitted to examine the photographs and documents concerning mysterious human sightings and flotsam found in the American island. Despite the discovery of a Soviet liferaft that was half-buried near a deserted beach, members of the National Guard's 1st Scout Battalion did not consider the physical evidence conclusive.

On February 1, 1988, Dan Howard, a Pentagon spokesman said, "There is no convincing evidence that the Soviets have landed on Saint Lawrence Island; no conclusive evidence." After talking with some of the Eskimo scouts, John Schaeffer of the Alaska Guard said, "We don't have a Soviet person on hand so we can completely verify this, but circumstantial evidence is that they're conducting some activity on this island." Spetsnaz units are active around the world; in Scandinavia and in the Philippines. "So why not here?" Schaeffer asked.[16]

The Soviet Union's strategy for a major war is keyed to methods of fighting that could make a nuclear response by the United States unlikely. The Soviets envision a sudden, massive, and lightning-fast strike into the stomach of the NATO alliance, essentially a blitzkrieg. Then, if NATO countries chose to retaliate against the Red Army with nuclear weapons, their own populations would share the brunt of the nuclear detonations along with the Russians.

Glavnoye Razvedyvatelnoye Upravlieniye (G.R.U.), the Main Intelligence Directorate of the Soviet General Staff, has been assigned the task of directing the Soviet Spetsnaz teams who are earmarked to precede Moscow's conventional armed forces into a theater of operations. Landed by minisubmarines—in recent years these submersibles have cruised about the coastal waters of Baltic nations—Spetsnaz units would destroy or immobilize European-based nuclear weapons just prior to the Red Army's massive assault.

Full-scale mock-ups of Western cruise missile installations in the NATO countries have been built in the Carpathian Mountains and in the Ural and Volga military districts. Resembling the countryside surrounding British and French nuclear bases, these Soviet groundforms afford Spetsnaz units an opportunity to rehearse their combat roles in conditions that approximate reality. Life-size inflatable models of NATO weapons' systems add realism to the Spetsnaz training program.

Spetsnaz units also contain intelligence agents and direct-action personnel who will be used to confuse the political and military leadership of NATO. Using phony passports and garbed in civilian attire, Spetsnaz terrorists would go to the residences of key NATO political and military leaders and assassinate them. Their deaths would coincide with the start of the Red Army's offensive.

Spetsnaz terror, supported by indigenous clandestine groups operating within the NATO countries, is a key component of Moscow's plan to blitz Western Europe. A key objective of Soviet support of terrorism is to establish in advance assets for facilitating optimal conditions for special operations. Soviet military theory necessarily requires the development of a diversified support and intelligence infrastructure before hostilities can begin. Thus, the Soviets have been developing a formidable global terrorist asset that is geared to strike a devastating blow in the heartland of Moscow's opponent just as the Red Army divisions unleash an attack. The G.R.U. has worked for years to build clandestine organizations in Western Europe and elsewhere and to maintain its control over these groups to enhance the Soviet grand strategy.

Louis C. Peltier and G. Etzel Pearcy in their book *Military Geography*, define grand strategy as follows: "the process of planning, coordinating, and directing the use of all of the resources of a nation or an alliance—social, political, economic, and military—toward the attainment and retention of a political objective." A grand strategy can be realized, he said, by "(1) amicable settlement of differences, (2) indirect pressures, (3) other unfriendly acts, and (4) war."[17] The Red Army is geared for war. Spetsnaz units are trained to conduct unfriendly acts in the vanguard of the Russian tanks and infantrymen, with assassination one of its specialties.

Spetsnaz forces have recently been in the forefront of the Soviet involvement in Afghanistan. Consequently, when the Russians blatantly used regular military forces to invade that country, they already had their Spetsnaz units there. Spetsnaz agents are not easily counteracted and they are trained to destroy objectives which are immune to other forms of attack. Armed with atomic, bacteriological, and chemical weapons, these special forces can cause untold damage to their enemy. Continued use of such forces could change the whole character of a future war.[18]

NOTES

1. John B. Wolf, *Fear of Fear: A Survey of Terrorist Operations and Controls in Open Societies* (New York: Plenum Press, 1981), pp. 108–132.
2. Colonel Charlie A. Beckwith, *Delta Force* (New York: Harcourt Brace Jovanovich, 1983), pp. 1–280.
3. Nicholas Daniloff, "Secret Report Assails Iran Rescue Raid Command," *The Star Ledger* (Newark, N.J.), June 6, 1980, p. 1.
4. Richard Halloran, "Military Is Quietly Rebuilding Its Special Operations Forces," *The New York Times*, July 19, 1982, p. 1.
5. Robert E. Osgood, *Limited War Revisited* (Boulder, Colo.: Westview Press, 1979), pp. 67–86.
6. William Stevenson, *90 Minutes at Entebbe* (New York: Bantam Books, 1976), pp. 55–111.
7. Stansfield Turner, *Secrecy and Democracy: The CIA in Transition* (Boston: Houghton Mifflin, 1985), pp. 114–137.
8. Steven Emerson, "Secret Warriors," *U.S. News & World Report*, March 21, 1988, pp. 24–32; Michael Kramer, "The Prisoners of Politics," *U.S. News & World Report*, p. 37; and Mortimer B. Zuckerman, Michael Kramer, and Richard Z. Cheshoff, "Israeli Leaders Square Off on Life-and-Death Issues," *U.S. News & World Report*, pp. 37–39.
9. Terrance Smith, "Israelis Staged Raid Rehearsal," *The New York Times*, July 9, 1976, p. 1.

10. Philip Taubman, "U.S. Military Tries to Catch up in Fighting Terror," *The New York Times*, December 5, 1984, p. 8.
11. Bill Keller, "Conflict in Pentagon Is Seen Harming Commandos' Unity," *The New York Times*, January 6, 1986, p. 1.
12. "Hybrid Aircraft," *The New York Times*, August 26, 1980, p. C2.
13. "A U.S. Ambush in the Gulf," *Newsweek*, October 5, 1987, pp. 24–27.
14. James Bamford, *The Puzzle Palace: A Report on NSA, America's Most Secret Agency* (Boston: Houghton Mifflin, 1982), pp. 155–279.
15. John B. Wolf, "Israel's Military Continues to Frustrate Arab Terrorists," *New York City Tribune*, August 25, 1987, p. 2.
16. "Soviet Spetsnaz Detected on Alaskan Island," *Free Press International Inc.*, February 12, 1988, p. 8.
17. Louis C. Peltier and G. Etzel Pearcy, *Military Geography* (Princeton, N.J.: D. Van Nostrand, 1966), p. 31.
18. John M. Collins, *Green Berets, Seals and Spetsnaz: U.S. and Soviet Special Military Operations* (Washington: Pergamon-Brassey's, 1987), pp. 39–62.

CLANDESTINE CHANNELS
AND NETWORKS

Soviet deliveries of arms to Third World countries began in 1954 in the form of a shipment of weapons from Czechoslovakia to Egypt. Shipments are usually accompanied by a high-profile military presence. Fifty-thousand Communist military advisers—instructors, technical personnel, and troops—are on assignment in the developing countries, and of these, approximately two-thirds are Cubans and the rest are from the Soviet Union and Eastern Europe.[1]

In 1980, the Soviet Union allocated $16 billion for arms to the developing world. A major portion of the tonnage of these military supplies was consigned to Cuba's regular armed forces and its territorial militia. The island-nation received about 56,000 tons of military supplies from the Soviet Union and Eastern Europe in 1981, the greatest annual shipment of weapons from the Communist bloc to Havana since the missile crisis of 1962. Most of the modern Soviet equipment remains in Cuba, but the new supplies permit Fidel Castro's government to ship large quantities of older weapons and related hardware to guerrilla groups operating in Central America.

American law-enforcement officials are concerned about the linkage between Cuban-inspired terrorism and movements that advocate independence for Puerto Rico. Soviet-made AK-47 assault rifles were once used in attacks on American servicemen stationed on the island. Unrest in Puerto Rico, it is believed, provides opportunities for recruitment by hostile intelligence agencies. Thus, island-based terrorism is a potential source of trouble for the United States. At least five Puerto Rican terrorist groups were, at one time, claiming responsibility for the bombings and shootings that were directed against American military personnel stationed there. The most dramatic acts were the ambush of a U.S. Navy bus in December 1979 and the bombings in January 1981 of nine jet fighters at an airbase by a group known as the *Macheteros*.

The insurgencies in Central America also disturb law-enforcement officials who are responsible for enhancing the security of the island. It is possible that terrorists might attack targets in Puerto Rico as a way to retaliate against the continuation of Washington's assistance to anti-Communist governments in Central America.[2]

"NARCO-TERRORISM"

Cuba is known to use narcotics rings to funnel arms and money to terrorists who are seeking to topple various Latin American governments. In 1982, Florida police discovered that the Castro government was helping a Miami-based drug trafficker smuggle weapons and money to a terrorist movement that was based in Colombia. Terrorists affiliated with a group known as the Movement of April 19th (M-19) attacked a police station near Medellin, Colombia, on March 12, 1982. When the terrorists opened fire, one police officer was killed and two were wounded.

It is believed that M-19, in exchange, protects drug cargos that move through Colombia and that are bound for Cuban-controlled ports. The Miami-based drug smuggler and other narcotics czars have used these facilities for refueling, repair work, marshalling cargos, and evasion of the U.S. Coast Guard. American authorities have solid evidence that Cuban MIGS (jet fighters) and patrol boats escort and protect shipments of drugs moving from Colombia through Cuba to the Florida Keys.

Three of Colombia's six terrorist organizations are used by the Cubans to eliminate officials who oppose their involvement in illegal commerce. The assassination of Colombia's Attorney General in January 1988 was a warning to Colombian officials who wanted to approve extradition of major cocaine traffickers to face trial in the United States.

South American terrorists are also often used to kill workers who are involved in the manual eradication of coca plants. (Formed into crews, the field hands are sent into the coca production areas of Peru, Colombia, and Ecuador to eradicate the plants by setting fires.[3])

Castro also has used his countrymen to enhance his control of the drug networks. On April 1, 1980, a group of Cubans, seemingly seeking political asylum but believed by some authorities to be controlled by Castro, crashed a bus through the gates of the Peruvian embassy in Havana. This incident was the precursor of a series of events that brought the *Mayombero Bandidos* to the United States.

Acting on orders of Fidel Castro, Raul Castro removed all police from the Peruvian embassy on April 4, 1980 (Good Friday). "Let Peru handle the lumpen" (contemptibles), Castro said, "Cuba doesn't have to feed them." On April 6, 1980, about 10,000 Cubans were within the confines of the embassy. Several countries, including the United States, offered asylum to the refugees. Students, physicians, and housewives were sprinkled among the refugees, who were mostly blue-collar workers. On April 20, 1980, Cuba released 37 of the refugees to a man who sailed freelance between Key West, Florida, and Mariel, Cuba. This marked the beginning of the great Cuban refugee tide that poured out of Mariel Harbor and inundated South Florida.

Mayombero Bandidos from Mariel

The term *Marielito* is associated with Mariel Harbor, the embarkation point for 125,000 refugees who left Cuba on the so-called Freedom Flotilla. After Castro closed the harbor on September 26, 1980, this exodus became known as the "Mariel Boatlift." Anxious to exploit the confusion created by the refugee tide and to save face, Castro chortled, "If they want *escoria* (scum) let's give them *escoria*." Unleashing his agents, the Cuban dictator flushed out the "undesirables" from neighborhoods throughout Cuba and herded them to El Mosquito, a heavily guarded plantation camp near Mariel.

According to the Associated Press, about 2,000 hard-core criminals left Mariel for Florida on the boatlift. An Immigration and Naturalization Service (I.N.S.) estimate supported the tally: 2,000 hard-core criminals among 24,000 of the refugees who had prison records for political or minor crimes. Many of the hard-core felons were mentally twisted or broken as a consequence of prolonged torment in prison. They worshipped the god Chango and were members of the Abaqua cult. Practitioners of Abaqua are called *Mayomberos*. Consequently, a formidable cadre of *Mayombero Bandidos* from Mariel came to the United States on the Freedom Flotilla.

Almost 50 percent of the Marielitos were released to family or friends from staging areas in Florida; the remainder were sent to military bases, where they remained until someone was located to sponsor them. Sponsors were obliged only to register their own names and addresses, guarantee lodging, and introduce the refugee to American life. Most sponsors simply wanted to help the Marielitos, whereas other tapped a large pool of unsponsored single males to form criminal gangs. Often a sponsored Marielito would sponsor others. An investigation in New York City uncovered details of how one Bandido sponsored prison associates, thus forming an instant gang.

Other Bandidos were sheltered by the *madrinas* (leaders) of the Mayombero sect, a black-magic cult. Under their auspices, Bandidos were told where to buy guns and how to conduct operations within a new world of civil rights. Quickly, the Bandidos realized that the National Crime Information Center (N.C.I.C.), maintained by the F.B.I., was of no use by those seeking to control criminals whose records were in Cuba.

In April 1984, the F.B.I. shelved a proposal intended to expand its national computerized files to include information about people who are considered suspicious but not wanted for crimes. A major role of the current N.C.I.C. system is to tell police officers on an almost instantaneous basis whether a particular car has been reported stolen anywhere in the United States. It also provides law-enforcement officers with information about an individual held by the police in one state and named in an arrest warrant in any other state.

In testimony before the Senate Judiciary Subcommittee on Security and Terrorism on March 14, 1984, William H. Webster, then director of the F.B.I., said he did not believe "that the mere capability is a justification in itself for putting names and facts into a massive computer file." He added, "I think we have to look very closely at information where somebody says, well, he pals around with the wrong kinds of people."

In the New York City area, the Mayombero Bandidos usually worked in gangs, often using eight or more men on a single robbery. But in Southern Florida, there was evidence of a central organization and leadership. Using sledgehammers and oxyacetylene torches, Florida gangs gained entry into warehouses. Clothing, sneakers, electronic equipment, airplane parts, and industrial thread were among the items which they stole. Informants told Miami and Dade County police that two brothers were the kingpins. The brothers, who were suspected of being Cuban intelligence operatives, had arrived from Mariel empty-handed.

Undercover police officers, many of whom are Cuban Americans with an intense desire to bring the Bandidos to justice, have been used to crack drug networks. These drug rings moved cocaine between Dade County, Florida, and Union City, New Jersey. Bandido drug dealers operated this network and other interstate drug rings that are engaged in trafficking narcotics between Las Vegas, New York, Miami, Washington, D.C., and locations in California. This marketing activity intertwined their cells. Most of the profits that are realized from the sales of drugs are believed to have been delivered to Castro.

In April 1983, a Drug Enforcement Administration (D.E.A.) informant testified about the Cuban-directed drug traffic at a New York State hearing. A former Cuban intelligence agent, the informant told officials that Castro had assigned 400 members of the Mariel boatlift solely to the task of smuggling and distributing drugs; he was one of them, he said. The informant mentioned that in 1981 he smuggled cocaine, marijuana, and Quaaludes into the United States. The profit of $7 million was used by Castro to bolster his sagging economy.

Some antiterrorist specialists believe that Cuban intelligence agents, who were sequestered among the boatlift refugees, have been assigned specific missions including: (1) the disruption of civil order by perpetrating robberies and homicides, (2) terrorism, (3) drug trafficking for the purpose of raising hard cash for the Cuban government, (4) sabotage, and (5) the unsettling of American prison populations if they become incarcerated. Some of the Castro operatives are believed to be "sleeper" agents.

The Mayombero Bandidos serve as "mules" (couriers), retailers, middlemen, and enforcers for sophisticated drug organizations. These drug networks are allegedly controlled by Castro's intelligence operatives.[4]

Santeria (Saint Worship)

Most of the Bandidos belong to a religious cult of African origin. In the June 15, 1986, edition of *Pueblo de Dios*, Ed Grant discussed the opinions and experiences of Catholic priests in the New York metropolitan area with *Santeria*. When coupled to a code of conduct resembling the pledge of fidelity sworn by a member of the Cosa Nostra upon being "made" (that is, "initiated" into an organized-crime family), Santeria is used by Cuban Bandidos to build the group fidelity needed to safeguard their cells from penetration by the police.

Popular among some Latins, Cubans in particular, Santeria is widespread within the Cuban-American population. Grant's article included observations of the cult by the Reverend Richard Rento, pastor of St. Brendan's Church in Clifton, New Jersey, and the associate pastor of St. Augustine's Church in Union City, New Jersey, the Reverend Pedro Navarro.

In Cuba, members of the Bandido cells are extremely street-wise people. Most of them have the savvy needed to avoid detection by Castro's agents, people who are specifically charged with the task of flushing out undesirables. Many Bandidos are veterans of the Cuban Armed Forces who fought in Angola and elsewhere in Africa and in Latin America. The Bandido's weapon is his status symbol, the measure of manhood, the key to survival. Trained and disciplined as a soldier in Cuban military camps through the medium of brute force, the Bandido understands the use of terror and its applications. Displaying a comprehensive knowledge of firearms, Bandidos prefer powerful 9-mm and .45 caliber handguns and use an assortment of other weapons—carbines, pump-action shotguns, rifles with night-vision devices, and machine guns. Some of these weapons have been modified to make them fully automatic, and others have been fitted with silencers.

While operating under the nose of Castro's henchmen, the Bandidos developed the sophisticated tactics and techniques that are needed to escape apprehension by the police, such as countersurveillance, intimidation, murder of witnesses and informants, establishment of safehouses, and the sequestering of firearms with associates when not in use. A Bandido on the run knows exactly where to go—which streets, which houses—to join his own kind. His associates, former prison acquaintances or military buddies, are also introduced to the safehouse network and admitted to the cells. Each cell is organized to commit a particular type of crime.

The omnipresence of the Cuban police forced the Bandidos to formulate ultrasophisticated security procedures—use of aliases, phony street names, forged I.D.s, and an unusual recognition system of their own. Keyed to a code of tattoos on the flesh between the thumb and the index finger and a series of numbers and letters on the inside of the lower lip, this classification system serves to identify a Bandido to those familiar with the cryptograms. Stickup men bear three vertical lines. Drug dealers use three vertical lines and two horizontal lines. Three vertical lines over a five-pointed star is the emblem of the kidnapper, whereas an enforcer is identified by a three-pronged pitchfork. An inverted cross is the mark of a gun merchant, and a heart bearing the word *madre* is the symbol used by an executioner.

This coding system of tattoos, which is part of Cuban prison culture, is used by an inmate to prove his machismo. In Cuba it is considered a disgrace among the legitimate people to have tattoos, a practice limited almost exclusively to the convict population. Among the Bandidos, however, tattoos are a useful identification tool.

Police pressure in Cuba has also forced the Bandidos to control their nonverbal expressions. Many of them are skilled at deception, realizing that a twitch of a leg or an arm, a nod of the head, or a sweaty palm print are signs of lying. Often only the scars on a Bandido's face, usually the sign of prison experience, betray his true identity. A few of them are remarkable liars, able to set their faces into an expression "that could have been stamped on a medal of a saint."

The psychocultural and intrapsychic aspects of Santeria also contribute to the social stability of the Bandido cells. Depicting tribal gods in the image of Christian saints, Santeria blends African religion and Christianity. Black slaves brought to the New World were often forbidden by their Spanish masters, who introduced them to Christianity, to practice their African religions. Consequently, the slaves amalgamated both religions, hence the name *Santeria*, which literally means "saint worship."

Santeria and its allied cults, Voodoo in Haiti and Espiritismo on the island of Puerto Rico, have many adherents in the United States. There are millions of law-abiding Cuban people, some highly educated, who partake in Santeria rituals. For many of them, the rites are a replacement for the Catholicism that lost its influence when Castro imposed Communism in Cuba.

Some Bandidos subscribe to *Palo Myombe*, an ancient African cult that is linked to black magic. Those who practice this cult are known as *paleros* or *Mayomberos*. Specializing in sorcery through the medium of the dead, a palero, for a fee, will use rituals to inflict misfortune, insanity, divorce, even (according to a legend) death on an enemy or on the enemy of a client. The *nganga*, which is a basic tool used by the palero, consists of an iron cauldron filled with sacred dirt, blood, coins, herbs, feathers, bones, and, invariably, a human skull—as police in South Florida have discovered. However, most of the human bones that are used in this rite are obtained from professionally prepared biological specimens or by grave robbing.[5]

NICARAGUA AND WEAPONS TRAFFIC

Nicaragua, like Cuba, also receives arms shipments directly from Moscow as it acts as the hub of the Communist logistics network in Central America. Its seaports, Puerto Cabezas on the northeast coast and Bluefields on the southeast coast, provide the unloading facilities for vessels that are transporting arms and ammunition from Cuba as part of their cargo. Three Nicaraguan ships—the *Monimbo*, the *Aracely*, and the *Nicarao*—are involved in this traffic. Military supplies remain stockpiled in Nicaragua until guerrilla groups, operating elsewhere in Central America, arrange for their shipment into "liberated zones." According to the United States Department of State, the timing of the resupply operations in the case of El Salvador appears to be coordinated with the tempo of the fighting. Large deliveries of weapons have been detected before each surge in the level of the insurgency in various areas of Central America.

Weapons deliveries from Nicaragua to El Salvador by overland routes pass through Honduras via at least five separate roadways. Honduran authorities have intercepted various shipments from Nicaragua in their country. The six persons who were arrested in January 1981 by Honduran police as they were unloading weapons from a truck, identified themselves as members of the International Support Commission of the Salvadoran Popular Liberation Forces (F.P.L.). The truck contained 100 M-16/AR-15 automatic rifles, 50 81mm mortar rounds, approximately 10,000 rounds of 5.56mm ammunition, machine-gun belts, field packs, and first-aid kits. Over 50 of the rifles were traced to American units assigned to Vietnam in 1968 to 1969. These weapons were left in Southeast Asia when United States troops departed. Because Nicaragua has a military assistance agreement with Vietnam, American weapons inventoried by the Hanoi government continue to be funnelled through Nicaragua into adjacent countries. In April and July 1981, Guatemalan security forces captured large caches of shoulder weapons at safehouses in Guatemala City. Traces made on the serial numbers of individual United States-made weapons indicated that 17 M-16/AR-15s had been issued to American units in Vietnam in the late 1960s and early 1970s.

It is often impossible to know with certainty which Central American guerrilla group has been designated as the final recipient of weapons uncovered in a clandestine shipment or confiscated from a safehouse. Using the same secret smuggling techniques and routes, Cubans and Nicaraguans are currently supplying lethal military hardware to terrorists and guerrillas in four countries—Guatemala, Honduras, Costa Rica, and El Salvador. In addition to ammunition and rifles, recent clandestine supply operations in Central America have included greater quantities of sophisticated weapons. Underground groups also regularly receive tens of thousands of dollars for routine purchases of nonlethal supplies on the open market and for payments, mostly bribes, to enable the clandestine pipeline to function.[6]

I.R.A. WEAPONS CHANNELS

American weapons, mostly M-16 automatic rifles and M-60 machine guns, are being smuggled to terrorist groups, often in mislabeled crates or stuffed into openings in machinery. A few years ago, British troops raided a building in a predominantly Roman Catholic district of Belfast and seized an M-60. The machine gun was one of seven that were taken from a National Guard armory north of Boston in 1976. Many of the illegal weapons used by the Irish terrorists are stolen from United States military bases in return for payments sometimes made with the proceeds of I.R.A. bank robberies. According to a spokesman for the United States Treasury Department, "when the I.R.A. is shipping guns, it's a couple here, a couple there." "To them," the spokesman continued, "one gun is a large item."[7]

Leaders of the Irish Northern Aid Committee (Noraid) insist that money they collect at bars, dances, dinners, and parties across the United States is used solely for the benefit of the wives and children of I.R.A. members. But numerous Irish and American officials maintain that Noraid is an important source of weapons for the I.R.A. On October 1, 1981, this latter view was confirmed when federal agents arrested Noraid's director in New York City on charges of conspiring to ship guns to the I.R.A. This was the first time that a Noraid official had been formally accused of illegally helping to arm the I.R.A. The arrest of the gunrunner stemmed from charges lodged in June 1981 against three other men. These men were taken into custody after one of them handed an undercover F.B.I. agent $16,800 in exchange for 42 automatic rifles, submachine guns, and handguns. The money used to make "the buy" was allegedly received from the Noraid official.[8]

OPERATION SHAMROCK

In a series of arrests in February 1982, five men were taken into custody at Niagara Falls, New York. Immigration inspectors attached to Operation Shamrock, an investigation into I.R.A. gunrunning, said they confiscated $10,000 in British currency and a diary containing a "shopping list" for weapons. The cash and the diary were in a car used by the arms merchants. Written on the shopping list were the following: 200,000 rounds of ammunition for an assortment of American, British, Soviet, and Czechoslovakian rifles and pistols, electronic devices capable of detonating bombs by remote control, and small remote-controlled aircraft capable of transporting 20 pounds of explosives as far as five miles. The diary contained the names of more than a dozen American companies that might have been able to supply the communications and electronic gadgetry. Federal investigators tried to find information that would tie sales from these companies to the clandestine I.R.A. supply channel, assuming such purchases were in fact made.

This secret pipeline was detected after a year of undercover work and investigations by federal agents assigned to Operation Shamrock.

Evidence had been obtained indicating that the pipeline stretched from Dublin through Amsterdam and Toronto to Buffalo, New York. Information pointing to the existence of this secret distribution channel was the telephone number of an I.R.A. "safe house," in the Toronto suburb of Mississagua, which was written on a piece of paper carried by an I.R.A. official who was arrested in New York City in 1980. When the house was staked out, it was found that people and automobiles arriving there were crossing the United States border regularly. American immigration inspectors had once encoded the license numbers of all vehicles entering the United States from Canada, storing the data in a computer. An interpretation of the patterns developed through computer analysis showed that the I.R.A. was regularly sending people across a bridge that links Canada to the Buffalo area.

In a typical case, a suspicious inspector refused entry to a car with a certain Ontario registration at a checkpoint on a bridge. Yet the computer printout showed that half an hour later, the same car was admitted at another bridge. Each day, tens of thousands of cars cross the four bridges linking the Buffalo and Niagara regions to Ontario. Consequently, it is almost impossible to make a thorough check.

An Irish citizen, however, must have a visa to enter the United States, but, if challenged at one of the bridges, he could state that he was unaware of that requirement. Procedures in this case would oblige the immigration inspector to deny the visitor entry and to mention that a visa must be obtained at the United States Embassy in Ottawa or the Consulate in Toronto. Federal officials said that the I.R.A. used the automobile bridges because airlines offering direct service from Europe to the United States demanded proof that the necessary visa had been obtained.

The group of men who were arrested in February 1982 at Niagara Falls included two who had been previously convicted on munitions charges and a 35-year-old resident of Belfast. In a copyrighted story, the *Buffalo Evening News* said that classified documents based on reports from the Royal Canadian Mounted Police (R.C.M.P.) and British authorities described the man from Belfast as a primary suspect in the 1979 assassination of Lord Louis Mountbatten. He was mentioned as the "brains" behind the killing of the distinguished war hero, diplomat, and elder statesman of Britain's royal family.

Held in the Erie County (New York) Correctional Facility, the alleged terrorist, after posting bail, was returned to Canada and was arrested by Canadian immigration officials. While being deported to Ireland from Canada, he slipped away from the Canadian immigration official who was escorting him at Orly Airport in Paris on March 4, 1982.[9]

IRISH NORTHERN AID COMMITTEE

Support for the Irish republican cause in the United States has always been strong. According to the publicity director for Noraid, his organization has ten chapters around the United States, including a Texas branch. The president of this chapter states that Noraid's purpose is to "raise money for dependents of Irish political prisoners."

The British government once claimed that 47 percent of all weapons seized from I.R.A. terrorists were of American manufacture. It believed that many of the guns were smuggled into Ireland by Noraid operatives.

Formed in 1970 by four Irish nationals who lived in Ireland, Noraid raised $250,000 in the first half of 1981, more than twice as much as in the same period of 1980. The most direct challenge to the organization's position that it raises only relief money was the Department of Justice's effort to force Noraid to register under the Foreign Agents Registration Act as an agent of the I.R.A. Provisionals.

Although Noraid has been registered as an agent of the Northern Aid Committee in Belfast since 1971, the Justice Department said in 1977 that it had failed to supply sufficient information under the registration act's rules. Also, federal officials stated that Noraid did not identify itself as the foreign principal of the I.R.A. Provisionals. Additionally, Noraid has been unable to supply the address of the Northern Aid Committee in Belfast. No canceled checks made out to the committee ever appeared in Noraid files.

As evidence of Noraid's link to the I.R.A., the Justice Department offered documents that included an undated flyer, with a Northern Aid Committee letterhead. It was signed by Joe R. Martin, Active Service Unit 3, Belfast No. 1 Brigade. The flyer said, "Remember—the Irish Northern Aid Committee is the only organization in America that supports the Provisional I.R.A."[10]

THE AMERICAN-MADE "STINGER" MISSILE

In addition to the American weapons that are funnelled through illegal channels and networks to terrorist groups, the United States supplies surface-to-air missiles to "freedom fighters," guerrilla groups opposing Communist-sponsored governments. These fighters need the SAMs to combat the helicopter gunships that are supplied to their opponents by the Soviet Union. These aircraft have had a devastating effect on guerrilla columns moving across open terrain.

Three persons, who are knowledgeable about American aerial support for anti-Communist freedom fighters in Central America and Africa, have revealed details about these clandestine "cargo drops" to their captors after escaping from plane crashes. In 1986, a Sandinista soldier used a Soviet SAM to shoot down a cargo plane carrying supplies to his adversary. An American survivor of that crash was captured by the Communists, whereupon he revealed to them details about his mission. Similarly, a U.N.I.T.A. (Union for the Total Independence of Angola) supply officer was seized by the Communists in Angola. He blew the cover placed on American resupply flights originating from an abandoned Belgian airfield in Zaire to Luciania, a dirt landing strip in Southwest Angola that was protected by anti-Communist guerrillas.

On January 25, 1988, the Sandinistas used their SAMs to down another cargo plane, a DC-6 that was ferrying supplies to the anti-Sandinista resistance. The plane was used in an aerial supply operation run by 50 Americans from Swan Island.[11] Situated about 100 miles off the Honduran Atlantic coastline, this island in 1954 was the site of a powerful radio station operated by the C.I.A. Its purpose was to support the agency's propaganda activities in the Caribbean Basin. According to Trumbull Higgins, author of *The Perfect Failure: Kennedy, Eisenhower and the CIA at the Bay of Pigs*, "the purpose of this new station was first to attack Rafael Trujillo, the gradually weakening dictator of the Dominican Republic, and subsequently to attack Fidel Castro, its real target."

During the Bay of Pigs expedition, the operators of Radio Swan, as the station was called, abandoned their propaganda format. Instead, the radio was used to direct the invasion force and to control the movements of anti-Castro guerrillas inside Cuba. At one time, the station had been operated by the Gibraltar Steamship Corporation, a New York company with a Miami address that allegedly fronted for C.I.A. activities.[12]

Alejandro Sanchez Herrera, who parachuted to safety when his plane was hit by the Soviet SAM in January 1988, was part of the aerial supply unit that dropped 11 bundles of military supplies for the Jorge Salazar Commandos, an element of the anti-Sandinista resistance. Sanchez's plane had dropped its cargo before it was hit. Speaking for the resistance from Miami, Marta Sacasa said that 12 crew members were aboard the DC-6; eleven of them were killed, including the pilot and the co-pilot.

Aerial resupply flights were used effectively in the China-Burma-India theater during World War II. Innovative American commanders, however, had to overcome the concerns of senior officers who believed aerial resupply was suicidal and impossible to achieve. In 1943, Colonel Philip G. Cochran, who inspired the character Flip Corkin of Milton Caniff's cartoon strip "Terry and the Pirates," organized the First Air Commando Force. Devising a new method of waging war, Cochran's command resupplied a force of corps strength behind enemy lines and maintained it solely by air. The air command was under the direction of British Major General Orde Wingate. Cochran and Wingate perfected the aerial supply tactics now used by armies all over the world.[13]

Flying from airstrips hidden in the jungle—so reminiscent of "Terry and the Pirates"—cargo planes piloted by Americans continue to resupply the freedom fighters in Central America and Africa. Replenishment items for U.N.I.T.A. are delivered by planes based at Kamina, a former Belgian facility in the Shaba province in southern Zaire. President Mobutu Sese Seko of Zaire denies that Kamina is part of the network used to resupply U.N.I.T.A. However, during September 1987, Angolan troops uncovered a U.N.I.T.A. arms cache and found munitions boxes bearing the stenciled label "MATADI." Located near the mouth of the Congo River, Matadi is Zaire's principal seaport.

In August 1985, all legal obstacles to providing American assistance to U.N.I.T.A. were removed when the United States Senate revoked the Clark amendment, a prohibition that had outlawed assistance to U.N.I.T.A. Aerial supply, however, has remained a dubious way to sustain anti-Communist guerrillas while simultaneously trying to mask the identity of the primary purveyor and its distributors. Poorly disciplined personnel moving cargo and careless freight handlers, for example, will not obliterate (sanitize) any and all markings that identify the country responsible for originating the shipment. Also, persons who are taken prisoner from air crashes or captured from back-country airstrips are apt to provide their interrogators with information that can be used to verify insights gleaned from packing crates and other evidence. The requirement, too, that dirt landing fields be lighted for operations after dark has increased the risk of detection, particularly when planes land with clockwork precision, as some observers claimed they did at Luciania.

Thus, the security of the Mobutu government was not enhanced when the munitions boxes labeled "MATADI" were uncovered by the Angolan soldiers. Covert operations cannot remain clandestine if those involved are careless and poorly supervised.[14]

Lit by lamps reportedly installed by Americans, Kamina currently serves as the nexus for the American resupply flights to U.N.I.T.A. Four weekly flights carry weapons from this airfield to Luciania.

In 1985, a detachment of soldiers from the Rapid Deployment Force, based at Fort Bragg, North Carolina, were flown to Kamina to conduct a program of counterinsurgency training for Mobutu's troops. According to Bob Woodward, "CIA ties with Mobutu dated back to 1960, the year the C.I.A. had planned the assassination of Congolese nationalist leader

Patrice Lumumba." He said, "Before the CIA plot could be effected, Lumumba was murdered by another group of Mobutu supporters."[15]

The American surface-to-air missile, dubbed the "Stinger," has been trickling into the arsenals of terrorists who oppose governments that are allies of the United States. Twenty of these weapons, which are capable of traveling about three miles, were included in a 50-ton shipment of machine guns and other weapons that were seized by the French Coast Guard when they intercepted the Panamanian-registered coastal vessel *Eksund* in 1987. Naming Libya as the supplier of the arms, the crew of the vessel told the French police that the weapons were consigned to the I.R.A. and were loaded on the night of October 14, in Tripoli, Libya. Five Irishmen were taken off the *Eskund* and charged in France with "trafficking in weapons for terrorism." At least three of the men, according to Irish police sources, were I.R.A. members.

Meanwhile, I.R.A. threats of escalating the clandestine fight to end British rule over Northern Ireland (Ulster) prompted Sir John Hermon, Britain's chief constable, in a New Year's 1987 statement to warn that the I.R.A. was planning to undertake a series of violent attacks in 1988. Mentioning that the terrorists had received SAMs in shipments other than the freight carried by the *Eskund*, Hermon believed that the I.R.A. would, once again, resort to car bombings and utilize the most deadly equipment.

Preparing for the worst, the Royal Air Force (R.A.F.) helicopters, used by the British to track I.R.A. movements in Ulster, are being fitted with the same antimissile system that is carried by American jet fighters. This system, which was built by American defense contractors, deploys an array of miniature high-intensity flares that confuses the infrared guidance system of a heat-seeking missile such as the Stinger.

The I.R.A. could use its SAMs to counter the aerial surveillance deployed by the British or to knock down a commercial jet bound to or from a British airport. The prospect of sophisticated weaponry in the hands of terrorists is terrifying. But American missiles are not the only SAMs in the clandestine pipeline. The British themselves have used a missile called the "Blowpipe" in their Falkland Islands campaign. Ironically, this weapon is produced by a firm situated near Belfast. If the British distribute this weapon to the allies, no doubt one of them could become part of an I.R.A. arsenal.

In December 1987, a Reuters photograph showed an Afghan Army soldier displaying what was reported to be a United States Stinger missile that was captured from resistance fighters in the district of Khost, the site of a fierce battle between the Soviet Army and the Afghan freedom fighters.[16] The Afghan guerrillas had great success in countering Soviet helicopter gunships when using this weapon. It is conceivable that the Soviets procured Stingers from their Afghan clients and transshipped the weapons to the Libyans, who then stowed them aboard the ship that was intercepted by the French.

In Panama, General Manuel Noriega once was asked by Salvadorian rebels to arrange an arms deal to help them buy the American-made Stinger and other sophisticated weapons. He agreed to help and established a contact with a Sandinista intelligence officer. Jose I. Blandon, a former close adviser to Noriega, disclosed to U.S. Senate investigators the details of this transaction, but he said he did not know for certain if the Stingers were delivered.[17]

Clandestine channels and networks, which are used to supply terrorist groups worldwide, underscore the hazards of moving munitions without being able to control their ultimate use. Meanwhile, the movement of drugs and, in some instances, weapons for profit underpins the terrorism of the 1980s. Motivations fueled by political ideology, which were responsible for sparking the terrorism of the 1960s and the 1970s, have become less important.

NOTES

1. J. C. Hurewitz, *Middle East Politics: The Military Dimension* (New York: Frederick A. Praeger, 1969), pp. 438–456.
2. Beatriz Ruiz de la Mata, "P.R. Terrorists Feared by U.S. Installations," *The San Juan Star* (Puerto Rico), August 31, 1985, p. 13.
3. Elaine Sciolino, "U.S. Finds Output of Drugs in World Growing Sharply," *The New York Times*, March 2, 1988, p. 1.
4. John B. Wolf, "Cuba Supplies U.S. Addicts in Destabilization Bid," *New York City Tribune*, May 13, 1986, p. 2 and idem, "Cuban-Colombian Narco-Terrorist Crop Flourishes," ibid., October 14, 1986, p. 2.
5. John B. Wolf, "Cuban Bandits Bound by Vows and Saint Worship," *New York City Tribune*, July 8, 1986, p. 2.
6. Stephen Engelberg with Elaine Sciolino, "A U.S. Frame-Up of Nicaragua Charged," *The New York Times*, February 2, 1988, p. 1.
7. William Borders, "3 British Soldiers Slain in Belfast," *The New York Times*, March 26, 1982, p. 2.
8. Bernard Weinraub, "I.R.A. Aid Unit in the Bronx Linked to Flow of Arms," *The New York Times*, December 16, 1975, p. 1.
9. Richard D. Lyons, "U.S. Says It Has Broken an I.R.A. Ring That Crossed from Canada to Buy Weapons," *The New York Times*, March 1, 1982, p. B1.
10. "Irish Aid Efforts in U.S. Still Strong," *The New York Times*, September 8, 1981, p. 11.
11. James Brooke, "Angola Guerrilla Describes U.S. Aid," *The New York Times*, December 15, 1987, p. 4.
12. Trumbull Higgins, *The Perfect Failure: Kennedy, Eisenhower, and the C.I.A. at the Bay of Pigs* (New York: W. W. Norton, 1987), pp. 24, 30, 51, 64.

13. John B. Wolf, "U.S. Aerial Supply Operations for Anti-Leftists Told to Captors," *New York City Tribune*, February 16, 1988, p. 2.
14. John B. Wolf, "Americans Said to Fly Aid to Central American, African Rebels," *New York City Tribune*, January 5, 1988, p. 2.
15. Bob Woodward, *Veil: The Secret Wars of the C.I.A. 1981–1987* (New York: Simon & Schuster, 1987), p. 268.
16. John B. Wolf, "SAM and Stinger Missiles Find Way to Hands of IRA, Others," *New York City Tribune*, January 26, 1988, p. 2.
17. Engelberg with Sciolino, "A U.S. Frame-Up," p. 1.

APPLICATIONS

ANTITERRORISM IN NORTHERN IRELAND

On the morning of March 25, 1982, gunmen hiding in a Belfast house on Crocus Street opened fire on an army patrol. Two British soldiers of the Green Jackets Regiment died instantly when a hail of machine-gun and automatic-rifle fire penetrated the rear of their Land Rover. A third soldier died of wounds within the hour.

Following the classic pattern of the clandestine struggle in Northern Ireland, this ambush, in a narrow urban street, was carried out effectively and efficiently as a consequence of prior planning. The assassins, terrorists of the Irish Republican Army (I.R.A.), spent the night waiting in a house across the street from a heavily fortified police station in the predominantly Roman Catholic Falls Road area of Ulster's largest city. Armed with a machine gun and two high-powered rifles, the killers burst into the house shortly after midnight and held its occupants at gunpoint, while they waited for their quarry.

When two Land Rovers drove out of the gate of the station and into the street, shortly before noon, the I.R.A. terrorists opened fire from windows. Immediately after unleashing their fusillade, the gunmen fled out the back door of the house and disappeared into the maze of small streets and alleyways that intersect to form a labyrinth.[1]

The Crocus Street ambush disturbed British Army strategists because it was evidence of an I.R.A. reorganizational move, a shift from neighborhood-based units to clandestine cells. Instead of the conventional military structure that was often unraveled by a single informer, the new I.R.A. cells contained people from different parts of a city or even of the province. Only the cell leader was authorized to contact higher authorities or other cells. This style of organization provided a "cut-out" that limits the damage caused by an informer or a terrorist who breaks under interrogation.

In 1982, I.R.A. attacks were being executed by cells designated as A.S.U.s (Active Service Units). Sophisticated and deadly weapons used by an A.S.U. were kept under leadership control until needed for a special attack. Armalite automatic rifles, infantry mortars, Soviet-bloc RPG-7 rocket launchers, booby traps, and the M-60 machine gun manufactured in the United States were the basic weapons used by the A.S.U.s.[2]

I.R.A.: ORGANIZATION AND OPERATIONS

The British government once pegged I.R.A. membership at 300 to 500 people in the A.S.U.s and an auxiliary force of 2,000 to 3,000 more who operated a safe-house network—certainly a disappointingly small force of revolutionaries after 13 years of struggle. I.R.A. gunmen are used sparingly because new terrorists are proving difficult to recruit. Its hit teams, however, are believed to be staffed by terrorists who are conditioned by up to ten years of operational experience. A few hundred of such well-armed terrorists could raise havoc anywhere in the United States. Thus, the British believe that the I.R.A. will convulse Ulster for some years to come. Northern Ireland, which has a population of approximately 1.5 million, is smaller than most American states and contains fewer people than a number of America's cities.[3]

Although the I.R.A. is no longer attracting the large number of people that it had recruited in the early 1970s, the British Army contends that it no longer needs them, because a small number of activists can maintain a disproportionately high level of violence. New recruits are often selected from the *Fianna*, a youth organization whose members eagerly seek promotion to full gun-carrying terrorist status. Furthermore, the prisons, pouring out "a steady stream of embittered and dedicated terrorists," are another dependable source of I.R.A. manpower.

A strip of hill country in south Armagh County has been the launching pad for many of the I.R.A.'s ambushes. The British call the region "bandit country" and the Irish have labeled it "the killing ground." A British garrison of about 1,000 troops has been stationed at Crossmaglen, a Catholic stronghold situated astride a network of clandestine routes that are used by terrorists traveling from the south into Belfast. Conceal-ment and escape for the A.S.U.s are easily managed in the towns and villages of bandit country, whereas elsewhere in Ulster it is difficult. Bands of terrorists are often spirited across the open border into the Irish Republic or they "disappear" among the Catholic farmers and the village residents of the region, who are openly hostile to the British garrison.

Attacks on the Judiciary

The populations of Belfast and Londonderry must be traumatized if the I.R.A. is to remain credible. Its leaders know that ambushes and fire-fights in Northern Ireland's heavily populated urban areas still provide the media attention that the I.R.A. requires. Consequently, they con-tinue to stage urban terrorist operations despite the great risks involved for their A.S.U.s.

For example, on March 2, 1982, Irish terrorists tried to assassinate Northern Ireland's top judge, Lord Lowry. Two gunmen, who slipped away through a backyard, fired four shots at him as he was getting out of his armor-plated car at Queen's University in Belfast. Police said Lord Lowry escaped unhurt when his bodyguards threw him to the floor of the car.

Judges have always been high on the I.R.A.'s hit list. The Lowry ambush, however, marked the first serious attack on a member of the judiciary in Northern Ireland in five years. It was initiated from a window of a vacant house opposite the university. In 1974, a magistrate had been shot dead at his home near the same university. Two years later, Judge Garret McGrath was shot and wounded while on vacation in North Antrim.[4]

Use of Explosives

According to sources in Ulster, the 1982 bombings in Northern Ireland were an I.R.A. attempt to show that the organization was still active despite a series of arrests of suspected terrorists. The authorities said the I.R.A. also gave advanced warning of four blasts in which no one was reported hurt. These bombs exploded in Belfast, Newry, Newtown-stewart, and Armagh. But a fifth blast, a car bomb, exploded without warning in Banbridge, 30 miles west of Belfast. Detonated on a crowded main street, the bomb killed a 9-year-old child and injured ten people, five of them seriously.

On Tuesday, April 20, 1982, explosive-packed cars blew up in five of Northern Ireland's cities. Police said that three or four people were wounded slightly in the explosion in Strabane, 14 miles southwest of Londonderry. However, no injuries were reported in the other bombings that took place in Ballymena, Bessbrook, Belfast, and Londonderry.

Attacks on the Royal Ulster Constabulary

The Royal Ulster Constabulary (R.U.C.) has been a primary target for terrorist gunmen. These attacks abated after a remote-controlled bomb, which was planted behind a corrugated fence, exploded and showered with shards of metal four R.U.C. officers who were sitting in a parked Land-Rover. This incident occurred in central Belfast shortly after midnight on November 28, 1981. One of the policemen was killed, and the other three were hurt, one of them seriously.

On March 28, 1982, the attacks on the R.U.C. resumed, however, when Inspector Norman Duddy, apparently shadowed by his killers, was assassinated as he left a church service in Londonderry. Another policeman was shot and killed in Londonderry on May 4, 1982, the eve of the first anniversary of the death of Robert "Bobbie" Sands. Sands was the first of 10 I.R.A. guerrillas to die in the prison hunger strikes of 1981. Police said that the officer died instantly when a terrorist machine-gun squad fired at close range on a police patrol. Another officer was wounded seriously in the attack.[5]

Ambush Tactics

The I.R.A. has continued to ambush British army units. On April 1, 1982, terrorists waited in ambush in a Londonderry apartment they had seized. When an unmarked van transporting two British soldiers in civilian clothes appeared in the gunsights of their weapons, they opened fire. The two soldiers, who were thought to be members of the Special Air Service (S.A.S.) on an intelligence mission, were killed. They were the fourth and fifth British soldiers killed in ambushes within a week.

Stephen Tiric, a British army captain who the I.R.A. claimed was also a member of S.A.S., disappeared earlier in 1982 after entering the Three Steps Inn, a crossroads pub in an isolated section of bandit country. Tiric was dressed in civilian clothes and was believed to be involved in undercover work when he vanished.

Information gathering on tactical subjects is a critical aspect for the two sides that are involved in the "shadow war" in Ulster. James Prior, Great Britain's Secretary of State for Northern Ireland, revealed that an I.R.A. informer once provided the government with information leading to the arrest of 24 suspected terrorists on firearms and murder charges.[6]

In mid-November 1981, the rate of killings in Ulster increased to nearly one a day, causing fear and bitterness among both the Protestant majority and the Roman Catholic minority. To counter the I.R.A., Britain began flying additional troops into Northern Ireland. This airlift of battle-ready paratroopers raised British troop strength in the province to just over 11,000, with most of the additional manpower being used to augment patrols in troubled areas and to conduct searches.[7] These searches of private residences, some of which were conducted without warrants under emergency legislation, were an important part of the battle against terrorism. Often suspected gunmen were flushed out of hiding or weapons were uncovered. Although the British Army did not divulge its reasons for selecting a particular house for a search, it was often thought to be "acting on information" (tips). The security force in Northern Ireland had a diverse network of informers of varying reliability. Also, the government maintained a special telephone number that the public could call to give information anonymously.

In 1980, there were over 4,000 searches of private residences in Ulster, including raids on houses that were unoccupied at the time. Many of these searches produced either an arrest or some contraband. Some Catholics, however, regarded them as random intimidation, harassment, and part of a grim mythology that dates back hundreds of years.

Usually, the British troops do not "toss" (breakup) a house when they enter it. "But am I supposed to be grateful for that?" "No," remarked a Catholic resident of Belfast. "I hate the Brits and I'll always hate the Brits. They should get out of my country just like they should stay out of my house."

The British paratroopers considered house searches as distasteful duty. As one young trooper put it, the job of searching a private house in Northern Ireland was something that soldiers should not have to do even in their own country.[8]

British antiterrorist operations did not target just Ulster's Catholic population. In an early morning raid on April 14, 1982, about 30 police officers arrested five officials of the Ulster Defense Association (U.D.A.), the most formidable of the Protestant self-help organizations, and seized submachine-gun parts and ammunition in a raid on the group's Belfast headquarters.

The legislation that gave the British police greater powers in searching people's homes also established a system of antiterrorist courts in Ulster. In short, Northern Ireland's antiterrorism courts look just like any other courtroom in the United Kingdom with one major exception: the jury box is always empty. The use of juries in terrorist trials was abolished as an emergency measure in the 1970s on the grounds that, in the

highly charged atmosphere enveloping the community, jurors were subject to intimidation and threats.

BRITISH MILITARY OPERATIONS

Although briefly augmented in the early 1980s, the British troop
strength in Northern Ireland has been greatly reduced. The reason for
the decline was twofold: (1) the trend in I.R.A. tactics was away from riots
to selective killings of security personnel, chiefly members of the constabulary, and (2) Ulster no longer was needed to provide the military
with experience in urban warfare once the large-scale attacks in Belfast
and Londonderry ended. All NATO forces to which the United Kingdom
provided a large contingent received intensive training in urban
warfare.[9]

Helicopter, electronic surveillance, and computerized systems have
also helped the British Army to reduce its force in Northern Ireland.
Streets are under electronic observation by night and day, reducing the
need to send infantry patrols into all of the byways simultaneously.
Similarly, helicopters have replaced infantry squads in patrolling the
borders.

At one time, regular British army battalions were stationed in Northern Ireland. Gradually the R.U.C. assumed the duties that were assigned
to these units. Most of the army battalions were in the province for four
and one-half months on rotation from British garrisons. Two of these
units were usually stationed in bandit country, watching the border with
the Irish Republic, another was deployed near Belfast, and a company
was positioned near Londonderry.

Personal information about the commanders of the various British
military units who are stationed in Northern Ireland has been classified
"utmost secret" by London. On October 17, 1981, Lieutenant General Sir
Steuart Pringle was severely wounded when a bomb went off in his car as
he drove from his home in southeast London. The I.R.A. claimed responsibility for the attack. Pringle had been appointed commandant of the
Royal Marines on April 2, 1981. After the explosion, he was taken to a
hospital where doctors amputated his right leg below the knee. Fully
recovered, he proceeded to direct his 9,000-member force from its London headquarters. Pringle once served two three-month tours in Northern Ireland, in 1972 and in 1973, as a Lieutenant Colonel in charge of 45
Commando, a unit which has been specially trained in mountain and
arctic warfare. General John Jeremy Moore, who took temporary command of the Royal Marines as Pringle recuperated, had commanded the

commando forces during the Falkland Islands campaign. He also had served in Northern Ireland.

THE ROYAL MARINES

The Royal Marine organization includes a small secret unit of crack commandos known as the S.B.S. Its activities are so clandestine that its exact name is not public: some members say it is short for "Special Boat Service," others say "Special Boat Squadron." But one thing about the S.B.S. is common knowledge: as seagoing sabotage experts, they are to the marines what the S.A.S. —the antiterrorist unit—is to the army. "We can do anything the S.A.S. can do," the S.B.S. boasts, "and walk on water, too." The service has an insignia—a frog and crossed canoe paddles—that is worn only at private dinners and celebrations. Their motto, too, is appropriate: "Not by strength, but by guile."

Founded during World War II, the S.B.S.'s most famous exploit was a raid involving ten men who paddled canoes 50 miles up the Gironde River, in occupied France, to blow up a group of German ships in Bordeaux. The landings that prepared the way for the British invasion of South Georgia and the Falkland Islands were also undertaken by S.B.S. units. Because of their special training, S.B.S. operatives have been used to defend Britain's North Sea oil rigs from terrorist attack. The group also made headlines in 1973 when members parachuted onto the ocean liner *Queen Elizabeth 2* after a caller threatened to blow it up.

Currently, the S.B.S. recruits its men from the toughest and most skilled of the Royal Marines, with only one man from every 30 who volunteer being selected. Recruits are trained in obstacle swimming, diving, minelaying, and parachuting. Marksmanship, mountaineering, hand-to-hand combat, and survival in enemy territory are also among their many capabilities. In combat skills, the 100 to 400 men that constitute the S.B.S. (their total strength is unknown and all estimates are at best wild guesses) are trained to use an assortment of weapons that include Uzi and Sterling machine guns and pistols of various makes. Each man chooses his own weapons, wears what he likes, and eats and drinks what he finds. He knows how to live in holes without hot meals for weeks.

Additionally, an S.B.S. paratrooper can jump from 25,000 feet, with a collapsible boat strapped to his body, and fall to 1,200 feet before his chute opens. Most jumpers use the HALO, a high-altitude, low-opening parachute. Upon hitting the water, the S.B.S. trooper has a special mask and a tank that recycles air and does not leave bubbles trailing on the surface.

Permitted to dress informally and to call their officers by their first names, the independent S.B.S. Marines avoid wearing snappy military uniforms but, instead, dress in stained waterproof jackets or jungle-green pullovers. Many of them wear soccer shoes. Their combat equipment includes weapons, a small pack of food, spare socks, a waterproof poncho, a fingertip-sized compass hidden beneath a bootlace eyelet, and a wire sewn into the waistband of their fatigues. Fastened to their belts are a canteen, a knife, a handgun, snares, a fishing line, and a food pouch—everything that is needed to survive for a week.

Some S.B.S. men carry a briefcase-sized radio that can "burp" out long coded messages in less than a second, making it almost impossible for trackers to pinpoint the source. Headquartered at Poole, a harbor town in the south of England, the S.B.S. men are allegedly capable of "sleeping under a general's bed for a month without even the chambermaid becoming aware of their presence."[10]

THE GARDA

The Irish army and its police force also have stepped up efforts to curb the I.R.A. When the army constructed barracks near the Ulster border, these facilities disrupted the I.R.A.'s cross-border traffic and impeded its staging operations. The *Garda*, the Irish Police, has been particularly effective in uncovering caches of prize weapons and explosives. Additionally, the Garda and the R.U.C. continue to exchange intelligence and the results of interrogations. As an unarmed police force, the Garda is particularly vulnerable to attack. Several of its officers once were murdered by terrorists running roadblocks.

THE ULSTER VOLUNTEER FORCE

Police officers, who are regarded by terrorists as the tool of the "forces of repression," continue to be targeted. On August 19, 1984, Protestant youths carrying firebombs clashed with the police in Belfast. The rioting was triggered by a courtroom brawl a few days earlier involving the police and 47 Protestant suspected terrorists. The defendants faced 227 charges, including the murders of Roman Catholics and membership in the outlawed Ulster Volunteer Force.

The Ulster Volunteer Force has developed considerable popular support within Northern Ireland's Protestant community. Thousands of its supporters marched on August 18, 1984 to protest police brutality and to demand an end to the police use of informers. "Things are getting out of control," said Andy Tyrie, allegedly the supreme commander of the U.D.A. "We've tried to cool down the hotheads, but we're talking about years of frustration at the failure of British policies," he said.

Rioting by Protestant elements flared in 1984, the first time in a decade. This outbreak, which was confined to the Shankill Road section of Belfast, demonstrated the ire of a handful of people who are ideologically linked to the terrorists. Although the R.U.C. is staffed overwhelmingly by Protestant officers, the supporters of the U.D.A. regard its efforts to administer justice uniformly and without reference to the religious preference of the terrorist offender as disloyalty to their "church."[11]

PROFESSIONALISM OF THE POLICE

Impartiality is not regarded as a laudable virtue by members of a community that is continually stirred by propagandists who are skilled in the art of transforming religious bigotry into terroristic violence. In Northern Ireland, the police officer's role is crucial to the preservation of order. Trained to perform their duties within the framework of the British legal system, the R.U.C. has quelled riots in Roman Catholic neighborhoods a few days before being asked to control violence involving militant Protestant youths.

The professional quality of the British style of antiterrorist policing in Northern Ireland is linked to the indoctrination and training of the R.U.C. These programs emphasize the development of community relations and other interpersonal and psychological skills. Consequently, it is most difficult for a propagandist to exploit any weaknesses of the police force.

The British also rely on internal affairs units to monitor police integrity. Through a process of periodic inspections, the failures and errors of individual police officers are identified and corrected before they become serious and subject to manipulation by terrorists, who are always watching for opportunities to discredit the police.

Additionally, the British police have recognized the compelling need for self-restraint and "evenhandedness" when combatting terrorists in a struggle for the hearts and minds of the people. They are always ready to charge members of their units with crimes when committed and bring them before the criminal courts.

STAKING OUT THE TERRORISTS

In February 1986, when British antiterrorists who were operating in mufti killed Francis Bradley in Toomebridge, Northern Ireland, people started asking questions. Bradley, a twenty-year-old nationalist, was accompanied by two other men. Although the police said that guns were found at the scene of the slaying, Bradley's companions were arrested but were later released without charges. Thirty-four killings have been attributed to British personnel working undercover during the period from late 1982 to February 1985. Bradley's death signaled the resumption of ambushes by British stakeout squads, a tactic that had not been used for almost a year.

In 1984, Frederick Jackson was killed by an antiterrorist plainclothes squad as he was driving away from a construction site at a trucking firm. His company had been engaged to upgrade the facility. Jackson, the police said, was hit by a bullet fired by a member of an S.A.S. undercover unit. S.A.S. was attempting to prevent the escape of a group of I.R.A. gunmen, who planned to bushwack a soldier as he reported for duty. Jackson's car apparently crossed the trajectory of a bullet that was fired by one of the British marksmen. The Jackson family, however, believed that their kinsman was killed because S.A.S. mistook him for an I.R.A. man who was to drive a getaway car for the terrorists who were assigned to the ambush operation. This incident added additional fuel to the fire stoked by those who urge the dissolution of the British undercover stakeout units.

In 1986, John Stalker, then deputy chief constable of the Greater Manchester Police in England, was asked to inquire into some shooting incidents in Northern Ireland in 1982. These involved antiterrorist operations and alleged members of the I.R.A. Stalker was recalled from the inquiry, which was continued by the chief constable of the West Yorkshire Police, and subsequently resigned from the police. At the time of this writing, the matter was still under investigation.

On February 23, 1988, Britain announced that the only British soldier who was sentenced to life imprisonment for fatally shooting an Irish civilian had been pardoned and restored to active duty. Prime Minister Margaret Thatcher defended this decision in Parliament. The British had also decided not to prosecute police officers who were found to have obstructed justice in an investigation into a series of fatal shootings by the police of civilians in Northern Ireland. National Security and the public interest were cited by the British attorney general as the rationale for barring the prosecutions. The inquiry into these killings was triggered by allegations that the police in Northern Ireland used shoot-to-kill tactics against unarmed I.R.A. suspects in 1982. According to the British soldier who was exonerated, the person he shot seemed to be reaching for a weapon in a jacket pocket during a street confrontation.[12]

There always remains the temptation for police or military units to act outside the law when conducting antiterrorist operations. Some police officers and soldiers insist that the normal safeguards in the law for the individual are not designed for a terrorist. Terrorists deserve to be treated as outlaws, comment some seasoned antiterrorists.

SPECIAL AIR SERVICES

Democratic societies must develop reliable and professional intelligence systems to furnish police and military personnel with the information they need to use proactive measures to control terrorism. Otherwise, the use of raw military force, regardless of the grave consequences of such action, could be the only legitimate option left to protect a free society from collapse.

Aware of the need for its troops to get to know the population of Northern Ireland on an intimate level, the British Army assigned a large number of men to undercover operations. Many soldiers were assigned to S.A.S., whose motto is "Who Dares Wins." S.A.S. operatives have been highly effective in disrupting the I.R.A. command structure and infiltrating Protestant paramilitary terrorist organizations. Cells of the U.D.A. have been penetrated by S.A.S. operatives. The determination of the British to use S.A.S. personnel to control both I.R.A.- and U.D.A.-inspired terrorism has contributed to the success of its antiterrorist initiatives in Northern Ireland.[13]

On May 9, 1987, British police revealed that three important I.R.A. gunmen, including the East Tyrone Province area commander, were killed in a firefight with police on the previous day. Notified by an informant of the I.R.A.'s intention to raid a police station in Loughgall, British police and troops lay in wait. Cocky after the car-bomb killing of Judge Maurice Gibson and his wife Cecily a month earlier, the I.R.A. was convinced that it had cleansed itself of infiltrators and informers. Using a bomb-laden bulldozer to ram the fence surrounding the police station, which was thirty miles southwest of Belfast, the I.R.A. succeeded in blowing the roof and a side off the building before the British opened fire. All the I.R.A. terrorists were killed in the shootout, including Jim Lynagh, described by police as one of the most wanted I.R.A. gunmen in Ulster. Patrick McKearney, who had escaped from a Belfast prison with 37 other I.R.A. terrorists in 1983, also was killed. The shooting of the

I.R.A. leaders was the worst single blow suffered by the organization since 1972, when four of its key members died while handling a bomb. Prior to this ambush, the I.R.A. had mounted an imposing campaign in Ulster, killing 13 police officers and soldiers and a senior judge. S.A.S., however, has always been the I.R.A.'s nemesis.

INFORMANT DEVELOPMENT AND CONTROL

In Ulster, the police claim that the I.R.A. cannot control defections from its cells. Informers, therefore, continue to be an important tool in the British antiterrorist campaign. The army, the S.A.S., and the police use them to monitor the I.R.A.'s intentions and operations. Acting on tips from informers, the British have made a number of arrests, uncovered arms caches, and emplaced ambush units.

Some people say that most Irish informers are "turned," that is, they are induced to betray the I.R.A. by police Special Branch agents and S.A.S. operatives during interrogations. The British claim that Catholics are increasingly disenchanted with I.R.A. methods and report that kneecappings are evidence of this dissension. The number of reported kneecappings, however, is not a valid indicator to measure the success of the British antiterrorist campaign in Ulster. In the ghetto, where police rarely venture except in convoys of armored vehicles, the I.R.A. uses kneecapping as a punishment for various forms of antisocial behavior. One young man, who was not accused of informing, was once found spread-eagled on a Belfast garbage dump, shot in the legs and arms. Informers, however, get a "headjob," the Belfast euphemism for a bullet in the brain. The traditional I.R.A. method of execution is to force the victim to kneel and then to shoot him in the back of the head.

A few years ago, Patrick Trainor, a member of the I.R.A.'s "Provisional" wing, was found dead in the Catholic Anderstown quarters of Belfast. Shot twice in the back of the head, he was one of the five informers the I.R.A. claimed to have killed in a purge of their ranks.

Conforming with the I.R.A. tradition of tracking down "touts" (ghetto slang for an informer) and settling old scores, the terrorists regularly comb their ranks for other traitors. I.R.A. veterans remember the story of one old-timer who fled to the United States during Ireland's 1921–1922 civil war. Finally tracked down in the early 1960s, he was slain for alleged betrayal. "A tout is a dead man wherever he is," the I.R.A. maintains. "We always get informers. Sometimes it takes years, but we always get them."

I.R.A. countermeasures designed to stop the flow of sensitive information to the police are not always effective. John Hermon, Britain's chief constable in Northern Ireland, spoke confidently of a breakthrough in the campaign against the I.R.A., when he revealed that "super-grasses"—as important informers are called in Belfast—continue to provide the police with significant information.

The I.R.A. once hunted for Christopher Black, a supergrass. Released from the Maze prison in 1981 after serving half of a ten-year term for armed robbery, Black was rearrested in Belfast's Catholic Ardoyne enclave while manning an I.R.A. roadblock. Terrorist sources said that Black broke under questioning and agreed to inform in return for immunity from prosecution on a possible murder charge. According to the I.R.A., he provided the police with the names of activists who have been charged with two killings and several attempted murders. Smuggled out of Northern Ireland by the police, Black is believed to have a new identity. Supposedly, he is being guarded in a Northern England hideout with his wife, two children, and mother-in-law.[14]

In November 1987, an offshoot of the Irish National Liberation Army (I.N.L.A.) critically wounded a Protestant city councillor in Belfast. In telephone calls to the press, the Irish Peoples Liberation Organization (I.P.L.O.) claimed responsibility for the shooting of George Seawright, who once said that Roman Catholics should be burned, and who was immensely popular among Protestant extremists. The I.P.L.O. had coalesced around the notion that the I.N.L.A., a militant Marxist faction of the Irish Republican Army, was no longer a viable organization. The I.N.L.A., it claimed, has been penetrated by the police.

In 1983, Dominic "Mad Dog" McGlinchey had formed the I.N.L.A. because he insisted that the I.R.A. had become too soft. Dubbed "Mad Dog" after his boast to the Irish press that he had killed 30 people, McGlinchey was perceived as having a matter-of-fact attitude toward killing, and participated himself in at least 200 acts of terrorism. He was captured in the Irish Republic and was extradited to Ulster in 1984.

The I.P.L.O. evade the police by moving often and disguising themselves. They have been known to dye their hair, grow or shave a beard, and dress as women. At their hideouts in the Irish Republic, the I.P.L.O. plans its attacks against police officers, soldiers, and politicians.

Irish terrorists have been controlled by the police, who use information obtained from their criminal accomplices to convict them. A nuance in the British judicial system permits prosecutors to offer convicted terrorists a "deal," usually consisting of one or more of the following: a reduced sentence, immunity from prosecution, a new identity, a job, a car, a house. In return, the informant must agree to testify in court against former comrades. Such informers are usually "disappeared" from Ulster to a life of anonymity and immunity from prosecution for their extensive criminal background.

Christopher Black was the first supergrass informer. During a courtroom session in 1983, he pointed his finger at 38 I.R.A. gunmen. This group was charged with 182 counts of terrorism, murder, bombing, gunrunning, and membership in an outlawed organization. Opponents to the use of supergrasses insist that trials involving their use may possibly convict defendants on the testimony of criminals that has not been verified for accuracy and reliability. The British government, which contends that reliance on the supergrass is nothing new in English common law, has stated that uncorroborated testimony from an accomplice is admissible evidence in any British court.

Claiming that the supergrass is not just a paid informer, police mention that the payments given the informers are a pittance, merely enough for food and rent. In 1984, the British government stated that it spent $730,000 to safeguard the supergrasses who were living incognito.

Although the use of informants has been institutionalized, the British use other methods to check terrorism in Ulster. The conduct of house searches without warrant but within the ambit of emergency legislation is an important part of their continuous battle against the terrorists. Often, in such search operations, gunmen are flushed out of hiding, or weapons are recovered by the searchers.[15]

POLICY GUIDELINES

The antiterrorist policy that is implemented by the British in Northern Ireland mirrors their experience with the techniques of exercising social control in both primitive countries and in advanced and pluralist societies on five continents. The maintenance of law and order and the reduction of the threat posed by a terrorist group within the United Kingdom are the fundamental objectives of this policy. Consequently, the philosophical orientation of the control measures, instituted by the government in Northern Ireland, is one that casts all extralegal terrorist acts—bombings, kidnappings, and assassinations—as morally wrong.

Anxious to safeguard the public's right to know, aware of the absolute requirement to have all citizens fully cognizant of the details of its antiterrorist laws, and resolute in its commitment to counter the claims of the terrorist offenders, the British continue to emphasize publicly that their antiterrorist measures are intended solely to remove dangerous people from the masses. However, the media continue to provide the I.R.A. with several million dollars worth of free publicity.

Atrocious acts, such as the assassination of Lord Louis Mountbatten on August 27, 1979, and the placement of bombs in two London parks that killed eight British soldiers on July 21, 1982, were contrived to focus media attention upon the I.R.A.'s cause. According to a statement issued by the terrorist organization in the wake of the July 1982 bombings in London, "the Irish people have sovereign and national rights which no task or occupational force can put down."[16] To protect against this sort of inadvertent cooperation by the press, the British have subjected their newspapers to the "D-Notice" system. Under the safeguards included in this system, the press is notified prior to publication when a particular news item could violate security laws.[17]

Emergency Legislation

Brian Crozier, director of the London-based Institute for the Study of Conflict and author of *The Rebels*, a pioneering study that examines how internal pressures could cause the breakdown of a state, discussed other legal concepts that provide the underpinning for the British antiterrorist effort in Northern Ireland. "It is very important to make it clear," he said, "that any emergency legislation that is introduced, including detention without trial, is temporary in nature and will be revoked as soon as possible."[18]

Four additional aspects of emergency powers legislation are characteristic of the British antiterrorist posture: (1) draft laws must be easy to understand; (2) the purpose of emergency legislation is to control an insurgent group that has demonstrated its absolute disdain for the law; (3) all "war measures" must be closely monitored and reviewed periodically; and (4) all laws must be effective and applied equally to all.[19]

Political Prisoner Status

Considered hypocritical by civil libertarians, Northern Ireland's antiterrorism courts still figure prominently in releases by the media. "These special courts with their conveyor-belt justice are a poison in this society," according to Paschal J. O'Hare, who has considerable experience in defending Irish nationalists. O'Hare and other Irish republicans insist that the very existence of the nonjury courts constitutes a special political status. The basic purpose of the prisoners who participated in the "blanket protest" and the hunger strike, all of whom were convicted and sentenced in the antiterrorism courts, was to compel the British government to grant them status as political prisoners.[20]

The "blanket protest," during which some prisoners who were incarcerated at Maze Prison near Belfast had worn nothing but a blanket since 1976, ended in 1981 when the government told the protestors that they could begin wearing civilian clothes as soon as their relatives brought them in. The Irish nationalists had maintained that they are political prisoners, fighting a war of independence, and not common criminals. That assertion was the basis of their refusal to wear prison-issued uniforms. The government made the concession on clothing without calling it political-prisoner status because it applied to all prisoners in Northern Ireland, including the small number who were serving sentences for ordinary crimes unrelated to terrorist activities.[21]

Just before Christmas 1980, a hunger strike was called off when an agreement between the prisoners and the government was about to be finalized. But the understanding collapsed in March 1981, when Bobby Sands started a second hunger strike. Ultimately, ten prisoners starved themselves to death in this protest.

After the second hunger strike collapsed on October 3, 1981, British Secretary of State James Prior announced that the British government would grant the prisoners the right to wear their own clothes at all times instead of any kind of prison-issued clothing. He also promised concessions regarding reduced sentences for good behavior and increased from 25 to 50 the number of other prisoners with whom an inmate could associate with in off-hours. Also, Prior promised that prison work might include education. Again, these concessions did not constitute a grant of political status, the government said, because the new rules were applied to all prisoners.[22]

Gerry Adams, once thought to be a high-ranking officer of the I.R.A., considered the changes in the British prison policy as yielding to the five demands on which the hunger strikers had based their action. These demands were the right to wear their own clothes, to free association, to receive more mail and visitors, to have a greater say in the work they do, and to have time off for good behavior. "What is certain is that the right by the prisoners to wear their own clothes has been won by the deaths of the ten H-block martyrs," remarked Adams.[23] (At the Maze, the prison buildings are called H-blocks because they are built in the shape of the letter "H.")

ANTITERRORISM COURTS

In 1981, the Haldane Society of Socialist Lawyers, a British group, reviewed the operations of the antiterrorism courts and issued this statement: "If Northern Ireland's problems are susceptible to a political solution, then civil and political liberties must be restored to its people. So long as the courts continue to play a clearly political role, so long will a political solution be impossible." Essentially, the aspects of the special courts that created the most controversy were the severity of the sentences, the number of people convicted, and the courtroom procedures.

Possession of explosives or firearms can bring a sentence of 5 or 10 years or more. Gun-control legislation specifies that a judge can presume that a person who is accused of possessing a weapon knew that the gun was there, unless the defendant can prove that he did not know about it.[24]

During the first six months of 1981, these nonjury courts convicted 292 people of terrorist crimes. Twenty-eight of these felons were sentenced to life imprisonment, the maximum sentence in Britain, and sentences of 10 years or more were levied on 35 others.

Procedurally, the antiterrorist courts lack drama. "You're not putting on a show for anyone," one British lawyer remarked. Furthermore, a judge often speeds the process along with a remark such as "you already told me that." Very serious cases, therefore, can be completed in a day or two, particularly when the defendant chooses not to take part. Asserting that the British courts have no legitimate jurisdiction in Ireland, many I.R.A. gunmen do not participate in their own trials.

These abridgements of civil liberties in Northern Ireland continue to make the government uncomfortable, although it claims that they are necessary. Parliament, however, regularly debates this issue because the government insists that emergency legislation be renewed every six months. Some debates have been particularly charged, with one member of Parliament after another rising to demand some kind of change.[25]

Hanging

Except for acts of treason, the death penalty has been abolished in the United Kingdom since 1965, even though, however, 104 members of the House of Commons had voted to keep it. In 1974, a motion to restore the death penalty, moved after the I.R.A. bombed a tavern in Birmingham, England, gained 217 backers. A similar recommendation, put forth in 1975 after a wave of terrorist bombings in London's West End, garnered 232 votes for the motion and 361 against.[26]

In July 1982, Prime Minister Thatcher, speaking in Parliament a few days after an I.R.A. bomb killed three soldiers of the Household Cavalry, rejected a new move to bring back hanging for those who commit terrorist crimes. Although she is a supporter of capital punishment, Thatcher noted that the House of Commons refused to restore the death penalty in May 1982 by a 357 to 195 vote.

Roy Jenkins, who as home secretary and cabinet minister was responsible for internal security, once cogently summarized the arguments of those members of the House of Commons who have opposed the death penalty. Jenkins argued that there is no evidence to indicate that the prospect of hanging will have a deterrent effect. He also believed that hanging might be the trigger for violent reprisals against the government while terrorists await trial and sentencing. Some terrorists, he noted, have scant regard for their own self-preservation. Most of the debates in the House of Commons during the past decades have concentrated less on the moral aspects of hanging than on its value as a deterrent to terrorist acts.[27]

Paul Wilkinson, author of *Terrorism and the Liberal State* and a professor at Aberdeen University in Scotland, advised that "if the death penalty for terrorist murder is to be reintroduced in Britain, the government, security forces, judiciary and penal system should all be fully prepared for a sudden and severe escalation in terrorist violence, at least in the short term."[28]

Torture

On February 8, 1977, the British government conceded that it had used five torture techniques on detainees in Northern Ireland, but gave a solemn pledge to the European Court of Human Rights, assembled in Strasbourg, France, that it would never do so again. Speaking before a preliminary hearing designed to establish the scope of the court's jurisdiction regarding a complaint lodged by Ireland, Sam Silkin, the British attorney general at the time, told a panel of 18 judges that British forces would cease to use the so-called five techniques of interrogation about which the Irish government had complained. These are hooding a prisoner, harassing him with noise, putting him on a bread-and-water diet, depriving him of sleep, and making him lean against a wall for long periods, off-balance with his arms outstretched.

Charging numerous cases of torture and other ill-treatment of prisoners by British security forces in Northern Ireland, in the months after the introduction of internment without trial in August, 1971, the Irish government submitted a voluminous account of these events to the European Human Rights Commission. Some of these allegations were upheld by the commission after a four-year investigation in which 119 witnesses were heard, among them senior security officers.

Silkin told the court that his government was not contesting the commission's findings. He said that, after an official inquiry into the conduct of the security forces in Northern Ireland, the use of these five techniques of interrogation had been halted in 1972, and compensation was paid to those who had suffered.[29]

Seven years later, a judicial commission, which was headed by former Crown Court Judge Harry Bennett, investigated Northern Ireland's prisons. The commission concluded that there were indications that an unspecified number of suspected terrorists were still being tortured during the course of police interrogations. Responding to torture charges made by Amnesty International, the 140-page report compiled by the commission recounted incidents of "bruising, contusions, hyperextension and hyper-flexion of joints, hair-pulling, jabbing, rupture of the ear drums and increased mental agitation."[30]

On March 16, 1979, the report was presented to Parliament and the government was placed on the defensive. Roy Mason, then the secretary of state for Northern Ireland, was called to his feet time and again by hostile questioning. Deeming the charges of police brutality as part of an I.R.A. propaganda campaign "to undermine the effectiveness and impair the efficiency of the force," Mason referred to what the report called "the classic dilemma" of how a liberal democratic society copes with terrorism. "On the one hand," he said, "that society is subject to violent attack aimed at its overthrow, and its people are killed, maimed and despoiled; on the other hand, that society seeks to assure to its people freedom under the law from violence and oppressive conduct."[31]

On March 19, 1981, the International League for Human Rights urged the British government to revise Northern Ireland's emergency laws for the interrogation and trial of suspected terrorists. Warning of a growing acceptance of the emergency legal measures imposed by the United Kingdom in 1973, the league made public a study entitled "Ten Years on in Northern Ireland: The Legal Control of Political Violence." This study was sponsored by the league and its British affiliate, the National Council for Civil Liberties. It offered a number of recommendations including the limiting of interrogation of suspected terrorists to one hour at a time, the disciplining of police officers who extracted confessions in violation of a legal code, and the banning of nighttime searches of homes unless a warrant has been obtained in advance. The league's report concluded by recognizing that there was little alternative for the British involvement in Northern Ireland until some more stable political settlement is achieved.[32]

House Searches

The emergency legal legislation, regarded by the British as the essential component of their effort to control terrorism in Northern Ireland,

permits police and soldiers to search private residences without warrants. A standard I.R.A. technique is to take over a house on a well-
travelled army-patrol route, hold the inhabitants hostage, and set up an
ambush built around an M-60 machine gun.[33] Once the squad has established its "fields of fire," an I.R.A. cell member calls the police and
reports an incident, such as a burglary or a traffic accident. As a police or
an army patrol approaches, the terrorist trap is triggered. The comment
of the I.R.A. gunmen involved in the slaughter is: "It don't mean nothing." Similar slogans were echoed in Vietnam by the American fighting
men who also understood the "horrible, hollow absurdity of the
cause."[34]

The government says its files do not store information on details of
the house searches, for example, which of these produced an arrest, but
often suspected gunmen are forced to flee their hideouts or weapons are
uncovered.[35]

Arrest Procedures

Under the emergency measures, it is legal for the police to arrest
without warrant any person suspected of being a terrorist and to hold the
suspect for 72 hours. But in a survey once conducted in association with
the National Council for Civil Liberties, a London-based group, two-
thirds of a group of 48 people arrested under the emergency measures
had never been asked about any particular incident. The surveyors concluded that the chief objective of the police arrests was to build up a
dossier on those who were arrested as a consequence of questioning and
not to develop a criminal case against them. Most of the reported police
interrogations involved the asking of specific questions that were intended to obtain details about the interviewee's family associations and
political views.[36]

Informant Development

Many of these arrests, called "screenings," occur in the early morning hours and are executed by the police, sometimes reinforced by army
units. I.R.A. leaders claim that, once arrested, some persons agreed to
provide information to the government in exchange for freedom from
prosecution. One such informer, a father of two, was being paid about
$11 per day for his services. Subsequently, he was shot through the head
by the I.R.A. and his body was found in a garbage chute.[36]

Security sources have said that informers often were "turned," that
is, induced to betray their colleagues, by police Special Branch officers

during the interrogation. (The Special Branch was formed out of the Irish Special Branch subsequent to the campaign of bombings by Irish revolutionaries from 1883 to 1885.)[37]

Extradition

The restrictions on civil liberties in Northern Ireland moved inexorably south to the Republic of Ireland. Irish politicians became aware that their constituents, who were 90 percent Catholic, had waved aside the Provisional I.R.A.'s call for a socialist secular state and the termination of the favored position of the Roman Catholic Church in any united Ireland. In 1972, Irish voters agreed to remove the church's special status that had been conferred in the 1937 constitution. But Catholic-accented aspects of life continue to dominate Irish society. The church, however, has condemned the I.R.A. because it has much to fear if its socialist, sectarian views ever become part of the value system of the power elite.[38]

Declining public support for the I.R.A. in southern Ireland is evidenced by a marked reduction, 60 percent to 70 percent, in the number of demonstrators that attend rallies in support of terrorist causes. Additionally, press releases by the Dublin government continue to emphasize that 20 percent of the Irish Republic's unemployment could be alleviated with the money it takes to police the I.R.A.[39]

In some cases, Irish laws are stricter than the British antiterrorist decrees that are enforced in Northern Ireland. In 1979, Ireland held approximately 150 terrorist offenders in its jails after convictions in Irish courts. Consequently, some Irish government officials are infuriated when the British talk about "safe havens," which, they say, the terrorists have in Ireland. The Offenses Against the State Act, a rigid piece of Irish legislation, requires a person, when asked, to account for his movements. It also provides that a senior policeman's sworn opinion that a man is a member of the I.R.A. is acceptable in court as evidence of his membership.[40]

After the murder of Lord Mountbatten, there was talk of even harsher laws, including restrictions on a suspect's right to remain silent or to get bail. The Irish are aware of the allegations that some of the terrorist convictions in Northern Ireland have been based on confessions obtained by police brutality in British jails.

Ireland is reluctant to extradite suspected terrorists even when it apprehends them, claiming that their crimes are politically motivated. Also, the Irish government has long maintained that few (if any) countries permit so-called hot pursuit or extradition of people who are considered to be engaged in political causes. Although the British and Irish police cooperate in their investigations and enjoy harmonious relations, the police from the north cannot pursue fugitives south across the border.[41]

On March 6, 1982, an Irish citizen who was suspected of being an I.R.A. terrorist became the first person to face trial in Ireland for offenses that were committed in Britain. Invoking a 1976 law permitting trial in Ireland for offenses said to have been committed abroad, the Irish charged George Tuite of "conspiring to cause explosions." The law was invoked at the request of the British government.

Tuite had spent fifteen months at large since escaping from London's Brixton Prison in December 1980. He was arrested by the Irish police outside Dublin in March 1982. During the course of his trial, the defense called no witnesses and argued that the state had not proved its case. The principal witnesses were members of Britain's antiterrorist squad from Scotland Yard. Ultimately, Tuite was sentenced by the Irish court to 10 years in jail.[42]

REFORM OF THE POLICE AND THE ARMY

At one time, regular British Army battalions were stationed in Ulster. However, as previously stated, the R.U.C. has assumed most of the operational duties once assigned to these military units. On October 10, 1969, the British adopted the recommendations of a report that was compiled by a Royal Commission which was established to review policing methods. As a result, the R.U.C. was absorbed into the regular organizational setup of British police forces. This arrangement ended the dependency that had developed between the Protestant-dominated Stormont government of Northern Ireland and the R.U.C. Also, it facilitated the interchanging of police personnel, the reinforcement of constabulatory units, and the standardization of policing methods throughout the United Kingdom.

Furthermore, the Protestant-dominated Ulster Special Constabulary (U.S.C.), known as the "B" Specials, who were once used on riot duty for which they were neither trained nor equipped, were disbanded. The Ulster Defense Regiment, a newly created bisectarian volunteer force, replaced them, and were placed under military command.[43]

During the autumn of 1978, as business activity in Belfast turned upward, the movement of people in Londonderry became less restricted as checkpoints and barricades were removed from the streets, and the British instituted a comprehensive antiterrorist program known as the "Way Ahead Policy." Forecasting the eventual transfer of all security duties, including riot control, to the police, this policy specified that the police officer and not the soldier would do all of the arresting and questioning of suspected terrorists.

Becoming aware of the need for its troops to get to know the local population on a more intimate level than they were able to in the past, the British Army in the late 1970s extended a soldier's tour of duty in Northern Ireland to 18 months. Formerly, a soldier completed a four-month tour of duty in Ulster before being rotated to regular assignments in Britain or West Germany. This revised manpower allocation scheme, based on the realities of British antiterrorist operations, permitted the army to deploy a larger number of plainclothesmen in sustained undercover operations. Many of these operatives were tied to the S.A.S.[44]

CONCLUSION

Essentially, the success of Britain's antiterrorist campaign in Northern Ireland can be measured by the following significant indicators: (1) a reduction in guerrilla strength—approximately 200 terrorists were active in all Northern Ireland in 1979 whereas 700 gunmen were ready for action in Belfast alone in 1972; (2) the incarceration of more than 1,200 I.R.A. terrorists, many of whom were arrested after the police received "tip-offs" from members of the Catholic community; and (3) a reluctance of the I.R.A. to involve itself in a sustained campaign of operations in Ulster's major cities, Belfast and Londonderry. Instead, I.R.A. members avoid capture by conducting operations almost exclusively in rural areas.[45] However, I.R.A. cells are difficult to uncover because they consist of only four or five people. Thus, they continue to have the capability to bomb in London and other major British cities.

Although they are prepared to use emergency powers to check terrorism, the British continue to prefer the civil courts. These facilities have functioned throughout the "troubles" in Ulster and have prevented the emergency measures from being used arbitrarily.

The British are imbued with the principle that the power used by their antiterrorist personnel to arrest and detain must be exercised within defined parameters. An arrested terrorist, therefore, is afforded an opportunity to appear before a tribunal that is presided over by a judge and be represented by counsel. It is the judge who will advise the government whether or not the case presented by the arresting authority is adequate.

The wisdom of the British approach to antiterrorism was highlighted by a message delivered in November 1981 by Tomas Cardinal O'Fiaich, the Roman Catholic Primate of all Ireland. The Cardinal urged Catholics to reject violence and abide by the law. "Let me state in simple language with all the authority at my command," O'Fiaich said, "that participation in the evil deeds of this or any other paramilitary organization is a mortal sin which will one day have to be accounted for before God in judgement." Speaking not so much to the gunmen themselves as to the people in the Catholic community who help and protect them, he reminded Catholics that cooperation "in any way with such organizations is sinful and if the cooperation is substantial the sin is mortal."[46]

The cardinal's pastoral advice was evidence that the British antiterrorist information program, which was designed to gain the loyalty of the people of Northern Ireland by countering the claims of the terrorist offenders, was correctly targeted. Still, an atmosphere of hopeless negativism continues to characterize the "troubles."

NOTES

1. "3 Soldiers Die in IRA Ambush," *The Star Ledger* (Newark, N.J.), March 26, 1982, p. 3.
2. John J. Farmer, "War without End: New IRA Sets Pace of Struggle in North Ireland," *The Star Ledger* (Newark, N.J.), April 25, 1982, p. 1.
3. John J. Farmer, "Serene Hills Mask Violence of Provo Country," *The Star Ledger* (Newark, N.J.), April 29, 1982, p. 1.
4. "Ulster Judge Unharmed in IRA Ambush," *The Star Ledger* (Newark, N.J.), March 3, 1982, p. 4.
5. "Gunman Kills a Police Officer in Clash in Northern Ireland," *The New York Times*, May 5, 1982, p. 5.
6. Farmer, "Serene Hills," p. 1.
7. William Borders, "600 British Troops Flying to Ulster," *The New York Times*, November 19, 1981, p. 13.
8. William Borders, "House Searches in Belfast Enrage Catholic Families," *The New York Times*, December 23, 1981, p. 11.
9. "Britain to Increase Ulster Forces," *The New York Times*, December 1, 1982, p. 11.
10. "13 Nations Training Commandos to Save Air Hijacking Hostages," *The New York Times*, October 22, 1977, p. 7.
11. Jo Thomas, "Thousands in Ulster March to Denounce Killing by the Police," *The New York Times*, August 14, 1984, p. 1.
12. Francis X. Clines, "Parole by British Stirs Irish Furor," *The New York Times*, February 24, 1988, p. 6.
13. Tom F. Baldy, *Battle for Ulster* (Washington, D.C.: National Defense University Press, 1987), p. 115.
14. John B. Wolf, "British Police Rely on Informers to Control the IRA," *New York City Tribune*, May 26, 1987, p. 2.
15. John B. Wolf, "British Police Use Informers in War against Irish Terrorists," *New York City Tribune*, December 8, 1987, p. 2.
16. "Scotland Yard Hunts IRA Bombers as Thatcher Vows Never to Give In," *The Star Ledger* (Newark, N.J.), July 22, 1982, p. 1.

17. John B. Wolf, "Controlling Political Terrorism in a Free Society," *ORBIS: A Journal of World Affairs* (Winter, 1976), p. 12.

18. Brian Crozier, *A Theory Of Conflict* (London: Hamish Hamilton, 1974), pp. 150–151.

19. Ibid.

20. "Rights Panel Bids Britain Revise Laws on Ulster Terror Suspects," *The New York Times*, March 19, 1981, p. 4.

21. William Borders, "Terrorism Courts Assailed in Ulster," *The New York Times*, September 13, 1981, p. 4.

22. Ibid.

23. William Borders, "IRA Vows to Press Struggle Despite Ending of Prison Fast," *The New York Times*, October 5, 1981, p. 1.

24. William Borders, "London Is Easing Rules in Ulster Prisons," *The New York Times*, October 7, 1981, p. 3.

25. Borders, "Terrorism Courts," p. 4.

26. Ibid.

27. Robert B. Semple, Jr., "British Continue Ban on Death Penalty," *The New York Times*, December 12, 1975, p. 3.

28. Paul Wilkinson, "The Pros and Cons of Hanging Terrorists," *The Police*, February, 1976, pp. 24–25.

29. "British Admit Irish Were Tortured," *The New York Times*, February 9, 1977, p. 3.

30. William Borders, "Torture of Ulster Prisoners Indicated in British Report," *The New York Times*, March 17, 1979, p. 3.

31. Ibid.

32. "Rights Panel Bids Britain Revise Laws on Ulster Terror Suspects," *The New York Times*, March 19, 1981, p. 4.

33. Borders, "House Searches," p. 11.

34. Joe Klein, "A Novelist's Vietnam: The 13th Valley by John M. Del Vecchio," *The New York Times Book Review*, August 15, 1982, p. 1.

35. Borders, "House Searches," p. 11.

36. John Conroy, "Ulster's Lost Generation," *The New York Times Magazine*, August 2, 1981, p. 72.

37. Ed Blanche, "I.R.A. Executing Informers," *The Home News* (New Brunswick, N.J.), January 17, 1982, p. 23.

38. John J. Farmer, "Revolution Rings Hollow in Halls of the Irish Republic," *The Star Ledger* (Newark, N.J.), April 30, 19082, p. 1.

39. John B. Wolf, "Assessing the Performance of a Terrorist and an Antiterrorist Organization," in *New Dimensions In Transnational Crime*, ed. Donald E. J. MacNamara and Philip John Stead (New York: John Jay Press, 1982), pp. 72–102.

40. William Borders, "Dublin Problem: Fighting Any Irish, Even Terrorists," *The New York Times*, September 16, 1979, p. 8.

41. William Borders, "Ulster's Fugitives Creating Problems," *The New York Times*, June 4, 1979, p. 9.

42. "IRA Bomb Plotter Gets 10 Years," *The Star Ledger* (Newark, N.J.), July 14, 1982, p. 9.

43. "Britain Beefs Forces as IRA Attacks Grow," *The Star Ledger* (Newark, N.J.), November 19, 1981, p. 4.

44. "Britain's Secret Army," *Counterforce: The Monthly Newsmagazine on Terrorism*, February, 1977, pp. 12–13.

45. Wolf, "Assessing the Performance," pp. 97–102.

46. William Borders, "In Ulster, Middle Ground Is Vanishing," *The New York Times*, November 23, 1981, p. 3.

TERRORISM IN THE PACIFIC REGIONS

Ethnic and religious diversity in the Pacific Basin and Indian Ocean regions is being manipulated by astute propagandists. Their communications are altering traditional life-styles by edging people who were previously disenfranchised to push their governments for change. Some of these alterations in past practices have been violent.

LIBERATION THEOLOGY

Liberation theology is a body of teaching recently expounded by primarily Spanish-speaking priests. Its tenets have influenced many Christians in Latin America and others whose history is rooted in Spain, as, for example, the people of the Republic of the Philippines.

When explaining this theology, the clerics advocate land and tax reform, better treatment of laborers and, in some instances, a rejection of the capitalist system. Marxism, emphasizing class struggle, is sometimes akin to the liberation theologians' political interpretation of the Bible and the papal encyclicals. The traditional Christian notion that each individual must save his own immortal soul and be accountable to his Creator for his actions receives but cursory treatment by these men who espouse the theology of liberation. Addressing a gathering of Latin American bishops in 1979, Pope John Paul II cautioned against the adoption of any interpretation of Jesus as a "political activist" or "even as someone involved in the class struggle."[1]

On September 3, 1984, the Vatican's Congregation for the Doctrine of the Faith issued a report which had been approved by Pope Paul VI (1963–1978) denouncing the use of Marxist principles in liberation theology. A portion of the report said: "Let us recall the fact that atheism and the denial of the human person his liberty and his rights are at the core of the Marxist theory." Entitled "Instruction on Certain Aspects of the Theology of Liberation," the congregation's 36-page document stated further that "this theory, then, contains errors which directly threaten the truths of the faith regarding the eternal destiny of individual persons."[2]

Strong differences of opinion, however, are apparent among the Catholic church's hierarchy regarding the meaning and application of liberation theology. Arturo Rivera y Damas, archbishop of San Salvador, has tried to avert an open dispute over its interpretation. Elsewhere in Central America, the church in Nicaragua was split by a conflict among those who advocate the radical theology and those who regard it as an anathema.

Clerics throughout the Hispanic world were advised by the Vatican's Congregation for the Doctrine of the Faith to use caution when making statements on liberation theology. The Salvadorian bishop insisted that liberation theology does not permit those who interpret the Gospel to use Marxism, class struggle, and violence as analytical tools. He reiterated the Vatican's call for a dialogue to end the conflict between the rival groups.[3] The impoverished portion of the Hispanic world, when exposed to a radical interpretation of church doctrine, becomes hypersensitive as a consequence of liberation theology's identification with the concept that the Scriptures favor social activism.

"Liberation Theology is a profoundly evangelistic Christian concept," said Bishop Leonidas E. Proano of Riobamba, Ecuador. "Christ came to earth to proclaim the good news to the poor. Christ was the liberator incarnate. We must continue to do the same thing." The Bishop has been a leader in organizing small Christian communities in his diocese. These hamlets are a vital part of the "liberation" concept of raising the spiritual conscience of people preliminary to liberating "the integral man."[4]

Nicaraguan Clergy

The Catholic Church in Nicaragua is split, divided into a pro-Sandinista nucleus of priests who preside over a "people's church" and a traditional group that is in accord with the Vatican. Several priests also hold key positions in the Sandinista government. The traditional hierarchy, however, continues to exert a strong influence on Nicaragua's Catholics and abhors the secularism of the Sandinistas. These bishops have been criticized by Sandinista officials for not condemning the rebel groups (the Contras), who are backed by the United States. Countering government innuendo, Nicaraguan bishops issued a pastoral letter in April 1984 criticizing the Sandinista government and urging it to open negotiations with leaders of armed insurgents.[5]

Some priests in El Salvador have also endorsed the theology of liberation. Five of them are part of the guerrilla movement that has attempted to wrest political control from the government. Joining the clandestine organization in 1980 and 1981, when the city of San Salvador was being buffeted by urban terrorism, the priests proclaim that their struggle is an appropriate Christian response to grave social injustice.[6]

In 1976, a priest in the Basque country of Spain, speaking of E.T.A. (*Euzkadi Ta Askatasuna*), the principal terrorist organization of the region, said: "Violence justifies counterviolence. Since we live in violence and the violence of the establishment is so great, so-called subversive violence is sometimes the only form of defense."[7]

Latin American Clerics

Infused with this same ideology, the Reverend Camillo Torres, as early as 1968, projected the image of the guerrilla priest across the continent of South America. Torres was killed while participating in a raid that was squelched by the Colombian Army.

Reverend Gustavo Gutierrez, a Peruvian cleric, is the author of *A Theology of Liberation*. The theme of this book, which was published in 1973, is related to the concept of poverty as an actual fact, and neutrality on this point as absolutely impossible. Gutierrez is thus credited with articulating the concept of liberation theology as a doctrine that emphasizes class warfare and engages the poor in Marxist fashion as "shock troops."[8]

Reverend Juan Luis Segunda, a Uruguayan priest and the author of *Liberation of Theology*, published in 1975, and Friar Leonardo Boff, a Brazilian, have sparked the expansion in Latin America of the notion of Jesus as a political activist. "His teaching," Friar Boff wrote, "was such a political threat that the authorities of Israel made use of Rome's authority to eliminate a dangerous political adversary. That is precisely what Jesus was."

Although the friar's writings have contributed to the growth of liberation theology in Latin America, his book, *Church: Charisma and Power*, which was published in 1981, was condemned by a religious tribunal in Rio de Janeiro shortly after it reached the bookstores.[9]

Vatican Analysis

According to Joseph Cardinal Ratzinger, the Vatican is determined to undercut theologies that "reduce the faith to a duty apart and use Marxist analysis to interpret not only history and the life of society but also the very Bible and the Christian message." Cardinal Ratzinger is the prefect of the Sacred Congregation for the Doctrine of the Faith in the Vatican.

On September 7, 1984, Father Boff had to defend his advocacy of the doctrine of liberation theology before the Sacred Congregation in Rome. Summoned from Brazil by the Vatican, the friar was directed to appear before the congregation and explain aspects of his book that "had created difficulties." The congregation believed that the friar's book contained doctrine unsettling "to the faith of the whole ecclesiastical community."[10]

BASE COMMUNITIES

Pope John Paul II, competing with the Communists for the support of the poor, does not identify himself with liberation theology. In 1984, he met with the South African bishops in Zimbabwe and warned them against using the theory of class struggle in their effort to help the poor. The Vatican was particularly alarmed over the extension of the *Communidades de Base* (base communities) in Latin America. There are about 70,000 of these basic Christian communities in Brazil which Father Boff claims are used to evangelize the poor. These communities, which are designed to organize people away from their church parishes, are the forum through which liberation theology is dispensed. Often consisting of poor villagers, the communities meet regularly, often secretly, to discuss the Scriptures in the light of existing social, economic, and political reality in Latin America. Guided by a priest and led by a lay preacher, or "Delegate of the Word," these communities sometimes form clandestine groups that fight openly for social change. These quasi-religious organizations take into serious consideration the socioeconomic and human conditions of the people and their need for freedom from want and oppression.[11]

Forming these communities was a theme at a meeting called in August 1976 by Ecuadorian Bishop Leonidas E. Proano. Fifty-six bishops from Latin America and the United States attended the meeting. On August 12, 1976, Ecuadorian police raided the bishop's office in Riobamba and jailed him for 24 hours, accusing him and others of possessing a loaded weapon. The next day, Ecuador's government asked 37 Roman Catholic clergymen to leave the country for having taken part in a subversive meeting. According to the Quito officials, the priests had been distributing subversive material and planned to interfere in the internal affairs of Ecuador and other countries.[12]

Revolutionary consciousness in Latin America has been ignited by the witting or unwitting activities of prelates, professors, trade unionists, and student activists. The susceptibility of the region's population to the idea of "direct action" (revolution) as an instrument of social change was further increased by the continuing migration of aroused citizens from rural areas to the cities. Unemployment and an enlarged gap between the elite and the poor are other responsible factors. Also a clandestine Communist-controlled propaganda network, resembling the apparatus used by Fidel Castro to fan unrest in Cuba, has continued to target the poor of Latin America and other parts of the Hispanic world, particularly the impoverished citizens of the Philippine Islands.[13]

THE AQUINO/SIN ALLIANCE

According to many accounts, Jaime Sin, the Roman Catholic Cardinal of Manila, is trusted by Corazon Aquino to advise her in her capacity as President of the Republic of the Philippines. Sin's advice provides Aquino with the insights she needs to counter the propaganda that is spouted by spokespersons for the Communist Party of the Philippines (C.P.P.). The Communist-led National Democratic Front (N.D.F.) has been negotiating with the government on behalf of insurgents to end a 17-year-old Communist insurrection.

Cardinal Sin recognizes that Aquino's religious-oriented education provided her with the philosophical base needed to appreciate the impact of ideology on those who toil daily for their sustenance. Coached by the Cardinal, Aquino has cast Communism as an anathema in her homeland. Both Aquino and Sin know that the basic principle of Communism is the utter denial of all spiritual reality. Almost thirty years ago, a book authored by Augustine J. Osgniach entitled *Must It Be Communism* was published. In his book, Osgniach said, "In Communistic thinking there is nothing real except matter. There is no God; consequently there can be no heaven nor hell. There is no such thing as the soul or sin."[14]

In 1564, soldiers of "the cross and the sword," who were dispatched from Spain, were instructed to Christianize the Philippines and to use force only when necessary. Their success accounts for the fact that approximately 85 percent of the Filipinos are Roman Catholic. These people are being informed about the impact of Communism on religious persons: primarily its destruction of individual and family rights and its effort to control the total activity of people including their philosophy and religion. Aquino's spokespersons in the slums and barrios include a large number of priests and nuns.

Aquino's Move to Isolate the People from the Communists

Delivering a cogent counterpropaganda message that has appealed to the people, Aquino's orators have cast the Communist agitators as servants of the devil. As articulated by these opponents of evil, Aquino's appeal has alleviated the frustration experienced by many Filipinos as their traditional society began a rapid transformation and their homeland assumed a strategic role in the Pacific Basin. Also, it neutralized the appeal of the liberation theologists.[15]

Mao Tse-tung, when writing about guerrilla warfare, said: "What is the relationship of guerrilla warfare to the people? Without a political goal, guerrilla warfare must fail, as it must if its political objectives do not coincide with the aspirations of the people and their sympathy, cooperation and assistance cannot be gained."[16] Communist leaders in the Philippines are aware that the ideological approach to antiterrorism as formulated by Aquino and Sin and delivered throughout the Philippines at the grassroots level by prelates and others has negated their own appeals. Communism, according to some of these Marxists, cannot cope with this religious-based ideology.

Rolando Bello, a spokesperson for the C.P.P., said: "It is not an immediate possibility that the C.P.P. can seize power or win a war." Assessing the strength of the rebels, Bello said: "The objective conditions as well as the subjective strength of the N.D.F. [a coalition of left-wing groups—the C.P.P. and the New People's Army] is not yet sufficient to be able to win the revolutionary struggle in the immediate future." The New People's Army (N.P.A.) is the military arm of the C.P.P. It has been neutralized by Aquino's approach to politics.

Tito de la Paz, a member of the N.P.A. general staff, is also pessimistic. He said that all N.P.A. commanders were under orders to abide by and protect the cease-fire in the 17-year-old insurgency.[17]

While preferring to use words and perhaps prayers to isolate the Communists from her people, Aquino is ready to fight if she must. On December 20, 1986, she spoke to troops at Camp Aquino, an army camp named after an ancestor of her late husband, Benigno. "Courage, loyalty, a democratic faith, an unflagging vigilance for the rights, liberties and safety of our people, an earnest desire for peace and a keen preparedness for war—these virtues will stand us in good stead in the weeks and months ahead," Aquino said. Praising the military for sharing her patience under provocation, she said: "Success can only crown our efforts, and no small measure of the credit and honor will go to the armed forces when an honorable and enduring peace finally reigns in our land."

Directing her 1986 Christmas message to all, Aquino said, "I ask you, in this first Christmas in pride and freedom, to forgive and forget, to give democracy a chance to work and peace the chance to work." With sincerity on both sides, Cardinal Sin, in his remarks, said, "The guns may be still, not just during the holiday season, but throughout the coming years."

The Aquino/Sin alliance has enabled Southeast Asia's only predominantly Christian country to celebrate Christmas in peace for the first time since the insurgency began nearly two decades ago. Guerrillas in some of the provinces came down from the hills and spent Christmas with their families for the first time in years.

But some Filipinos have continued to grumble over Aquino's inaction in the economic sector, particularly her New Deal-type jobs program; apparently, the government does not have enough managers to run it. Cardinal Sin has retorted: "You cannot harvest your rice the day you plant it."[18]

The Unseen General

In Manila, the capital of the Philippines, Cardinal Sin is called "the unseen general." It was he who had urged the people to gather in the streets and safeguard the breakaway elements of the military who had assisted Aquino to assume the presidency. The defectors were led by heads of the reform movement that was spawned within the Philippines armed forces while Ferdinand Marcos was president. Marcos's tanks, it is conjectured, would have crushed the military revolt if Sin's followers had not positioned themselves between the armored column and the breakaway faction that was led by Juan Ponce Enrile and Lieutenant General Fidel Ramos. The new president of the Philippines selected Enrile as her defense minister and appointed Ramos chief of staff of the armed forces. Without the massing of Sin's faithful flock in the streets, Enrile, Ramos, and perhaps Aquino herself would today be deceased.[19]

Eighty-five percent of the population of the Philippines is affiliated with the Roman Catholic Church. Observers have reported that Catholics had carried placards with images of saints and the Holy Family when they stood between the tanks and the military reformists in 1986. Marcos had a choice, either to kill Christians waving a sign emblazoned with an image of the Mother of God or order his tanks to withdraw. Finessed by the unseen general, the tanks pulled back, and shortly thereafter, the Marcos regime collapsed.

Cardinal Sin's adroitness, and his outspoken support for the new government, enabled Aquino to overcome the objections that were voiced by some military officers regarding the release of political prisoners, including Jose Maria Sison, the founder of the C.P.P. Enrile, however, was cautious. Having fought Sison's followers for over fifteen years, he regarded the Communist guerrillas as tough hombres who were determined to seize political power. Furthermore, Sin was aware that leftist priests, the advocates of liberation theology, had sparked unrest throughout the Hispanic world by preaching sermons laced with tirades condemning violence, injustice, and poverty. Even Aquino's campaign was assisted by the invective of these clerics when they criticized the Marcos regime.

Cardinal Sin's strategy included cooptation of the radical clergy and the avoidance of conflict with them. Pope John Paul II had advised the cardinal that the ideology of the Catholic Church in the Philippines was moral and not political. The cardinal said, "The Pope smiled because he understands. He came from Poland."[20]

Thus, Cardinal Sin and other clerics have moved to halt all attempts to connect Marxist ideology with the Bible. By casting liberation theology as deception, the unseen general's steps to control the radical clerics of the Philippines is apt to prolong the hegemony of the Aquino government as it tries to reduce the conflict that has engulfed relations between church and state in Latin America.

CONTEST FOR THE *BARANGAYS*

In its attempt to counter the Aquino-Sin alliance, the C.P.P. tightened its control of the *barangays* (villages) and expanded its networks in the cities. Meanwhile, Sotero Llamas, an N.P.A. commander in Southern Luzon, has advised his "Sparrow Teams" (Communist assassination squads) to unnerve the Filipino soldiers who oppose them by hitting them while they relax in towns. Supposedly in control of 20 percent of the hamlets, the N.P.A. adopted the Communist tactic of encircling the urban areas to tighten the noose before they unleashed urban warfare in the streets, where the army and the police are strong.

Numbering about 24,000 members, the N.P.A. upgraded its propaganda apparatus to counter Aquino's "pro-poor" policies and to appeal to members of leftist labor movements and social-action groups. While proselytizing among the disenchanted and attempting to split the conservative coalition, the N.P.A. upgraded its propaganda by targeting the unemployed, college graduates, professionals, anti-Americans, and the poor.[21]

THE SPARROW TEAMS

Additionally, the C.P.P. organized and placed in the field the Sparrow Teams, which are assassination squads that are a key component of its campaign to destabilize the Aquino government.

Sparrows are a large family of hardy birds. Encircling the earth, these avians are cosmopolitan creatures, comfortable in both rural and urban settings and able to withstand adversity. They are interdependent, consequently, they survive in environments that are detrimental to other creatures—a life-style shared by those who deem themselves the wretched of the earth.

Sparrow Teams were active in Manila during the fall of 1986, when two senior police officers and a former national assemblyman were assassinated in November. Widely interpreted as left-wing killings, these deaths were viewed as an effort to push Aquino into declaring martial law; a move that could undercut her administration. In 1972, a spate of almost daily terrorist attacks had triggered numerous political rallies and provided former President Marcos with the justification for declaring martial law.[22]

In March 1986, Jose Maria Sison was released from prison by Aquino. She also freed Bernabe Buscayno, commander of the armed wing of the C.P.P., Alex Berondo, and Ruben Alegre. Buscayno is also known as Commander Dante.

Berondo and Alegre were both said to be members of a Sparrow Team. Berondo was wounded in a shootout in the Manila slum area of Tondo in June 1985. Alegre, who was active in student movements in the 1970s, was arrested in August 1984 in a Manila suburb.

THE "REFORM THE ARMED FORCES" MOVEMENT

While Corazon Aquino attempts to neutralize the C.C.P.'s appeal to the masses, she must simultaneously placate her military establishment. Officers in the Filipino Armed Forces, who were associated with the Reform the Armed Forces Movement, were in the vanguard of the uprising that brought Aquino to office. Since her inauguration, this group of soldiers has expressed its dissatisfaction with the government's handling of the Communist insurgency in the Philippines. They claim that this largely clandestine struggle has expanded and that the guerrillas, equipped with modern weaponry, are capable of inflicting more serious economic and political damage to the country.[23]

On November 7, 1986, observers in Manila feared that a coup by military officers was imminent. General Fidel V. Ramos, the armed forces chief of staff, ordered his commanders to neutralize any such action by disaffected elements in the officer corps. Placed on full alert by Ramos, the military moved to protect broadcast stations, public utilities, and other key installations that rebels usually seized to announce a takeover and demonstrate their efficacy.

ROLE OF GENERAL RAMOS

With the backing of Ramos, who stressed military neutrality and strict observance of the chain of command, the Roman Catholic Church, and the United States, Aquino said, "I am confident that when I leave there will be no coup, and even while I remain abroad there will be no coup." She was planning a four-day visit to Japan that was to begin on November 9, 1986.

Ramos, closely monitoring the insurgency in his country, recognized that any substantive negotiations with the leadership of the N.P.A. through the Communist political organization, the National Democratic Front (N.D.F.), must lend itself to measurement. For example, is support for the N.P.A. in various forms, money, silence, trending up or down? Are N.P.A. military operations, unleashed for the purpose of achieving rational cooperation in the hinterlands, arousing inactive members and garnering support among the rural population?

Ramos has apparently developed an organizational goals-assessment program that he uses to determine the efficacy of the N.P.A. and the threat it poses to specific targets and areas of the Philippines. Similar to the body-count formula used by the American commanders in Southeast Asia, the Ramos program is a form of "management by objectives."[24]

The N.P.A.'s objective is to influence political behavior by armed actions in the countryside and a campaign of bombings, assassinations, and kidnappings in urban areas. Thus, the effectiveness and efficiency of the N.P.A. are measurable in terms of the progress it makes toward realizing its objectives. If negotiations with the Aquino government merely permit the N.P.A. to gain the time it needs to achieve its objectives, then Aquino was wrong and the members of the Reform the Armed Forces Movement were right.

Ramos didn't pull his punches. His systems of measurements revealed that nearly one fifth of the towns and villages in his country were in some ways affected by guerrilla activity. He advised Aquino to set a deadline on talks with the N.P.A. Previously, the guerrillas had employed the familiar Communist strategy of conducting and prolonging inconclusive talks while strengthening forces. Reconciliation, Ramos said, should be the keystone of the government's approach as the army moves to reduce the guerrillas' stranglehold on the countryside.[25]

A member of the Philippine contingent in the Korean War and attached to the noncombatant Philippine Civic Action Group in Vietnam, Ramos understands the strategy and tactics of Communist guerrilla warfare. He recognizes that civilian and military reforms are needed to separate the N.P.A. from the people. He is therefore prepared to unleash an offensive against the guerrillas with an assortment of revitalized and reformed military units if the Communists refuse to negotiate peace with the Aquino government.

Unlike Marcos, President Aquino is attempting to reform local government whose abuses lend credence to N.P.A. propaganda. By directing private armies, some local officials wield power akin to that of the *samurai* (the military class of feudal Japan). Aquino is committed to ending corruption at all levels of government and intends to stress fairness over favoritism. She is determined, she said, to "begin the process of flushing clean the putrid stables of bureaucratic corruption and cronyism."

Ramos, meanwhile, is aware that the Aquino victory has destabilized the N.P.A. However, he must continue to enforce procedures that eliminate the abuses once characteristic of the Philippines armed forces, including the rousting of villagers, the plundering of farm harvest, and the killing of suspected opponents.[26] As commander of the Philippine Armed Forces, Ramos also is charged with managing a campaign of antiterrorist warfare in a jungle setting. His army contains an elite regiment tailored to combat insurgents. Consisting of three infantry battalions, this unit has airborne support for redeployment anywhere in the Philippine Islands. Its primary opponents are the Moro Liberation Front and the N.P.A. The front, which operates on Palawan Island, the Sulu Archipelago, and roughly half of Mindanao, is openly backed by the Libyan leader, Colonel Muammar al-Qaddafi.

THE NEW PEOPLE'S ARMY (N.P.A.)

The N.P.A. has conducted terrorist operations since 1972 for the purpose of forcing the Manila government to grant autonomy to the historic Muslim regions in the southern Philippines. Active in Davao Del Norte Province and elsewhere in the islands, the N.P.A. has shifted its targeting from underground political activities to direct military operations. It has formed unique "arms snatching" teams that try to snare the civilian militia members of the Home Defense Forces, concentrating on capturing weapons as the prime objective. In Northern Luzon, the N.P.A. once enlisted rural support by skillfully exploiting popular dissatisfaction with the Marcos government. Aquino's policies are regarded consequently as an attempt to separate the Communists from the people.[27]

Brigadier General Samuel B. Griffith, United States Marine Corps, retired, in his introduction to *On Guerrilla Warfare* by Mao Tse-tung, referenced an early Chinese essay on guerrilla war. The general said: "Mao has aptly compared guerrillas to fish, and the people to the water in which they swim." If the political temperature is right, Mao said, the fish will thrive and proliferate.[28]

PARAMILITARY VILLAGE ORGANIZATIONS

The Filipino military, determined to cleanse its island-nation of Communism, has established and is supporting paramilitary organizations in the countryside. Consisting of civilians, these groups are being deployed for the purpose of preventing villagers from being influenced by a left-wing party, known as *Partido ng Bayan*, by eliminating its leadership.

In the 1987 campaign for seats in the local legislatures, Partido ng Bayan had but a handful of official candidates. Vera Razon, a member of the party's staff, said: "Our attitude is, if we can secure the lives of our candidates, it's okay to field candidates." Her party was being targeted by the paramilitary groups that are backed by the military.

Unrelenting N.P.A. violence has prompted the army to recruit, organize, and arm civilians for the purpose of joining with them in the conduct of counterinsurgency operations. A recent report has stated that Alsa Masa, a paramilitary group, has purged a former Communist enclave in southern Mindanao of guerrillas.[29]

After World War II, the Communist guerrillas, known as the Huks, were not popular in the Philippine countryside. Ten percent of the villagers opposed them, another 10 percent favored them, and the rest stood unaligned. By using their physical and armed presence and a finely tuned propaganda apparatus, the Huks tried to woo active support from those who remained neutral.

Utilizing armed propaganda, expressed in the form of armed attacks on rural police stations and small government outposts, the Huks tried to intimidate the peasantry, but the leaders of Aquino's armed forces remembered this Communist ploy. Consequently, they have tried to neutralize Communist strength in the rural areas by keeping their paramilitary forces on the offensive. Thus, the N.P.A. is finding it most difficult to cope with this strategy, and its raids, which were designed to intimidate the citizenry, have been reduced.[30]

The Huks of the 1950s and the N.P.A. of today do not seem to have a strategy that permits them to move the focus of their campaign from the rural environment to Manila and other urban areas. The killings by a few Sparrow Teams make sensational news, in particular, when a prominent person is gunned down in Manila. But these murders, which are intended to help bring victory to the Communists, are potentially damaging to the C.C.P. because they disrupt commerce and other activities that the people depend on for sustenance.

In the Philippines, the Communist elements use coercion as a means to sway the masses, even though Communist ideology itself has little appeal in the villages. In the meantime, the Filipino armed forces are prepared to capitalize on the mistakes the N.P.A. will surely make as it uses force to control the people it must have on its side. To date, the military's paramilitary organizations have prevented the N.P.A. from obtaining the broad-based support that it needs to isolate the people from the government in Manila.

Since many Filipino officers have studied revolutionary warfare in the United States, most of them recognize that the struggle against the N.P.A. will be won or lost in the villages. Seeing certain similarities between N.P.A. tactics and those used by the Vietcong in South Vietnam at the beginning of the insurgency in that country, a retired Filipino general has said, "The Government placed its trust in weapons and failed, while the Vietcong placed theirs in the people and won. We must not make the same mistake."[31]

AMERICAN BASES IN THE PHILIPPINES

On November 7, 1987, President Reagan said that the Communist insurgency in the Philippines remains the single most serious threat to the survival of democracy there: "It continues becoming more violent as it becomes more desperate." Corazon Aquino has faced five coup attempts since becoming the island-nation's President in February 1986.

American bases in the Philippines were also endangered by the Communist-directed Sparrow Teams. Three Americans and a Filipino were shot dead in Angeles City, the Filipino community that harbors Clark Air Base. This facility and the naval installation at Subic Bay are the United States' largest and oldest overseas military complexes. Two-thirds of the 26,000 Americans linked to the base, including servicemen, civilian employees, and dependents, live in Angeles City, which is situated about 50 miles north of Manila.

In the wake of the killings, the commander of the 13th U.S. Air Force imposed restrictions on travel. Major General Donald Snyder said, "I'd be kidding you if I didn't tell you it may be a long haul." Americans were advised to use major arteries when moving about, and military police enforced off-limits curbs that were placed on bars situated near the gates to the airfield that cater to service personnel.[32]

LIBYA'S ROLE IN THE SOUTHWEST PACIFIC

Augmenting its effort to influence insurgents in the Muslim areas of the Philippines, Libya is bent on spreading subversion and terror elsewhere in the Southwest Pacific. Port Vila is the focal point of life in Vanuatu (formerly called New Hebrides) until its independence from joint French-British colonial rule. In 1986, Vanuatu established diplomatic relations with Libya and the Soviet Union. Port Vila is presently the site of embassies of four countries: the United Kingdom, France, Australia, and New Zealand. It also could be selected by the Libyans as the host municipality for one of their "people's bureaus" — Qaddafi's term for a diplomatic-type facility.

A strategic hub for the region, Vanuatu is apt to be used by the Libyans to spark and finance ethnic and religious unrest in the surrounding atolls and archipelagos. Vanuatu-based subversives could net with the Melanesians who oppose the French in New Caledonia, the aborigines who are dissatisfied with the Australian government, the natives who are opposing the elected officials in New Zealand and the leadership of the Moro Liberation Front, and the Muslim zealots who are trying to neutralize the government in Manila.

On December 1, 1984, the Kanakan Socialist National Liberation Front (K.S.N.L.F.), representing the Melanesian independence movement, declared a provisional government on New Caledonia, a luxuriant island and a Mecca for tourists administered by a French territorial government. At one time, Eloi Machoro, the front's military organizer, and twenty other K.S.N.L.F. militants had visited Libya to seek support from the Qaddafi government.

The Moslem uprising in the Philippines, which was directed by the Moro National Liberation Front, has had a continuing association with Qaddafi. In the mid-1970s, representatives of former Philippine President Marcos met with leaders of the Moro National Liberation Front in Tripoli, Libya. They agreed on partial autonomy, but not independence, for heavily Muslim parts of the Philippines. Libyan agents and propaganda continued to spark Muslim resistance to the Aquino government.

Communicating through leftist travel unions in New Zealand and Australia, the Soviets offer free air travel to subversive training centers for an assortment of South Pacific agitators. Vanuatuans and Caledonians have accepted free plane tickets from Qaddafi's agents and have boarded airplanes for Libya. Some of them were trained in clandestine warfare in the North African country, although officials in Port Vila have said that the instruction the Vanuatuans received was in the areas of public relations and public service.

Barak Sope, secretary-general of the ruling Vanuaaku Party and the foremost anti-West politician in Vanuatu, uses some of the Libyan-trained people as bodyguards. Sope arranged for a visit of Qaddafi's associates to Vanuatu. His bodyguards prevented customs officials from inspecting cargo that was delivered to his home, which is situated on an island in Port Vila Bay.

Vincent Boulekone, leader of the parliamentary opposition in Vanuatu, in his warning of Soviet moves to infiltrate the South Pacific said, "The Soviets want to control the South Pacific. If they get a base in Vanuatu, they will use it to interfere directly in the affairs of New Caledonia, the Solomon Islands, Fiji and other countries."[33]

The first military takeover in the Pacific Islands took place in Fiji a few years ago. Harboring a population of 715,000, this republic has a variety of domestic problems, including unemployment, crime, and poor health. These conditions are being manipulated by Libyan meddlers.[34]

In Australia, Prime Minister Bob Hawke has expelled some Libyan diplomats from the country. He accused them of interfering in domestic Australian affairs that were tied to issues associated with rights for the aborigines. Hawke said that the diplomats from Tripoli were trying to destabilize the region.

Belau, formerly called Palau, which is 700 miles off Guam and a part of the Trust Territory of the Pacific Islands that is administered by the United States under a United Nations mandate, is also within the ambit of South Pacific unrest. On June 30, 1985, Hauro I. Remeliin, the president of this western Pacific island republic, was shot and killed by an unknown assailant as he walked from his car to his home in Koror, the capital city. Political and economic problems have troubled Palau for several years. The islanders fault the United States for failure to establish such things as electric power plants and other essential components of a viable infrastructure. Designation of certain land areas for military purposes has created another dispute between Palauans and Americans.

The Southwest Pacific, which was once a place for relaxing on a sunny island in a quiet environment, is fast becoming a focal point for Communist-sparked terrorism. Soviet fishing trawlers and fishing experts, which are an integral part of Moscow's intelligence apparatus, ply the blue Pacific. Personnel abroad these ships are bent on counterbalancing the American presence in the region.[35]

INSURGENCY ON NEW CALEDONIA

New Caledonia's territorial government, when troubled by terrorism, declared a state of emergency in January 1985. This declaration followed a spate of violence that left three people dead and 33 injured, including 29 police officers.

A French colonial possession, situated about 750 miles east of Australia, New Caledonia was acquired by France in 1853. On January 12, 1985, the French Prime Minister Laurent Fabius announced that his government was sending additional security elements to France's South Pacific territory. According to French sources, the contingent included 600 military police officers and 480 individuals assigned to the antiriot division of the national police. This contingent bolstered the units already serving on the island. Approximately 5,000 French military police and regular army troops were already stationed on the island. These units, although equipped with helicopters and armored vehicles, were unable to check terrorism on this luxuriant island in the South Seas.

The troubles on the island evolved from an impasse similar to the conflict that precipitated the struggle in Algeria in the 1950s and 1960s. This dispute pitted the Christian French settlers, known as *colons*, against the Muslim population. New Caledonia's European settlers want the island to remain a part of France. But the majority of the island's Melanesians, who are known locally as Kanakans, representing about 40 percent of New Caledonia's 142,500 inhabitants, claim that they are victims of colonization and demand independence. On December 1, 1984, the Kanaka Socialist National Liberation Front, representing the Melanesian independence movement, declared a provisional government. Eloi Machoro, a leader of the front's hard-liners, was named minister of internal security. According to officials, it was Machoro and other members of the K.S.N.L.F. who visited Libya in 1984 and 1985.

In November 1984, Machoro and his supporters seized weapons from a police station on the island. Equipped with these guns, they took control of New Caledonia's hinterlands and encircled the European enclaves on the island's east coast. White settlers engaged in farming left their homes for safety, resettling in towns dominated by families of European origin and in Nouméa, New Caledonia's capital.

K.S.N.L.F. combat units, the strongest on the east coast of the island, continued to conduct raids for weapons. On December 2, 1984, one of these groups invaded the village of Thio, breaking into houses to seize guns and ammunition. French helicopters attempting to resupply the village were met with a fusillade of rifle fire. The K.S.N.L.F. terrorists were eventually forced to flee the area. In the interim, the French settlers set up a militia and established a system of night-watches to defend themselves.

According to sources in New Caledonia, the French troops have been immobilized. Many people on the island say that Paris has ordered the soldiers to take only minimal action against the K.S.N.L.F. because of the anticolonial attitude of powerful French socialists. But the island's European population was being intimidated by K.S.N.L.F. propagandists. In December 1984, the terrorists posted a letter, which was addressed to 14 French settlers, at a local post office. It said, "Independence is near. It will be for you to make your choice before the clock strikes an hour that will be fatal to you."

On January 11, 1985, a 17-year-old farmboy was murdered on his family's cattle ranch, igniting a round of violence in Nouméa. This killing, in the view of many French settlers, reduced the chances for New Caledonia to function without a partition scheme of some sort being imposed by the government. Shortly after the youth's death, security forces surrounded a house occupied by Machoro and his band of terrorists. The police demanded that the K.S.N.L.F. throw down their weapons and surrender. Instead, the terrorists began to snipe at the security unit. Police sharpshooters immediately assumed firing positions. Machoro was shot in the chest and killed. Marcel Monaro, his lieutenant, was wounded in the shoulder and died later of shock. After seizing control of the redoubt used by the terrorists, the authorities arrested 33 Kanakas and confiscated a supply of weapons.

French conservatives and moderates have criticized the Paris government for its failure to prosecute K.S.N.L.F. terrorists, particularly individuals who have injured police officers and barricaded roads. These critics insist that France's scheme to expedite the process of self-determination in New Caledonia can only encourage hostile elements throughout the French overseas possessions—in Polynesia, in the Caribbean, and in Guiana. Paris has tested nuclear weapons in Polynesia and currently operates a space-satellite launching center in Guiana.[36]

In November 1985, French police arrested Luc Reinette, the leader of the Caribbean Revolutionary Alliance, and another separatist, Henri Amedien. After the arrest, the radio station of the Popular Union for the Liberation of Guadeloupe described the police action as intended, because of the disturbances in New Caledonia, to reassure "the partisans of colonialism."

Reinette had spent a year living in the underground and had vanished after the Caribbean Revolutionary Alliance exploded a bomb outside the French administrative headquarters in Basse-Terre. The November 1983 explosion in Guadeloupe's largest city wounded 23 people.[37]

SRI LANKA INFLAMED

Besides the French colonial areas, the former British colony of Ceylon, now dubbed Sri Lanka, continues to be tormented by ethnic violence regardless of the presence of an Indian peacekeeping force numbering about 50,000 troops. Tamil militants have been fighting to establish a separate homeland for their people in the north and east of Sri Lanka.

"While our leaders talk, we act," said one guerrilla, a member of the Eelam Tigers. The Tigers are directed by a handful of terrorists trained by the Palestine Liberation Organization. Approximately 2,000 Tamils have been introduced to guerrilla warfare in camps in southern India and equipped with weapons furnished by "foreign groups," reports *India Today*—an investigative journal published on the subcontinent. Once formed, a Tamil state would include about one-third of the island and would be called Eelam. The Sri Lankan government says it is willing to give the Tamils "almost everything except a separate state."

On May 11, 1984, the People's Liberation Army, the military wing of the Tigers, kidnapped an American engineer and his wife in Jaffna, a city populated mostly by Tamils. The group demanded that the Sri Lankan government, situated in Colombo, the capital, pay a ransom of $2 million and free 20 imprisoned Tamil rebels or accept responsibility for the deaths of the two Americans. According to a spokesman for the Colombo government, Sri Lanka responded to the ransom demand with a "deafening silence." After five days of captivity, the couple were released unharmed. Apparently, the Tigers recognized the futility of their strategy to prompt the United States into pressuring Sri Lanka to ease its repression of the Tamil revolutionary organization and thereby secure the release of its citizens.[38]

Sri Lanka's Strategic Position

In the 1970s, the British Royal Navy left its patrol areas in the Indian Ocean. The British ships were to be replaced by an American naval squadron about a decade later. As hostilities between Iran and Iraq intensified in the Persian Gulf, the mission of the United States Navy was stretched to permit it to safeguard the free world's interests in the region.

Ports for ships and shore leave for crews at locations near ocean-operating areas are a desirable requirement for any fleet, particularly one that is assigned to sea-surveillance missions for extensive periods due to the scarcity of ships and trained seamen. Sri Lanka offered the United States Navy three advantages that would enhance its operating missions, including a rigid anti-Communist policy imposed by the government, an excellent fleet anchorage at Trincomallee, and close proximity to the Arabian Sea.

A close association between Sri Lanka and the United States would undoubtedly foil Moscow's machinations in the region. Consequently, the Soviet Union sabotaged the connection. The Russians, who are masters of subversion and skilled in masking their presence, acted through Sri Lanka's Communist party to manipulate the traditional animosity between the country's major ethnic groups. Hostility between Tamils and Sinhalese escalated to a level that made it risky for the American Navy to use the port at Trincomalee and other facilities on the island.

Ethnic Discord: Tamils versus Sinhalese

The government of Sri Lanka has insisted that the trouble within its borders was foreign inspired. In 1983, more than 400 Tamils were murdered and 150,000 made homeless during an outbreak of ethnic violence on the island. According to the government, the unrest was being systematically targeted against the Tamils by a "hidden hand" directing a conspiracy designed to undo Sri Lanka's political system and economy. The weapons used by the 500-member People's Liberation Army included the Kalashnikov rifle (AK-47), a standard Russian weapon. The island's police stations, depositories for small arms and ammunitions, were favorite targets of the insurgents.

The government has also accused Communists of plotting to over-throw the island's democratically elected government and manipulating unrest in the Army. Pro-Marxist army officers, it reports, once hoped to use the turmoil as a "smoke screen for a coup."[39] In August 1983, the government banned all three of Sri Lanka's Marxist-oriented parties: the Communist Party, the Janatha Vimukthi Peramuna Party (J.V.P.), and the Nava Sama Samaja Party. All three, according to official sources, were directly involved in the bloodbath that left hundreds of Tamils dead and 110,000 to 125,000 homeless.[40]

A youth-oriented party, the J.V.P. is blamed for much of the vio-lence. Rohana Wijeweera, its leader, went underground after the killings in 1983. At one time, he had attended Moscow's Patrice Lumumba Uni-versity and also had led the island-wide insurrection against the govern-ment in 1971.

The direct cause of the killings of the Tamils was the bushwacking of 13 Sinhalese soldiers in July 1983 by Tamil extremists. Very much aware of their potential to disrupt government operations, the Tamils claim their actions are needed to balance police and army harassment and the favoring of the majority Sinhalese in the disbursement of development resources and government jobs. Consequently, relations have deterio-rated between the Hindu Tamils, who make up about 22 percent of Sri Lanka's population of about 15 million, and the Buddhist Sinhalese majority.

Since March 28, 1984, Tamil guerrillas have operated with impunity. They have killed two off-duty air force men in Jaffna, ambushed an army convoy with a car bomb, murdered two civil servants, and have assassi-nated two police officers. All their victims were Sinhalese. Countering the Tamil terror, Sinhalese soldiers have set fire to Hindu-owned busi-nesses and have arrested, interrogated, and killed Tamil youths who they believed were terrorists.

Estate Tamils, the descendants of the people who were brought to Ceylon from southern India to pick tea on British plantations, live in enclaves completely surrounded by the Sinhalese. Invariably, they are victimized by their Buddhist neighbors as retribution for assaults un-leashed by Tamil terrorists against Sinhalese. Rivalry between the Tamils and the Sinhalese is ancient. Beginning more than 2,000 years ago, it has been exploited by Portuguese, Dutch, and British colonizers. Tamils, for example, enjoyed educational and other preferences under the British. However, the Communists are not like the colonizers; they are not inter-ested in enhancing the life-style of the island's people for the purpose of exploiting its riches. Instead, they are seeking to destabilize Sri Lanka by using the tactics of subversion specifically tailored to create another hostile environment in a region that is seething with unrest.[41]

The Eelam Tigers continued to use armed propaganda to upset the Sri Lankan Army as discipline among the troops engaged in the antiterrorist campaign was lost. On August 11, 1984, they killed at least five people and burned 139 stores and homes in retaliation for the ambush and killing of six soldiers. The army and navy were accused of using indiscriminate force to intimidate the inhabitants of Velvethurai, a fishing village used as a sanctuary by the terrorists. Gunboats fired on the village, and the soldiers were accused of burning homes and shops that are situated in the hamlet, which was previously the home of a Tamil terrorist commander who lived in self-imposed exile in Madras, India.[42]

The bombing tactics of the Tamil terrorists are similar to those used by an assortment of European terrorist organizations. Linked by training, weapons, and ideology to the Soviet Union, these groups favor the use of remote-controlled bombs that are placed in old vans parked by the roadside. These devices are used because they can be exploded at the right time and place. Scarce bomb components, often assembled with considerable peril by an explosives expert, are not wasted in an unscheduled explosion.

UPGRADING SRI LANKA'S ANTITERRORIST CAPABILITY

The antiterrorist skills of Sri Lanka's security forces have been upgraded to counter the terrorism. Courses of study that are designed to enhance the organization of information gathering for use in the intelligence process—collation, evaluation, and processing—were organized. The Sri Lankans also attempted to build an effective information-gathering network and to train a paramilitary unit to combat the Tamil terrorists.

According to Junius Jayawardene, President of Sri Lanka, Israeli intelligence agents and former members of the British Special Air Service (S.A.S.), now employed by a private security company, were engaged to teach the required antiterrorist skills. Jayawardene said that his government selected the Israelis because they agreed to provide the requisite instruction, which took place in Colombo, the capital. Sri Lanka's request for assistance in improving its intelligence system and in upgrading its military's antiterrorist skills was rejected by the United States, Britain, and West Germany.

The Israeli training contingent did not participate in military matters beyond the classroom. Sri Lanka's Muslims, however, were offended by the presence of the Israelis, and ambassadors from governments espousing nonalignment from the Middle East were upset. But the Colombo government had no alternative because its armed forces lacked the antiterrorist capability needed to prevent partition of the island.[43]

Israeli intelligence personnel are skilled in providing hit teams and other special operations units with the information they need to uncover, identify, and eliminate terrorist offenders who are engaged in clandestine warfare. S.A.S. veterans are knowledgeable in the skills needed by small antiterrorist units to conduct special operations. A merger of Israeli and S.A.S. expertise and techniques eventually provided the direction for Sri Lankan security forces. These groups were organized to arrest hardcore cadre members of the Tamil terrorist organization for their crimes against public order.

Although pushed to the brink of collapse by the terrorists, the government of Sri Lanka used its developing antiterrorist forces within the parameters established by its legal codes. The use of counterterror to combat terror, especially when it was directed indiscriminately against random targets, imposed a psychological strain on all the people who were exposed to its use, forcing many of them to seek protection from the terrorists themselves.

Sri Lanka has recognized that it needed a police intelligence capability to augment the Israeli approach to control the terrorist offender. Only a properly organized police intelligence unit would contain the components that are required to gather, evaluate, interpret, report, record, and disseminate analyzed information relative to such things as the infrastructure, modus operandi, membership, and management practices of the Tamil terrorist organization. This information could then be used by the authorities to prepare a case for presentation in a Sri Lankan courtroom that would publicly identify the terrorists as criminals.[44]

CONCLUSION

Utilizing a pro-Christian and anti-Communist appeal, the Aquino government in Manila has attracted and held the popular support of the masses. This alliance has enabled it to neutralize factions in the armed forces that oppose its liberal policies. Meanwhile, the Soviet Union has benefitted from Libya's propaganda that is being preached among the Muslim population of the Southwest Pacific. In Sri Lanka, ethnic discord has contributed to the expense of sustaining the U.S. Navy in the Indian Ocean region, requiring it to resupply at sea rather than within the safe anchorages once used by Britain's Royal Navy.

Recent events in the Pacific Basin and Indian Ocean region indicate that terrorism continues to have a geopolitical perspective.

NOTES

1. Cesar Jerez, S.J., "The Mission of the Society of Jesus Today and Our Common Struggle for Justice," *Studies in the International Apostolate of Jesuits,* December, 1978, pp. 35–46.
2. Marlise Simons, "Vatican Reported to Have Sought Rebukes for 2 Other Latin Clerics," *The New York Times,* September 11, 1984, p. 14.
3. Stephen Kinzer, "Sandinista Priests Told They Could Be Defrocked," *The New York Times,* September 29, 1984, p. 4.
4. George Vescey, "Activist Prelates Assess Pope's Trip," *The New York Times,* February 4, 1979, p. 7.
5. Alan Riding, "Religion Becomes a Political Weapon for Both Left and Right in Nicaragua," *The New York Times,* May 29, 1981. p. 4.
6. "Church in El Salvador Denies a Leftist Slant," *The New York Times,* March 30, 1981, p. D1.
7. Henry Kamm, "A Priest in the Basque Country of Spain Tells of Trying to Understand Violence," *The New York Times,* May 17, 1976, p. 2.
8. George Vescey, "The Bishops' Meeting Begins," *The New York Times,* January 28, 1979, p. 18E.
9. George Vescey, "Pope Warns Bishops against Political Role by Clergy," *The New York Times,* January 29, 1979, p. 8.
10. "Key Sections from Vatican Document on Liberation Theology," *The New York Times,* April 6, 1986, p. 14.
11. R. J. Gore, "Liberation Theology: Deliverance or Deception," *New Reformation,* Spring, 1981, p. 4.
12. Vescey, "Activist Prelates," p. 7.
13. Henry Kamm, "Philippines Expelling U.S. Priest Apparently Because of Teachings," *The New York Times,* June 16, 1981, p. 12.
14. Augustine J. Osgniach, *Must It Be Communism?* (New York: Joseph F. Wagner, 1949), pp. 3–68.
15. Fox Butterfield, "Bold Growing Communist Drive: Test for the Aquino Government," *The New York Times,* February 28, 1986, p. 1.
16. Mao Tse-tung, *On Guerrilla Warfare* (New York: Frederick A. Praeger, 1965), pp. 3–19.
17. Butterfield, "Bold, Growing Communist Drive," p. 1.
18. Lee Lescaze, "As Terrorism Spreads Mrs. Aquino's Tenure Appears in Jeopardy," *The Wall Street Journal,* October 19, 1987, p. 1.
19. Lescaze, "As Terrorism Spreads," p. 1.
20. John B. Wolf, " 'Unseen General' Now Stands Guard in Philippines," *New York City Tribune,* March 25, 1986, p. 2.
21. Steve Lohr, "Quelling the Philippine Insurgency No Easy Task," *The New York Times,* May 13, 1985, p. 1.
22. John B. Wolf, " 'Sparrow Teams' Forcing Aquino to Take Tougher Stand," *New York City Tribune,* December 9, 1986, p. 2.
23. Seth Mydans, "4 Key Communists Freed by Manila; Military Objects," *The New York Times,* March 6, 1986, p. 1.
24. John B. Wolf, "Insurgency Growing in Philippines, Ramos Claims," *New York City Tribune,* November 18, 1986, p. 2.

25. Barbara Crossette, "Manila Chief of Staff Seems to Side with Defense Minister on Rebels," *The New York Times*, November 1, 1986, p. 4.
26. Eduardo Lachica and Anthony Spaeth, "Philippine Guerrillas Steadily Gain Ground as Economy Falters," *The Wall Street Journal*, March 18, 1985, p. 1.
27. John B. Wolf, "Filipino Communists Seen Set to Tighten Control of Villages," *New York City Tribune*, November 24, 1987, p. 2.
28. Mao Tse-tung, *On Guerrilla Warfare*, p. 8.
29. John B. Wolf, "Rural Filipino Paramilitary Groups Assist against Communists," *New York City Tribune*, January 19, 1988, p. 2.
30. Robert A. Asprey, *War in the Shadows: The Guerrilla in History* (Garden City, N.Y.: Doubleday, 1975), pp. 88–832.
31. Wolf, "Rural Filipino," p. 2.
32. John B. Wolf, "U.S. Servicemen in Philippines on Alert against Assassins," *New York City Tribune*, December 19, 1987, p. 2.
33. John B. Wolf, "Libyans Spark Unrest in the Southwest Pacific," *New York City Tribune*, June 30, 1987, p. 2.
34. James P. Sterba, "Army Coup in Fiji Tarnishes Its Image as Big-Brother State," *The Wall Street Journal*, May 29, 1987, p. 23.
35. "U.S. Gears up to React to Soviet Inroads in the Western Pacific," *New York City Tribune*, November 23, 1987, p. 2.
36. John B. Wolf, "Caledonia Liberation Group Using Terrorism in Attempt to Oust French," *New York City Tribune*, March 6, 1985, p. 2.
37. John B. Wolf, "Corsican Terrorism Said to Be Allied with Caribbean, Pacific Insurrections," *New York City Tribune*, March 20, 1985, p. 2.
38. John B. Wolf, "Soviets Fomenting Animosity in Sri Lankan Ethnic Groups," *New York City Tribune*, June 20, 1984, p. 2.
39. "Sri Lanka Rounding up Communists," *The New York Times*, August 3, 1983, p. 3.
40. Orville H. Schell, "Sri Lanka's Abuse of Human Rights," *The New York Times*, August 24, 1983, p. A23.
41. "In A Neighbor of India, Unending Tension, Too," *U.S. News & World Report*, July 2, 1984, p. 40.
42. "Sri Lanka Death Toll Climbs in Rebel Strife," *The Star Ledger* (Newark, N.J.), December 3, 1984, p. 4.
43. Sanjoy Hazarika, "Israel Said to Aid Sri Lanka Forces," *The New York Times*, August 26, 1984, p. 19.
44. Dalton de Silva, "Israel Secret Service to Train Sri Lankans to Oppose Rebels," *New York City Tribune*, June 14, 1984, p. 3.

9

COVERT CUBAN INTELLIGENCE OPERATIONS IN THE AMERICAS

The Americas department is a division of the Cuban General Directorate of Intelligence (D.G.I.) that manages all of Havana's covert activities in the Western hemisphere, especially its moves to undercut democracy and capitalism. A handful of strategically placed D.G.I. operatives are assigned the task of implementing programs that are formulated in cooperation with the Kremlin. These agents execute measures intended to divert American society from the orderly pursuit of its national purpose. Cuban intelligence is skilled in manipulating the terrorist groups that are lodged in a targeted country, edging them into using armed propaganda to highlight significant economic and social grievances. The objective of these Communist-contrived terrorist acts is to advertise that the American system of government is in shambles and that Americans lack the will to protect their vital national interests.

Moscow calculates that acts of terror by its surrogates, that is, the groups which are used for the purpose of masking its own involvement, will cause the citizens of the United States to question the determination and foresight of their government and business leaders. Once this process begins, the Kremlin conjectures, any American approach to protect its interests will be characterized by indecisiveness and failure.[1]

The Soviet Union forecasts that the American people, upon being confronted with danger and riddled with discord, will abandon democracy and accept some form of dictatorial rule in its stead. According to

Karl Marx, dictatorships are eventually transformed into socialist systems through an inevitable historical process that is keyed to violence, its catalyst for change. Italy's Red Brigades, West Germany's Baader-Meinhof Gang, and various Latin American terrorist organizations have served as instruments for the Communist bloc in its campaign of surrogate warfare directed against the United States and its Allies.

The dimensions and characteristics of this form of warfare have received scant attention in the popular media. American officials admit that their country can wage nuclear war, or participate in a large-scale guerrilla war, but has not yet developed a comprehensive strategy to protect itself against acts of terror unleashed by the Kremlin's surrogates.

The Communists have skillfully contrived a scenario of terror that is designed to constrict the economic system of the United States. The plan involves the use of terrorist action in overseas areas vital to American interests, particularly in Central America. Among the significant components of this strategy are:

1. The disruption and eventual severance of the trade connections between the United States and Western Europe by creating an insecure environment for commerce.
2. The reduction of the American corporate investment and involvement in Central and Latin America, Asia, and Africa as a consequence of the high risk and vulnerability of business assets.
3. Denying the United States safe access to oil produced by the OPEC countries, while simultaneously increasing its dependency on foreign oil. The American antinuclear movement and advocates of environmental stability are unwitting but vital components in this portion of Moscow's analysis.[2]

The D.G.I., while acting as Moscow's surrogate, manages intelligence operations specifically contrived to assist the Communists to realize their objectives in the Americas, particularly by acts of terror and trade in narcotics.[3]

CUBA'S ROLE IN THE NARCOTICS TRADE

The American deployment of air and ship patrols to stifle the Cuban-supervised drug traffic that flows north to the United States from the Caribbean Basin has been ineffective. Some Latin American drug merchants have connected with the D.G.I. for the purpose of helping them elude surveillance by American patrols. The Cubans use the smugglers and their extensive clandestine connections to move weapons to terrorist groups in Latin America. Castro's agents reciprocate by securing the anchorages and providing access to the networks needed to safeguard drug-smuggling operations into the United States.

American agents have set back marijuana traffickers by seizing a number of boats used by the smugglers. Because these vessels are often loaded to the gunwales with tons of the narcotic, each seized shipment represents the loss of a huge investment.

The D.G.I. agents facilitate the smuggling of drugs into the United States when a mother ship's cargo, under Cuban protection, is transferred into speedboats in Cuban waters. Although the drug merchants continue to lose a handful of these boats to the American patrols, some of the faster vessels manage to reach the Florida coast. Transferring such huge loads from a big ship to small boats on the high seas is difficult, so the use of Cuban ports simplifies this task. The bulk of the Latin American drugs is thought to be shifted from a cargo ship to the speedboats at Cayo Largo, a Cuban navy base. The Cubans get a "piece of the action" (money) for the services they provide.[4]

It is inferred that the D.G.I. manages Cuba's connection with the narcotics traffickers with Castro's permission. By helping the smugglers, Cuba obtains hard currency while simultaneously hastening the deterioration of American society. Most of the cash funnelled into Cuba is being used to bolster the D.G.I. Created and funded by the Soviet intelligence service (K.G.B.), this agency has been controlled by the Russians since 1967. Until Castro has the financial wherewithal to finance Cuban intelligence operations, Moscow will continue to control the D.G.I.'s purse strings. Some American observers conclude that Castro wishes the D.G.I. to be loyal only to him.

Building an independent intelligence agency requires much ready cash but money is scarce in Cuba. Operating his government with a dole from the Kremlin, Castro needs access to the large amounts of money that are needed to finance and operate an intelligence service free of Soviet control and influence. His connections with the drug merchants provide him with the needed extra income.

Castro, meanwhile, continues to boast of his agents' capability to foment urban violence in the United States. According to D.G.I. defectors, some of Castro's agents did infiltrate into the United States as part of the 1980 boatlift from Mariel, Cuba. On November 5, 1982, four high-ranking Cuban officials were among the 14 people who were indicted in Miami on federal charges of smuggling narcotics into the United States. Prior to 1982, Cuban officials had not been directly linked to the drug traffic. But in April of that year, Thomas O. Enders, then serving as assistant secretary of state for Inter-American Affairs, revealed that the

United States had evidence of drug trafficking being used as a cover for Cubans who were running guns to guerrillas in Latin America.

The Cubans indicted in Miami, all of whom were presumed to be in Cuba, included Vice Admiral Aldo Santamaria Cuadrado, Rene Rodriguez Cruz, Fernando Ravelo Renado, and Gonzalo Bassols Suarez. Cruz and Cuadrado were members of the Central Committee of the Cuban Communist party. Renado and Suarez, as members of Cuba's diplomatic corps, were assigned to its mission in Colombia; Renado as ambassador, Suarez as minister counselor.

Jaime Guillot Lara, a Colombian, also was indicted. Reputed to be an international drug trafficker, he was once arrested in Mexico and charged with smuggling. A wanted man in Colombia, Lara has been accused of smuggling arms from Cuba for leftist guerrillas.

Nine Cuban-born Americans were among those named in the indictments. These papers asserted that all those who were indicted had conspired "to commit certain offenses against the United States." This conspiracy included an arrangement to use Cuba as a loading station and as a source of supplies for ships transporting methaqualone tablets and marijuana from Colombia by way of Cuba to Florida. In two separate operations between the fall of 1979 and January 1981, the conspirators smuggled more than five million methaqualone tablets and more than 1,000 pounds of marijuana into Florida. The Cuban navy's role in the conspiracy was to protect and resupply the ships that were transporting drugs from Colombia to the United States.

Cuadrado and Cruz were part of Castro's inner circle. Both men were members of the cadre that was responsible for directing the guerrilla force that overthrew the Batista government in 1959.[5]

Responding to the indictment of the four Cuban officials, Miguel Martinez, the press officer of the Cuban Interest Section in Washington at the time, said, "It is all lies. There is not a single truth in those allegations and that's that."

REVELATIONS FROM INFORMERS

Mario Estebes Gonzalez was arrested by the United States Coast Guard on November 29, 1981, as he was transporting 2,500 pounds of marijuana in a speedboat off the Florida coast. He cooperated with federal authorities in return for immunity from prosecution for his previous involvement in narcotics trafficking. Estebes told law-enforcement officials that he delivered between $2 million and $3 million to Cuban officials. These amounts were the proceeds of drug trafficking in the United States in a 15-month period. Estebes' revelations confirmed previous information alleging that D.G.I. agents were among the people who left Cuba on the Mariel boatlift. These agents, he said, had a variety of assignments, including drug trafficking, economic espionage, and disrupting Cuban exile groups.

According to Estebes, narcotics were brought by ships from Colombia to the small port of Paredon Grande on the north shore of Cuba. At this location, the drugs were unloaded and reloaded into small boats for shipment to Florida. Drugs obtained by Cuban agents in Florida, he said, were shipped to the New York area inside vans furnished with concealed compartments to hide the drugs. Dealers in New York City, and in Newark, Elizabeth, and Union City, New Jersey, became the distribution funnels for the Cuban-procured cocaine, marijuana, and methaqualone tablets.

The New York City Police Department noted that from 1980 through 1982 individuals who are believed to have entered the United States in the Mariel exodus were arrested for an assortment of felonies and misdemeanors. Information developed by other American law-enforcement agencies support allegations that Cuban officials facilitated the movement of narcotics in the Caribbean Basin.

On August 4, 1983, the *Miami Herald* printed comments by a Cuban defector who told American officials that Raul Castro, Fidel's brother and the second highest government official in Cuba, once accepted money from drug smugglers in exchange for an agreement to use Cuba as a base for drug running. Perez was chief of the Overseas Community Department of the Cuban Institute of Friendship with the Peoples, an agency that handled the Cuban government's relations with Cuban emigrants. He was also a captain in the D.G.I. After landing at Miami International Airport, Perez told a U.S. Customs official that he wanted to speak to "state security." F.B.I. agents were called to the scene and debriefed the Cuban.[6]

Additional information about the Cuban government's connection to drug trafficking and arms smuggling was revealed by a man identified as "Mr. B." On September 10, 1983, while testifying before a United States Senate Treasury Appropriations Subcommittee hearing into drug smuggling, Mr. B. mentioned that Cubans funnelled heroin into the United States through Mexico. Proceeds from the sales, he said, were used to finance arms shipments to Central America. A self-proclaimed professional informant, Mr. B. said that weapons and heroin are shipped from Cuba to ports in Mexico. There, they are separated, he said; the heroin moves north to the United States and the weapons travel south to Central America.[7]

TERRORISM IN PERU

Sendero Luminoso (Shining Path) is a Peruvian terrorist organization that finances its operations with revenue it derives from the cocaine trade. This commerce links it to Castro's drug merchants. Organized by Abimael Guzman, Shining Path initiated a Maoist insurgency high in the Peruvian Andes on May 17, 1980. At the outset of its campaign, the terrorist group burnt ballot boxes in remote hamlets and destroyed pylons in the hydroelectric grid that feeds electrical power to Lima. Peruvian politicians once scoffed at information attributing these crimes to an incipient terrorist movement, instead blaming the destruction on bandits.

Occasionally, Shining Path mirrors the Chinese Maoist movement of the 1930s. It needs little money, and its members live off the land. A member of the group once said that "shortages will always be overcome if the path is right." Previously, Shining Path obtained weapons and dynamite by raiding police stations and construction sites. They fabricated bombs out of tin cans and used llama-hair slings, a weapon used by Indian herdsmen, to toss dynamite sticks.[8]

The savage tactics that were executed by the Shining Path terrorists have placed a barrier between themselves and the Indians. On December 31, 1984, terrorists armed with machine guns and clubs swept into two Andean hamlets and beat to death 40 members of a home-defense squad. These people were protecting their village from intrusion by criminals bent on transforming the region into a Maoist-style enclave.

Peru's president, Alan Garcia, recognized that Sendero Luminoso was a major threat to the stability of his country. Afoot in his land for a decade, Shining Path had killed over 10,000 people and, in 1985, it accelerated its campaign in Lima. Speaking to the press about Shining Path, Garcia said, "It is not like a bad tooth that one can locate and extract. It is a virus that attacks the whole body."[9]

Although Peru's Indian population, who are the descendants of the Incas, are desperately poor, they do not heed the Maoist appeal communicated to them by Shining Path's propagandists. Instead, the $400 million promised by the Peruvian government for land reform, agricultural assistance, and social services for the 3.5 million Indians that inhabit the Andean highlands has neutralized Shining Path's attempt to articulate a cause in the Andes.

The terrorists, trying to win the "war of words" in the Andean villages, blocked the civic-action moves made by the Garcia administration. A United States official assisting the Peruvians in administering the aid program said, "It must be the only insurgency in the world that assassinates engineers and development specialists instead of C.I.A. officers and political attachés."[10]

Stymied in the Andes, the terrorists rebuilt a guerrilla network in Lima that was weakened in 1986 by the arrest of key leaders. Targeting banks, neighborhood offices of Garcia's Aprista Party, retail stores, government offices, movie theaters, embassies, restaurants, and factories, Shining Path once prompted officials of the U.S. State Department to rank Lima as one of the two most dangerous capitals in Latin America; Bogota, Colombia was the other.

Deploying "annihilation squads" to execute a program of selective assassinations, Shining Path killed 39 prominent personalities in Lima in 1986. In 1987, assassinations increased as Shining Path began targeting foreign businessmen. In March 1987, an annihilation squad wounded a manager of the Bank of Tokyo and killed the industrial relations director of a canning plant. Consisting of about 200 zealots in leadership positions and about 1,000 other terrorists throughout the Andean nation, Shining Path continues to try to manipulate Garcia into taking repressive measures. These moves, according to terrorist sources, will eventually make him unpopular and polarize the country.[11]

CUBA'S ROLE IN CENTRAL AMERICAN REVOLUTIONS

Drug trafficking to North America is but one of the D.G.I.'s key responsibilities. It has also trained the guerrilla cadres that managed the insurgencies in Central America. On March 20, 1981, Luis Alvarado Saravia, a Salvadorian guerrilla, surrendered to government forces. He told them that he had been trained in Cuba, and that Cubans and Nicaraguans were fighting alongside the insurgents in El Salvador. Both Nicaraguans and Cuban authorities have denied giving help to the Salvadorian guerrillas. However, in July 1980, Nicaragua's Deputy Defense Minister Eden Pastora, and Deputy Interior Minister Jose Valdiva resigned their posts because they felt obliged, they said, "To give active aid to the revolutionary struggles of others." According to Sandinista sources, their destination was either El Salvador or Guatemala.

The intelligence agency, seeking to merge its assets, had tried to amalgamate the two major groups fighting the Sandinistas, but Pastora opposed this strategy. He wanted Somoza's national guard leaders expelled from the coalition. An investigation addressing the charge of C.I.A. involvement said, "It's not their style."[12]

The K.G.B.'s activities in Central America were once believed to be coordinated by operatives assigned to the Soviet embassy in San Jose, Costa Rica, Moscow's only diplomatic facility in the region. On August 21, 1979, in the midst of a violent strike by some 5,000 public employees in the port of Limon, Costa Rica ordered two high-ranking Soviet diplomats to leave the country, charging that foreigners had incited the cargo handlers.

According to a report issued by a congressional committee in San Jose, about 60 percent of the 450 tons of arms that entered Costa Rica in 1979 came from Cuba.[13] Most of these weapons were used to overthrow the government of General Somoza in Nicaragua. Two terrorist bombings in March 1981 signaled the onset of political turmoil in Costa Rica. In one of the incidents, three United States Marines were injured when terrorists bombed their jeep. The other explosion damaged the Honduran embassy in San Jose. The Costa Rican authorities believed that foreign terrorists, linked to Salvadoran guerrilla groups, were responsible for both blasts.

A communiqué signed by the Carlos Aguero Echeverria Command, a leftist group, said that the bombings were in reprisal for United States and Honduran support of the El Salvador junta. The document also called for the formation in Costa Rica of a "political-military organization," a leftist euphemism for a guerrilla group.[14]

Cuban Involvement in Nicaragua

The Sandinista National Liberation Front (F.S.L.N.) derived its inspiration from Fidel Castro's model of insurgent warfare and conducted main-force guerrilla activity in rural areas that meshed with urban terrorists operations. These tactics complemented acts of armed propaganda that were undertaken by Marxist elements operating in Managua and other cities.

The urban terrorist groups were known as the Proletarian Tendency and The Prolonged Popular War. These clandestine bands were engaged in political efforts among workers and slum dwellers and prepared the masses for participation in the armed struggle that resulted in the establishment of a socialist state. These urban clandestine groups had a network of cells in most of Nicaragua's largest cities. The Tertiaries concentrated in fronting with the bourgeois and agrarian opponents of Somoza in the countryside for the purpose of isolating the government from the rural areas.[15]

The F.S.L.N.'s strategy for conquest was predicated on the advice Fidel Castro gave to the Sandinista leaders during a conclave in Havana in September 1978. Castro advised the Nicaraguans to refrain from a frontal attack against the national guard and concentrate on hit-and-run attacks and other guerrilla activities. He suggested that they avoid large-scale offensives until they had acquired the needed logistical and organizational apparatus to sustain conventional operations against Somoza's National Guard.

Havana avoided direct involvement in a situation that could have required the large-scale use of Cuban military units. Instead, it was alleged that Panamanian Air Force planes airlifted Cuban arms to Sandinista units that were positioned in Costa Rican bases for guerrilla forays into Nicaragua. Further, a Cuban military unit consisting of 200 troops was involved in logistical functions. Stationed in Costa Rica, the Cubans stockpiled arms and shipped them to Nicaragua. Some of these weapons shipments were seized by Somoza's forces. They consisted mostly of machine guns, recoilless rifles, mortars, Belgian-made FAL automatic rifles, M-1 rifles of American manufacture, and an assortment of Soviet items. The Russian gear consisted of rocket-propelled grenades, ammunition, uniforms, medical supplies, and communications equipment. This cargo was hidden in trucks entering Nicaragua from Costa Rica.[16]

CUBAN STRATEGY IN CENTRAL AMERICA

Havana was convinced that the prospects for revolutionary upheaval in Central America in the 1980s were enhanced by the success of the Sandinistas. Also, the Cubans believed that unification of the various antagonistic revolutionary factions in Guatemala and El Salvador into a united front for armed attacks against the established governments of these Central American democracies was possible. Consequently, they prepared local insurgent groups in Central America for the long haul by recommending that they organize a united front.

A Guatemalan once said that a Cuban emissary met in the capital of his country with the leaders of two terrorist groups and a dissident wing of the Communist party. The Cuban urged them to combine their efforts within the parameters of a movement similar to the Sandinistas.

Cuba constructed its support for Central American revolutionary groups by using an analytical assessment developed by its intelligence service. This report described the revolutionary environment in each of the Central American countries the Cubans sought to influence. D.G.I. personnel were used to train terrorist cadres and to place ideological pressure on Marxist elements in Nicaragua, asking them to aid guerrillas who were fighting military governments in adjacent countries. A Sandinista said, "For the next year or longer I will be teaching a political orientation to new cadres." "You may, in time, see me in El Salvador or Guatemala fighting their dictatorships," added another.[17]

The E.G.P., *Ejercito Guerrillero de los Pobres* (Guerrilla Army of the Poor), is a leftwing terrorist group in Guatemala. Its founder was Valentin Ramos, who was killed in January 1976. The E.G.P. was linked to the Cubans, along with another Guatemalan terrorist group known as the Rebel Armed Forces (F.A.R.), *Fuerzas Armada Rebeldes*.[18]

CUBA'S LINKS TO PUERTO RICAN INDEPENDISTA FACTIONS

Havana endorses the activities of the Puerto Rican Socialist Party (P.S.P.) and has sponsored pro-independence activity for Puerto Rico in Cuba. The United States, however, has no concrete evidence of Cuban support for the Puerto Rican terrorist groups that utilize armed force for the purpose of severing Puerto Rico's tie to the American mainland.

At one time, Castro sponsored free trips to Cuba for interested leaders of the Puerto Rican *independista* movement. P.S.P. members traveled to Havana and other Cuban locations to receive training. Additionally, *Claridad*, a P.S.P. newspaper, was partially financed by Havana. The demands of the party, as printed in this publication, were synchronized with a bombing campaign conducted by Puerto Rican terrorist groups in New York and Chicago. The F.A.L.N. (*Fuerzas Armadas de Liberacion Nacional*) was responsible for over 100 bombings in American cities, most of them in New York City and Chicago.[19]

Ambush near Sabana Seca

About 6:40 A.M., on the morning of December 3, 1979, a band of men armed with automatic rifles ambushed a busload of American sailors shortly after it left a communications center at Sabana Seca, 10 miles west of San Juan. Two sailors were killed and ten were injured, two of them critically. This was the first fatal attack on American military personnel by terrorists in Puerto Rico since 1970.

Hours later, a communiqué was found in a bus station in the Santurce section of San Juan and was handed over to the F.B.I. Signed by the "joint forces" of the Macheteros, the Armed Forces for Popular Resistance, and the Organization of Volunteers for the Puerto Rican Revolution, the statement said that the attack was in retaliation for the deaths of activists while in custody.

The ambush occurred as a green truck, resembling a type commonly used by utility companies of the island, pulled in front of the bus and forced it to halt. As the driver of the truck jumped out of his vehicle and ran toward a parked van, several men leaped out of this vehicle and opened fire with handguns and automatic rifles. Although the strafing of the bus lasted only about 15 seconds, more than 40 bullet holes punctured its body. On disengaging, the terrorists fled in the van leaving the truck behind. A few hours later their getaway vehicle was found in a San Juan suburb, about a 20-minute ride from the site of the ambush.[20]

A Possible Cuban Link and Ghosts

Ballistics experts determined from spent shells found inside the van and other evidence that the assassins used shotguns, a commercial version of the M-16 rifle, and a Soviet-designed AK-47 automatic rifle to "shoot-up" the bus. Utilization by the terrorists of a Soviet-made weapon raised speculation among investigators of the possibility of a link between nationalist groups on the island and organizations outside Puerto Rico. Although there was no evidence of such a tie, investigators did not ignore the possibility. Police of the island contended that radical *independistas* receive guerrilla training in Cuba.

Concerning the identities of members of the groups claiming responsibility for the attack, one person close to the investigation said, "We're dealing here mainly with ghosts. They could be small cells; they could be large. We don't know."[21]

One sign that the ambush was planned and executed by professionals was that the terrorists used their own vehicles. This tactic avoided their possibly being stopped by the police for a traffic violation in a stolen vehicle. Such an incident would have aborted the operation or created a fiasco if the assailants tried to flee.

On December 9, 1979, unidentified gunmen also targeted Americans when they fired at a U.S. Navy patrol. According to a U.S. Navy spokesman at Roosevelt Roads Naval Base in Eastern Puerto Rico, "two individuals fired at a Navy sentry vehicle." No other details were made available regarding the incident, excepting a statement that the attack occurred inside the compound at the naval base.[22]

DESTRUCTION OF MILITARY AIRCRAFT
AT THE MUNIZ AIRBASE

On January 13, 1981, a spokesman for the Puerto Rico National Guard said that the guard and the F.B.I. were investigating the possibility that security personnel of the Muniz Air National Guard base, a field adjacent to San Juan's International Airport at Isla Verde, had given terrorists information on the base's security procedures. The guard had deployed two sentries to protect the 45-acre base, one at the main gate and another patrolling in a car. The Colonel's statement was issued in the wake of an attack by the Macheteros at the airfield.

As the watch at the airfield changed, authorities suspected that a terrorist raiding party gained access to the runways from either a lagoon or a swampland bordering the facility and then placed pipe bombs attached to 60-minute timers in the intakes and exhausts of over two dozen military aircraft. Three unexploded pipe bombs were retrieved from two of the planes by a navy bomb squad. Eight of a complement of 20 A-7D Corsair II fighters that were assigned to Tactical Squadron 198 of the Puerto Rico Air National Guard were destroyed. Two additional Corsairs, which cost $4 million each, were damaged. Rescue equipment and a pickup truck parked on the tarmac were also bombed.[23]

ROLE OF ARMED PROPAGANDA

Puerto Rican terrorists advertised their program of armed attacks against military installations and personnel as acts undertaken in retaliation for the deaths of three advocates of Puerto Rican independence who were "assassinated" by "Yankee intelligence." These men were killed by the Puerto Rican police on July 25, 1978, in what has become known as the Cerro Maravilla incident, and Angel Rodriquez Cristobal, an officer of the Puerto Rican Socialist League who was found hanged in a federal jail cell on November 11, 1979.[24]

The Cerro Maravilla incident involved the shootings by policemen of Rosado and Arrivi, on a mountain about twenty miles northeast of the city of Ponce. Several commercial and government-owned communications towers are situated on this terrain feature, which is known as Cerro Maravilla. The police contend that the two slain men were preparing to sabotage one of the towers. The men were accompanied by a police undercover agent who had infiltrated the Armed Revolutionary Movement, a group in which the alleged terrorists were members.

According to officials of the Federal Detention Center in Tallahassee, Florida, Cristobal's death was the focus of an investigation by the prison and the F.B.I. Spokesmen for the 8,000 mourners who crowded into the town of Ciales, Puerto Rico, for Cristobal's funeral, charged that he was killed by the federal authorities to force the F.A.L.N., which was operating in New York and Chicago, to make ill-planned retaliatory strikes that would lead to the capture of its cells.[25]

Serving a six-month sentence for trespassing on navy property while military maneuvers were under way, Cristobal was one of 21 demonstrators who were arrested on May 19, 1979, by naval policemen. They were taken into custody, after wading ashore from small boats onto Vieques, a small island which is situated off the coast of Puerto Rico.

THE D.G.I. AND THE "DIALOGUE"

Initiated by Havana and moderate Cuban-American exile leaders in 1978, the "dialogue" was a program that facilitated the departure from Cuba of roughly 4,000 political prisoners and their relatives. In reciprocation, Castro allowed about 220,000 exiles to visit the island. Negotiations that were linked to the dialogue involved conversations between the Cuban government and 75 exiled representatives who had not been involved in anti-Castro activities.

Composed of a group that included Protestant and Roman Catholic clergy, members of a pro-Castro exile group (the Antonio Maceo Brigade), selected Cuban-American businessmen, and exiles from organizations based in Costa Rica, Puerto Rico, and Venezuela, this "Committee of 75," as it came to be known, helped to arrange the release of political prisoners. The committee also processed applications from exiles who wished to visit relatives in Cuba.[26]

The D.G.I., who were responsible for monitoring Cuban exile activity worldwide, took advantage of the tourist and other airline flights that were linked to the dialogue to gain easy access to the United States. According to the F.B.I., the D.G.I., on gaining entry to the United States, successfully penetrated two anti-Castro groups, the Abdala and the Alpha 66.

D.G.I.-directed anti-exile intelligence-gathering activity in the United States was believed to be conducted under the cover of travel agencies and other private organizations that handled the dialogue flights to and from Cuba. These agents provided Havana with the opportunity to compile a dossier on almost any outspoken exile leader.

According to La Cronica, a weekly tabloid published in Puerto Rico, most of the employees who were tied to the travel agencies handling dialogue business were D.G.I. agents. In 1979, Carlos Muniz Varela, director of Viajes Varadero travel agency in San Juan, and Eulalio Jose Negrin, the only travel agent Havana would deal with in northern New Jersey, were assassinated by gunmen of Omega-7. A militant but miniscule anti-Castro group, Omega-7 purportedly killed the businessmen for furnishing the D.G.I. with information. These killings were efforts to deter Cubans from cooperating with Castro.

Under the guise of travel agents, the D.G.I. was able to conduct surveillance of exiled groups in a way that was denied them when Cuba was quarantined by Washington. Havanatur, a Panamanian-registered company based in Miami, was given a monopoly on the exile flights by Cuba. It was identified as an agency of the Cuban government by the Department of State and expelled from the United States on December 31, 1979. Carlos Alfonso, a former security adviser to the toppled Chilean government of Salvador Allende and a colonel in the D.G.I., owned Havanatur.

According to police sources, about 200 names on a list of 300 persons revealed publicly by the Reverend Manuel Espinosa of Miami were also D.G.I. agents or Castro collaborators. By February 1980, Reverend Espinosa had become the head of the Committee of 75. His dramatic transformation from the leading proponent of the dialogue into an anti-Castroite, according to some law-enforcement officials, came when Cuban authorities refused to finance his operations any further.[27]

C.I.A. NETWORKS IN CUBA

Clair E. George, formerly C.I.A.'s deputy director for operations, left the agency voluntarily and for personal reasons on December 31, 1987. Responsible for the clandestine services of the agency, George was not enamored by the American involvement in paramilitary operations in Afghanistan and Angola and the concept of establishing a "counterterrorism center" within the C.I.A. Former Agency Director William Casey sought to interface antiterrorist analysts and field operatives to enhance the efficiency and effectiveness of operations that were established to monitor international terrorist activities. Deputy Director Robert Gates supported Casey's antiterrorist initiative and the center was established. During George's tenure, the C.I.A.'s clandestine operations in Cuba were hamstrung, because most of its undercover operations on the island were compromised by Castro's agents.

A D.G.I. officer who surfaced in Czechoslovakia in June 1987 revealed that about 90 percent of the C.I.A.'s covert operations in Cuba were penetrated and then controlled for years by Castro's agents. "The

Cubans fed bogus intelligence to almost all the agents who weren't actually working for them." According to a press release, double agents directed by Cubans channelled inferior intelligence to selected targets.

During the summer of 1981, five members of Alpha-66, a broadly based anti-Castro group of Cubans, were seized as they disembarked from a launch on the coast of Matanzas Province east of Havana. They had trained surreptitiously in Florida to undertake this operation. Perhaps the dialogue was the wedge that the D.G.I. used to penetrate the anti-Castro Cuban groups based in the United States.

After the seizure of the Alpha-66 team by the Cubans, the Federal Bureau of Investigation launched an investigation of possible violations of the Neutrality Act—the law that forbids private citizens from conducting foreign policy. The F.B.I. had not been aware of the Alpha-66 operation until Havana radio announced the arrest of the landing party.[28]

Cuban support for Latin American drug dealers who moved their wares into the United States has undercut the domestic tranquility of America. Furthermore, Cuban assistance to Latin American revolutionaries has also diverted Americans from undertaking with gusto the tasks that are required to upgrade their nation's productivity.

NOTES

1. "Cuba Literally Bristles with Soviet Operation," *The Star Ledger* (Newark, N.J.), September 28, 1979, p. 1.
2. Kenneth B. Noble, "Official Ties Cuba to U.S. Drug Traffic," *The New York Times*, May 2, 1983, p. 3 and idem, "Excerpts from the Administration Paper on Central America," ibid., May 28, 1983, p. 6.
3. Selwyn Raab, "A Defector Tells of Drug Dealing by Cuba Agents," *The New York Times*, April 4, 1983, p. B1.
4. Stanley Penn and Edward T. Pound, "Smugglers of Drugs from Colombia to U.S. Are Protected by Cuba," *The Wall Street Journal*, April 30, 1985, p. 1.
5. George Volsky, "U.S. Drug Charges Cite 4 Cuba Aides," *The New York Times*, November 6, 1982, p. 1.
6. "Ex-Cuba Agent Bares Secrets," *The Star Ledger* (Newark, N.J.), August 5, 1983, p. 3.
7. "Cuban Drugs, Guns Tied," *The Star Ledger* (Newark, N.J.), September 11, 1983, p. 11.
8. Raymond Bonner, "A Reporter at Large, Peru's War," *The New Yorker*, January 4, 1988, pp. 31–35, 41–58.
9. Jonathan Cavanagh, "Peru's War against Guerrillas Drags on amid Charges of Mass Killing, Torture," *The Wall Street Journal*, February 27, 1984, p. 30.
10. "Targeting Americans," *U.S. News & World Report*, September 14, 1981, p. 31.
11. "Peru's President, in Reversal, Orders Tank Units to Quell Rising Terrorism," *New York City Tribune*, February 17, 1986, p. 3.
12. Richard J. Meislin, "Attack on Pastora: Much Intrigue but Few Facts," *The New York Times*, June 14, 1984, p. 4.
13. "Costa Rica Boots Two Soviets," *The Star Ledger* (Newark, N.J.), August 21, 1979, p. 51.

14. Alan Riding, "For Costa Rica, 2 Bombs Bring a Taste of Fear," *The New York Times*, March 22, 1981, p. 17.

15. Carl J. Migdail, "Nicaragua: Cuba All over Again?" *U.S. News & World Report*, September 11, 1978, p. 37; Stephen Kinzer, "War Memoir by Sandinista Is Best Seller," *The New York Times*, August 12, 1974, p. 7.

16. "Costa Rica Ties Cache to Leftist Guerrilla Plot," *The Star Ledger* (Newark, N.J.), March 20, 1982, p. 3.

17. Graham Hovey, "U.S. Fears Unrest in Central America," *The New York Times*, July 22, 1979, p. 13 and idem, "U.S. Study Says Cuba Plays Cautious Role in Nicaragua," ibid., July 4, 1979, p. 3.

18. Alan Riding, "Fearful Guatemalans Seek Closer Ties to Guerrillas," *The New York Times*, January 21, 1980, p. 2.

19. John B. Wolf, *Fear of Fear: A Survey of Terrorist Operations and Controls in Open Societies* (New York: Plenum Press, 1981), pp. 146, 168–169.

20. Clyde Haberman, "Search for Nationalist Terrorists Pressed in Puerto Rico," *The New York Times*, December 5, 1979, p. 24.

21. Clyde Haberman, "A Soviet-Type Rifle Tied to Bus Ambush," *The New York Times*, December 6, 1979, p. 23.

22. "Navy Patrol Is Attacked at a Base in Puerto Rico," *The New York Times*, December 10, 1979, p. 10.

23. Jo Thomas, "Puerto Rico Groups Says It Struck Jets," *The New York Times*, January 13, 1981, p. 1.

24. "Jury in Puerto Rico Studies 2 Slayings," *The New York Times*, January 21, 1979, p. 43.

25. "Puerto Ricans Vow to Avenge Death in U.S. Prison," *The New York Times*, November 18, 1979, p. 33.

26. Wendell Rawls, Jr., "Exiles Rallying in Miami in Hopes of Castro Ouster," *The New York Times*, April 4, 1980, p. 9.

27. R. Bruce McColm and Francis X. Maier, "Fighting Castro from Exile," *The New York Times Magazine*, January 4, 1981, pp. 28–34; Jeff Stein, "Inside Omega 7," *The Village Voice* (New York, N.Y.), March 10, 1980, p 1.

28. John B. Wolf, "CIA Official to Resign; Wasn't Enamored of Some U.S. Policies," *New York City Tribune*, December 22, 1987, p. 2.

10

UPGRADING THE AMERICAN ANTITERRORIST CAPABILITY

Vehicles which are packed with explosives are a standard bomb-delivery method that is used by terrorists in urban areas. In 1983 and 1984, these conveyances were employed in the Lebanese capital to demolish facilities utilized by Americans. In April, 1983, one of these trucks exploded, wrecking the United States Embassy in West Beirut. Eighteen months later, another vehicle, filled with explosives, was detonated near a building that was occupied by a garrison of American Marines at Beirut International Airport. This facility was wrecked by the blast.

BEIRUT BOMBINGS

The U.S. Department of Defense (D.O.D.), when commenting on these bombings, said that the assault on the Marine compound was undertaken with the knowledge of the Syrians. A spokesman for the Damascus government, however, denied that the Arab state was tied to any of the Beirut bombings. A group that called itself Islamic Holy War took responsibility for the explosion at the airport.[1] However, the identities of those who drove the "kamikaze" bomb vehicles that wrecked the American facilities were obliterated when the bombs in their trucks exploded,[2] precluding the use of fingerprint classification as a means of positive identification.

Sheik Muhammad Hussein Fadlallah, a Shiite Imam in Beirut, has been tied to various bombings that are claimed by the Islamic Holy War group. Western newspapers said he did not know if the terrorist group was real or imagined. "As an organization we could not discover even one percent that it exists," he said. "It may not represent only one thing. It may represent several structures using it as a cover. They could be Islamic...or some people who want to give Islam the brand of terrorism."[2]

Israel maintains an intelligence service that is replete with sources of information at all levels of Middle Eastern society. Consequently, it has the information needed to fix its opponents in time and place. This information permits the Israeli Defense Forces to unleash the surgical armed strikes that counter the terrorists.[3]

ATTACKS IN GREECE

Elsewhere in the Eastern Mediterranean region, Americans were also targeted by terrorists. On April 24, 1987, 18 people were wounded in a terrorist attack on a bus near Hellenikon Air Base, an American facility that abuts Athens International Airport. Twenty-five American servicemen and dependents were aboard the bus as it swerved out of control, hitting a tree, when a bomb connected to a 960-yard detonating cord exploded. Sixteen American military personnel and dependents and two Greeks were injured when the device detonated.

Nikon Arkoudeas, the chief of Greek police, described the bombing as a well-planned crime. Investigators reported that two men, dressed as public-utility employees, stretched the cord along the bank of the Kifissos River, hiding it under grass and sand, and connected it to a van. Awaiting the arrival of the bus in a van which was tagged with stolen license plates, the terrorists exploded the bomb when the bus moved by them, as it made its daily round-trip with no security escort, from a small Greek base at Elevsis to Hellenikon. The bombing demonstrated that the 4,500 American service personnel and dependents who were stationed in Greece were vulnerable to armed attack, particularly those housed in the vicinity of the four major United States bases.

Within 24 hours of the attack near Hellenikon, a left-wing group, known as the Organization of November 17th, claimed responsibility for the blast. It stated in a communiqué that its bombings were part of its effort to force "American imperialism" out of Greece. Deriving its name from the date when students revolted against the Greek military government in 1973, a move that was crushed at the time but eventually served as the catalyst for the junta's collapse, November 17th claimed responsibility for the assassination of the deputy chief of the Greek police antiriot squad in Athens on January 16, 1980. The same group said it had also murdered Richard S. Welch, the C.I.A. chief-of-station in Athens, in 1975.

Identifying with the extreme left and committed to the "struggle to rid Greece of the forces of fascism and imperialism," November 17th has used stolen vehicles to block the passage of cars through the narrow streets of Athens. Once halted at an obstacle, the terrorists approach the stopped vehicle and then fire automatic pistols into its passenger compartment. Seventeen bullets were fired at the vehicle that was carrying the antiriot squad commander.

In December 1976, November 17th murdered Evangelos Mallios, a former police officer who had been convicted of torturing political prisoners when the military government ruled Greece. Although Greek sources have reported that the C.I.A. official and Mallios might have been killed by the same gun, a .45 caliber automatic, that report has never been confirmed.

November 17th is not the only Greek terrorist organization that threatens to kill Americans. In January 1980, Greek police uncovered a terrorist group calling itself the Popular Frontal Initiative (P.F.I.), while investigating the death of two police officers who were murdered in Athens. While searching the homes of eleven left-wing P.F.I. extremists who were linked to these killings, the police found plans and sketches of the American embassy in Athens, and the United States Ambassador's residence. They also discovered notes referring to both places as potential bomb targets.

In February 1980, an Athens prosecutor charged P.F.I. terrorists with conspiracy to assassinate ambassadors from the United States, West Germany, Israel, Turkey, and Cyprus. Some of the arrested terrorists confessed that they had been trained by the Popular Front for the Liberation of Palestine (P.F.L.P.). Kostas Zyrinis, a 37-year-old publisher and the group's ringleader, went to Lebanon in 1978 for guerrilla training, a police spokesman said. Four other P.F.I. terrorists, including Zyrinis' girlfriend, were also sent to Lebanon for three months of terrorist training to become tutors for "freedom fighters," a Greek government source revealed.[4]

IDEOLOGY OF THE ARAB TERRORISTS

The ideology of the Arab terrorist groups who are active in Lebanon is a curious blend of the ideas of not just one theorist but many. The

Palestinian groups, particularly, display their faith in the Marxist doctrine that the revolution will emerge after a period of armed struggle, mostly kidnappings and assassinations. Meanwhile the shadowy elements that control the Lebanese hit teams and "snatch gangs" disregard the Marxist caution concerning involvement in revolutionary warfare without sufficient strength to defeat a well-organized and disciplined force. Militarily, these groups are no match for a U.S. Marine landing team or an armored attack supported by infantry that might sweep across the Lebanese frontier from Israel.

The radical Muslim terrorists, who are active in the vicinity of Beirut, regard the tactics of terror as positive virtues. Violence, their messages reveal, promotes the manhood of oppressed people and leads to freedom and unity. This notion was formulated by the Algerian existentialists, Albert Camus and Frantz Fanon.

In Lebanon, Fanon's ideas have been implemented by radicals who are responsible for a spate of political kidnappings. But Fanon explained the move to violence by the Lebanese terrorists as actions triggered by frustration. Palestinian violence, he would be apt to say, is the result of decades of neglect and failure. Having nothing to lose, some Arab terrorists are committed to the idea that violence is the only language that can be understood in the world.[5]

Albert Parry, author of *Terrorism: From Robespierre To Arafat* said:

> There were also Fanon's angry exhortations to the blacks, the browns and the swarthy (such as Arabs) to rise and attack not only in the name of nationalism, so as to form their own sovereign states, but also, and more importantly, in the name of a socio-economic revolution that would give true power to the masses.[6]

Today, the Israeli people and their supporters everywhere, particularly Americans, are the primary target of Fanon's disciples in Lebanon. The motivation triggering these outlandish acts that are undertaken by assassins and kidnappers is an effort to force the world community to see things their way by raising the cost of maintaining the status quo.

THE UNITED STATES EMBASSY NETWORK

The embassy network of the United States is a target for the armed propaganda—bombings, rocket salvos, and other atrocious acts—used by terrorists and mobs. Staging these multimedia image-building incidents to recruit members and attract financial support, many of these groups conduct their operations with impunity because some foreign governments do not have the resources to control them.

American diplomatic posts are situated around the world, some of them in countries bemired in civil war or plagued by other forms of unrest. The protection of these facilities—missions to international bodies, consulates, liaison offices, and embassies to 103 countries—involves security aspects of overwhelming proportions. Approximately 6,000 foreign-service employees staff these posts, all of them protected by U.S. Marines attached to the Security Guard Battalion that maintains its headquarters in Quantico, Virginia.[7]

Security Guard Battalion

Because of the small number of personnel, from 32 in Paris to as few as six in many smaller posts, the American Marine security detachments usually can do no more than fight a delaying action, if an embassy is attacked, and wait for help from local police. The mission of the U.S. Marines, who are scattered in 118 detachments around the world, is to protect Americans and others inside American embassies and to safeguard secret materials and government property. Total protection of an American diplomatic facility is only possible when the marine guards are assisted in their protective role by a host government.

The safeguarding of an embassy beyond its grounds is primarily the responsibility of the host government. The marine guards, for example, may not return fire outside the confines of the embassy compound, even at snipers, except on orders from Department of State officials. Concerning the rules relative to the use of deadly force, marines are advised to obey the orders of the ambassador or the chief of the mission to whom each detachment is responsible.

Equipped with a .38 caliber revolver, each embassy guard is familiar with the rules governing its use. Members of the detachments are instructed never to draw the revolver unless it is going to be fired. Each marine, however, has the "absolute right" to fire his side arm if his life or someone else's in the embassy is threatened. Marine guards are also trained to use a 12-gauge pump shotgun. The order to fire this weapon, however, must be issued by embassy officers representing the Department of State.[8]

Trained to conduct delaying actions so as to give the embassy time to "button up," to evacuate some personnel, and to move others to safe havens, Sergeant James M. Lopez held off the Iranian demonstrators in Tehran for nearly three hours. The lone U.S. Marine guard on duty at the consulate, Lopez herded the embassy staff to the more secure second floor of the building, destroyed visa stamps, and hurled teargas grenades at the invaders.[9]

Replacements for the marine detachments are trained at a full-scale replica of an American embassy. This building, which is situated in Quantico, contains all the Department of State's security equipment that is used at overseas diplomatic posts—closed circuit television systems (CCTV), automatic doorlocks, and electric quick-closing entry gates. Dedicated on November 7, 1980, the facility was named Marshall Hall, in memory of Corporal James C. Marshall, of Monroeville, Alabama, who was killed defending the American embassy in Saigon in January 1968. The library at the headquarters and training school of the Security Guard Battalion is dedicated to Corporal Steven Crawley, of Port Jefferson, New York, who was killed in an attack on the embassy in Islamabad, Pakistan, on November 2, 1979.

Approximately 100 Marines are enrolled in each training session conducted at the school. They are taught to recognize bomb threats, to take evasive action while driving, to use riot sticks and teargas, and to handle a shotgun and a revolver. Only those marines who are able to demonstrate excellence when performing their assigned military duties and who show an aptitude for learning and applying interpersonal and intercultural communication skills are selected to attend the school.[10]

Avoiding "the Honey Trap"

Foreign nationals often are used to perform tasks inside an American embassy, a practice that can prove to be hazardous. In 1987, agents of the Naval Investigative Service asserted that a U.S. Marine guard was romantically involved with a Soviet woman who was employed as a cook in the embassy. The woman was later identified as a K.G.B. "swallow," that is, a female agent, in the language of the espionage trade. Sometimes a swallow can serve as the bait in a "honey trap" (a mistress who is planted by an unfriendly intelligence service).[11]

The Soviets probably were aware of the State Department's prohibition on socializing for guard personnel, and took advantage of the fact that the marines at the embassy in Moscow were in need of someone to relax with. Therefore, the K.G.B. sent its swallows in whose company the American security guards relaxed for a few hours, compensating for their lack of contact with the opposite sex.

Wolfgang Lotz has written a book entitled *A Handbook For Spies*. In the chapter entitled "The Spy and the Opposite Sex," Lotz said:

> Love is blind, they say, and so is infatuation. It is surprising just how blind and gullible even a shrewd, well-trained agent can be under certain circumstances. Just let him meet someone who really turns him on, and you'll have a truly hazardous situation.

Lotz advises the spy to be wary of a woman "who is too good to be true." She is a woman who understands, a person who is helpful and selfless, catering to every whim and tolerating bouts of bad temper. She never probes, wanting to know only as much as you are willing to tell her. "No spy should have anything to do with such a woman. I will give you twenty to one that she is an agent of the opposition. Nothing else could account for this kind of feminine perfection," said Lotz.

Training for Embassy Guards

Lotz's observations could be incorporated into the training received by U.S. Marines who are assigned to serve a 15-month tour of duty at embassies and diplomatic missions around the globe, including inside the Soviet bloc, where the K.G.B. controls hundreds of swallows. Usually the K.G.B. permits a swallow to conduct her love affair any way she thinks best, always offering to help her whatever the outcome of the affair.[12]

Instructors reportedly have advised the Marines (whose average age is 24) to avoid associations with Soviet women and to report any advances to superiors. "I look to the leadership," said Brigadier General Walter Boomer, director of U.S. Marine public affairs and formerly commander of the security guards. "These young Marines for the most part will not let you down if it's clear to them what it is they're supposed to do."

Peter Hamilton, who discusses sex and character weaknesses in his book entitled *Espionage, Terrorism and Subversion in an Industrial Society*, believes that:

> Men and women in the civil and military services who are given access to military and political secrets are usually long-term public servants, carefully chosen for their security reliability and trained in the security arts. They are taught to guard against the sex approach by spies and their agents, and are not usually given access to vital material until they are sufficiently mature.[13]

In the aftermath of the revelation of lax security at the U.S. Embassy in Moscow, some of the Marine guards and other embassy personnel were sent back to the United States for violations of security regulations. Involvement with Soviet women or with the black market were among the alleged breaches of security regulations that triggered these reassignments.

In the embassy in Moscow, Soviet citizens were engaged by the Americans to perform routine tasks, such as auto repairs and clerical duties. Officials in the State Department defended this practice, stipulating that the Russians provided needed and inexpensive service. Furthermore, they believed that this practice was not responsible for any of the misdeeds of the embassy guards, whom they did not regard as a potential weakness in their security setup. Eventually, American workers were used to replace some of the Russian tradesmen at the embassy in Moscow, when nine American staff members were sent back to the United States for security violations.[14]

Monitoring the Terrorist Threat

Confronted with the problems posed by a lack of personnel, an embassy is often unable to monitor groups that have a terrorist bent; some terrorists give no warning, others mask their identity by using an alias. The first group to claim credit for the bombing on April 18, 1983 of the American embassy in Beirut was a pro-Iranian faction that had previously boasted of responsibility for a grenade attack against a United States Marine patrol.[15]

Beirut is a prime example of a city where surprise assaults by terrorists against American property cannot be prevented no matter how strongly an embassy is fortified. Between 1978 and 1982, factions who were tied to Palestinian guerrillas and who issued communiqués under fictitious names fired rockets at the United States Embassy on four separate occasions. In June 1976, they assassinated American Ambassador Francis Meloy and his economic counselor.

Safeguarding Information

The need to protect classified information from hostile elements is another imperative of embassy security. Shortly after the takeover of the Tehran embassy, Iranian militants said they had found documents confirming their belief that the hostages were spies. As the embassy was being penetrated, three embassy employees set about destroying sensitive documents in the vault, but the immense number of papers involved prevented them from finishing the job. Supposedly, one document linked three of the Americans to the C.I.A. Other papers contained the names of a few Iranians who visited the embassy.

Seven years after the Iranian embassy was seized, the classified documents taken by the pro-Khomeini students provided an insight into the C.I.A.'s Iranian operations, particularly its attempts to recruit sources of information: high-level Iranian officials, ayatollahs, foreign journalists, and diplomats.

Communications Security

Emergency disintegrators, which are used to destroy classified infor-mation when the security of a diplomatic post is penetrated by a hostile element, and an assortment of electronic measures also help safeguard diplomatic activity.

Although the American embassy employees in Tehran had tried to obliterate sensitive documents in the vault, they were forced by the Ira-nian militants to open the vault door. The documents that remained intact gave the militants tips they could use in their interrogations of the Americans and an insight into embassy operations.

United States officials, however, did manage to destroy their most sensitive communications equipment. Codes were not compromised be-cause encoding was done by computers that change their combination every one-hundred-thousandth of a second. The increased use of such automatic coding devices and satellites enables an embassy to rapidly retrieve information, thus permitting the U.S. State Department to pre-vent information from falling to unfriendly hands in the event of an embassy takeover.[16]

Conversion of existing embassy record-keeping systems to elec-tronic data banks permits equipment operators to request a document from a central file instantly, display it on a cathode ray tube (CRT), modify its format, and send a copy to Washington via satellite. Also, electronic office systems that are geared to the latest telecommunications technology permit the instant erasure of records when an embassy is threatened. After the crisis is over, electronics also enables an operator to resurrect data by enciphered satellite transmission. Officials from a host government could be apprised of these capabilities for the purpose of having them inform the populace at large that sensitive information in the form of hard copy (documents) would not be available to any group planning to seize an American embassy.

Highly sophisticated hierarchical computer systems, comparable to the one tested for use in West Germany's videotex system, also could be used to enhance embassy operations and safeguard the information that is its plasma. This system, transmitting text, graphic material, or data, has the ability to go beyond its own data banks, linking users with com-puters containing information not frequently requested.

An embassy that is tied into a regional system and that needs data from another electronic subsystem could be switched to a large central computer. This central processing unit (C.P.U.) could be staffed by De-partment of State personnel based in Washington, D.C.

Additionally, voice-message systems, electronic mail, teleconferenc-ing via satellites, computer-controlled heating, ventilating, and air-conditioning systems, and lighting arrangements would enhance embassy security. Buildings with these advanced features have been dubbed "intelligent buildings." The electronic age, therefore, facilitates effective relations between states without the physical presence of an embassy and its staff in high-risk areas.[17]

Electronic Emanations

Electronics equipment is not necessarily a panacea. Computers, word processors, and related data-processing equipment emit radio waves. Often, a spectrum analyzer and other devices that are designed for electronic espionage can glean enough textual information from these emanations to aid in the breaking of codes. It is important, therefore, that individual computer rooms be shielded with sheets of metal. Minicomputers can be protected by covering their external parts with metal and their screens with a fine mesh. But regional electronic data-processing systems, requiring more complicated installations, are difficult to protect.

The Department of Defense believes problems linked to "Tempest"—"an unclassified short name referring to investigations and studies of compromising emanations"—are multiplying. A computer security expert comments, "When you handled classified information manually there was no problem. With automation, it's another story."[18]

Bolstering security at its diplomatic facilities is one of the antiterrorist initiatives undertaken by the United States during the years of the Reagan administration. Revamping and upgrading its antiterrorist force were other moves.

DELTA FORCE: ITS OPERATIONAL AND TECHNICAL DEFICIENCIES

After the failed attempt to rescue the hostages in Tehran, the American Delta Unit, which consists of about 100 men, had never been bloodied in an antiterrorist operation, although it had been positioned for an attack in a few instances. During the Grenada operation, the unit was the core of a joint task force and was supported by helicopter gunships from the Army's 160th Special Task Force. The Delta air unit is part of the 101st Army Division, which is based at Fort Campbell, Kentucky. An element of the Air Force's Special Operations Squadron, coordinated from Hurlburt Field in Florida, has also been detailed to support the Delta unit.[19]

UPGRADING SPECIAL OPERATIONS

A review of low-intensity operations that were conducted by Delta-Force-type units during the last decade has revealed that tactical command and control systems must be devised that have practical worldwide applications. Additionally, specialized programs must be developed to train selected individuals to function independently and as a group without access to an extensive supply system. Also, these operations must be capable of handling intelligence collected from a variety of sources and covering everything that a special operations unit ought to know. The presence of an assortment of vexing and omnipresent considerations underscores the complexity of organizing and executing a long-range hostage expedition in an age of technological sophistication, particularly, when the terrorists have advance information of a pending strike against them. The acquisition by small nations of modern weapons is among the factors to be considered by Pentagon planners as they draft a scenario for a hostage-recovery operation, especially a foreign expedition.[20]

SMALL NATIONS WITH POWERFUL WEAPONS

American military commanders must realize that small nations have powerful weapons, superb training, and advice. Consequently, American soldiers, dispatched to quell turmoil in a foreign land, must be equipped with weapons that are low cost, easy to handle, uncomplicated, and reliable. An elite antiterrorist unit, for example, the highly touted American Delta Force, might not have a clear technological advantage over a band of terrorists who are equipped with weapons obtained from NORINCO or some other source.[21]

REAGAN'S HARDLINE: "GO TO THE SOURCE"

Terrorism is a reason for the democracies to develop and implement programs of comprehensive countermeasures to deal with the seemingly demented, but always calculated, actions of individuals who are engaged in this barbarity.

President Reagan has said that the United States would "go to the source" if foreign governments are involved in the sponsorship of terrorist acts. Secretary of State George P. Shultz supported this statement. He once mentioned that the administration is ready to retaliate against international terrorism. The United States is prepared, he said, to "take steps that have repercussions." However, he advised that Washington must guard against lashing out ineffectively.

For the Reagan and the Carter administrations, terrorism and its implications became a nightmare, particularly when the terrorists issued demands in exchange for the release of American hostages. Is the safety of the hostages to be secured at any cost? Must their lives be risked to discourage other terrorists and save future victims?

Forced to confront this issue, through a heavy overlay of politics, emotion, and history, different countries have found different answers. Israelis argue that hijackings and other extortion attempts would escalate if they complied with terrorist threats to release hostages. However, Israel is also interested in the well-being of the hostages as its primary concern. But when the murderers of the Israeli athletes at Munich were freed after the plane was hijacked, it was obvious that terrorists thrive on taking advantage of the common decency of peoples and governments.

The official United States government hostage policy closely resembles Israel's policy of no deal with the terrorists. This policy was formulated in 1973, when an American diplomat was slain in the Sudan by Arab terrorists. At the time, President Richard Nixon declared that the United States would not meet any demands for the release of hostages, saying such action would encourage political kidnapping and terrorism. Thus, the United States will not yield in any way to extortion or blackmail for the release of any of its citizens anywhere in the world. Its policy, therefore, is that it is the responsibility of the host country to take every step possible to assure the well-being of American diplomats and other citizens.[22]

INTELLIGENCE SHORTFALL

Weakness in the American intelligence process, particularly collection by agents in various parts of the world, impedes the effectiveness of the American response. The gathering of information from human as opposed to technical sources will continue to trigger debates between proponents of these systems for the remainder of this century. According to Eugen F. Burgstaller, "technical collection tends to bear more often and qualitatively more dependably on foreign capabilities." Regarding human collection sources, he said these "will properly be focused to the maximum feasible extent on the area of foreign intentions."[23]

The intelligence requirements associated with rescue operations differ significantly from the contingencies associated with urban antiterrorist operations, involving as they invariably do at least two and possibly three of the military services. Lacking the capacity to retaliate surgically as the Israelis did at Entebbe, the American antiterrorists could be embarrassed.[24]

CONGRESSIONAL RECOMMENDATIONS

Noel C. Koch, commenting about the American antiterrorist capability while serving as principal deputy assistant secretary of defense for International Security Affairs, said, "We've got bands that are in a higher state of readiness than some of our special operations assets." Shocked by the helicopter breakdowns and other aspects of the aborted attempt in 1980 to rescue the Americans who were held hostage in Tehran, the Reagan administration strengthened military units that were organized to perform commando-type hostage-rescue and antiterrorist chores.

Some members of Congress recommended the creation of a single agency to handle all military special-operations tasks. Senator William S. Cohen, a Maine Republican, is an advocate of a centralized special-operation command reporting directly to the Secretary of Defense. It would be responsible for planning, training, and equipping all of the military's specialized units.

Congressional criticism of the existing special forces configuration includes:

1. *Response time*: according to a House Appropriations Committee report, half the forces were not combat-ready half the time.
2. *Recognition*: lacking the "spit and polish" of the traditional American Armed Forces, individuals attracted to the clandestine units were regarded as poor material for staff billets. Many are passed over for promotion.
3. *Innovation*: according to Representative Dan Daniel, Democrat of Virginia, the armed forces do not want elite forces. He said: "The problem is, they're trying to conduct unconventional warfare with conventional plans and commanders."
4. *Flexibility*: dispersing the special-operation units among the armed services rather than unifying them under a separate agency impedes the planning process and delays field deployment. Six months of planning preceded Eagle Claw (the code name for the Iran rescue mission).
5. *Attitudinal problems*: special operations and special operatives are viewed with suspicion by some military commanders.

COVERT ACTION

Adequately equipped, American antiterrorist units should be capable of undertaking hostage-relief operations. But will these special-operations forces be able to chill and deter terrorists? Unless the terrorists who are responsible for these barbaric acts are punished, and others who are bent on undertaking similar atrocities are intimidated by the surprise, speed, and success of Delta Forces, Americans are apt to be targets of terror. The motto of the U.S. Marine Corps First Reconnaissance Battalion is "swift, silent and deadly." This slogan contains the appropriate watchwords for an antiterrorist outfit.[25]

Key military and political advisors in the Reagan administration suggested that the United States prepare itself to undertake covert action against terrorists. In May 1986, Secretary of State Shultz, in a speech at the American Jewish Committee's 80th Annual Dinner in New York, said:

> The United States will use such measures legally, properly, and with the due involvement of designated legislative committees. What is crucial is the ability to take some initiatives quietly in situations where the more measures are known, the less effective will be their results.

INTELLIGENCE LEAKS

Shultz's remarks have created a paradox. The need to brief certain designated individuals in the legislative branch of government, prior to unleashing a covert move, is seemingly inconsistent with the requirement that a security blanket be placed over an operation until its agents are secure and its task completed.

The directors of the C.I.A. and the National Security Agency (N.S.A.) asked news organizations to cooperate in efforts to check intelligence leaks. William Casey and N.S.A. head Lieutenant General William Odom claimed that leaks were expensive in terms of both human lives and billions of taxpayer dollars.

Although he did not provide any details, Robert Gates, Casey's deputy, said that there were agents who had not been heard from after disclosures in this country.

INTELLIGENCE SHORTCOMINGS

The shortcomings of American foreign intelligence, as identified by the press, include deficiencies in three critical areas: organization and management, analysis, and collection. The organizational and managerial faults include the revised organizational design implemented during the administrations of Presidents Ford and Carter and the reduced staffing and utilization of units assigned to perform covert activities in foreign areas.

The C.I.A. has devised numerous innovations and methods related to the processing of information. Press accounts, however, also have criticized the agency's analytical methods. As mentioned in the media, C.I.A. shortcomings in the past in this area included:

1. The inability of the designated bureau of the C.I.A. to provide the Carter administration with precise, cleanly focused responses to policy questions needed to formulate a response to foreign situations.
2. The publication of scholarly reports that often violated the most important principles for the production of intelligence. The readability and the convincing quality of reports are highly important.
3. The difficulty experienced by C.I.A. in assessing the key political, economic, and military issues associated with overseas problems. During the Iranian troubles, agency analysts were criticized by the press for placing too much reliance upon United States Embassy reporting and relegating other available resources to secondary roles.
4. The failure of managers associated with the analytical function to alert policymakers to alternative forecasts that existing intelligence information would also have supported.[26]

EXILE ORGANIZATIONS

Exile organizations, rather than American antiterrorist units, are the primary threat to governments opposing the United States. In 1985, the Mujahedeen Khalq claimed credit for attacks against Iranian targets. The Mujahedeen Khalq, which is the main underground opposition to the Khomeini regime inside Iran since the Islamic revolution, mounted a grenade attack on a government building in Tehran. The explosive devices killed two men and injured three who were adjacent to the target, identified by the anti-Khomeini faction as a center of "military suppression and torture."

IRNA, the official Iranian news agency, blamed the attack on the United States. It said, "two United States mercenary agents" riding a motorcycle hurled two grenades into the building. In an interview in

New York, Ali Safavi, a spokesman for the Mujahedeen, told the Associated Press that the group planned to attack Iranian government officials and facilities in an extensive effort. The group was involved, he said, "in a life and death struggle against Khomeini."

The Mujahedeen were in the forefront of the revolution that led to the overthrow of the Shah and the Ayatollah Khomeini's return from exile in February 1979. Members of the Mujahedeen, however, were opposed to the preachings of the Islamic fundamentalists. After clashes with these puritanical followers of Khomeini, the Mujahedeen were forced underground.

In Libya, Hamid Bakoush, King Idri's last prime minister before Qaddafi overthrew the monarchy in 1969, is general secretary of a group of exiles calling themselves the Libyan Liberation Organization. In November 1984, Qaddafi's agents recruited a death squad, through the Libyan Embassy in Malta, to kill Bakoush, who has lived in Cairo since 1977. However, the Egyptians learned of the plot and foiled it.[27]

In Central America, the United States supplied the Nicaraguan Contras by parachuting cargo from planes based at secret airstrips. These resupply missions were tricky. In November 1986, a Sandinista soldier shot down over Nicaragua a cargo plane with a shoulder-fired Soviet missile. An American, named Eugene Hasenfus, who was engaged as a "kicker" for the aerial resupply flight, survived the crash. Captured by the Sandinistas, he told them that supply planes made drops to United States-backed rebels who were fighting the leftist government near the Costa Rican border in southern Nicaragua.

Besides the possibility of a shoot-down by a portable missile equipped with an infrared sensor, some crews flying air-drop missions also get too relaxed. The deceased American pilot and co-pilot of the downed cargo plane were carrying highly revealing secret documents in violation of most basic security procedures. They had even refused to wear parachutes.

Captain Rosa Rasos, a spokesperson for the Sandinista army, was appalled by the apparent lack of security measures taken by the American aircrew. Rasos said, "To us, this shows the arrogance of imperialism. They didn't believe this could happen to them."

American aviators are aware of the efficacy of portable missiles that are manufactured in the Soviet Union. U.S. Air Force planes, equipped with sophisticated sensors to spot North Vietnamese trucks at night and rapid-fire guns to attack them, were used to fly reconnaissance missions over the Ho Chi Minh Trail. Some of these planes were destroyed by the Soviet missiles.

RESUPPLY FROM THE SEA

On August 11, 1985, the Chilean government announced that its security forces had intercepted ten tons of arms and explosives that were landed by Communist guerrillas on a beach in northern Chile. The terrorists used rubber dinghies to move the cargo from Soviet trawlers to the landing site near a fishing village, 412 miles north of Santiago. Six members of the Manuel Rodriquez Patriotic Front, an armed branch of the illegal Communist Party, were arrested after a shootout on the beach. Three of those who were captured by the police were trained in guerrilla warfare in Cuba, returning to Chile clandestinely.

Some years ago, the I.R.A. was supplied with Libyan arms. On April 7, 1973, British newspapers revealed that Qaddafi's government had forwarded, since 1971, three weapons shipments of between 3 and 7 tons apiece to the Irish terrorists. The newspaper accounts were triggered by a police seizure of 5 tons of armaments aboard a Cypriot gunrunning ship off the coast of southeast Ireland on March 29, 1971. Although it appears easy to parachute supplies to irregular forces, a less dangerous and more secure method would be to use fishing trawlers for resupply missions.[28]

CONCLUSION

Vexed by terrorists who target its personnel and its facilities around the globe, the United States continues its search for a formula that will allow it to check terrorism without compromising the standards and values of a free society. Its proactive approach to the use of high technology to safeguard its diplomatic posts has been exemplary. However, the record of its antiterrorist military forces was stained, nevertheless, by the debacle in the Iranian desert. The effectiveness and efficiency of its presently reconstituted special-operations units, although highly touted in the media, are unproved. Even though its ability to coalesce with disgruntled exiles and other factions who oppose its adversaries is indistinct, its naval effort, however, to protect shipping in the Persian Gulf has been noteworthy.

NOTES

1. Philip Taubman and Joel Brinkley, "The Marine Tragedy: An Inquiry into Causes and Responsibility," *The New York Times*, December 11, 1983, pp. 49–50.
2. "Key Sections of Pentagon's Report on Attack on the Marines," *The New York Times*, December 29, 1983, pp. 11–14.

3. Michael Bar-Zohar, *Spies in the Promised Land* (Boston: Houghton Mifflin, 1972), pp. 211–224.
4. John B. Wolf, "Greek Terrorists Target Americans Near U.S. Bases," *New York City Tribune*, May 5, 1987, p. 2.
5. Frantz Fanon, *The Wretched of the Earth* (New York: Grove Press, 1968), pp. 7–147.
6. Albert Parry, *Terrorism: From Robespierre to Arafat* (New York: Vanguard Press, 1976), pp. 302–303.
7. "After Iran Millions to Make Embassies Safer," *U.S. News & World Report*, March 2, 1981, pp. 52–53.
8. "Marine Guards Are Trained for a Limited Mission," *The New York Times*, November 11, 1979, p. 12.
9. John M. Crewdson, "Actions of Marine Guard in Takeover Enabled Five to Escape Diplomats Say," *The New York Times*, January 22, 1981, p. 5.
10. Philip W. Smith, "Marines Ready Opening of Embassy Guard Training Center...1 Year Later," *The Star Ledger* (Newark, N.J.), October 21, 1980, p. 6.
11. Lev Navrozov, "U.S. Intelligence Keeps Repeating a Fool's Mistakes," *New York City Tribune*, April 8, 1987, p. 2.
12. Wolfgang Lotz, *A Handbook for Spies* (New York: Harper & Row, 1980), pp. 77–93.
13. Peter Hamilton, *Espionage, Terrorism and Subversion in an Industrial Society* (Surrey, England: Peter A. Heims, 1979), pp. 78–79.
14. "Crawling with Bugs," *Time*, April 20, 1987, pp. 14–18.
15. Ihsan A. Hijazi, "Attackers Described as Pro-Iran," *The New York Times*, April 19, 1983, p. 12.
16. "Learning to Keep a Secret," *Time*, January 9, 1981, p. 19.
17. Andres Pollack, "Military Computer-Program Success," *The New York Times*, April 11, 1983, p. D1.
18. William J. Broad, "Every Computer Whispers Its Secrets," *The New York Times*, April 5, 1983, p. C3.
19. John J. Fialka, "In Battle for Grenada, Commando Missions Didn't Go as Planned," *The Wall Street Journal*, November 15, 1983, p. 1.
20. Richard Burt, "Report Charges Major Mistaken on Iran Mission," *The New York Times*, June 6, 1980, p. 1.
21. Tim Carrington, "Pentagon Buildup Called Long on Big Weapons, Short on Aid for Special Anti-Terrorist Units," *The Wall Street Journal*, June 10, 1986, p. 60.
22. Robert D. McFadden, "Terror in 1985: Brutal Attacks Tough Response," *The New York Times*, December 30, 1985, p. 8.
23. Eugen F. Burgstaller, "Human Collection in the 1980's," in *Intelligence Requirements for the 1980's: Clandestine Collection*, ed. Roy Godson (New Brunswick, N.J.: Transaction Books, 1982), p. 73.
24. Francis X. Clines, "Weakened Intelligence-Gathering Cited by President in Beirut Blast," *The New York Times*, September 27, 1984, p. 1.
25. John B. Wolf, "U.S. Anti-Terrorist Forces Hampered by Controversy," *New York City Tribune*, February 11, 1986, p. 2.
26. John B. Wolf, "An Underground War on Terrorism?...It Depends on Keeping Secrets," *New York City Tribune*, July 2, 1986, p. 2.
27. "Tehran Points to Guerrillas in Aftermath of Blast That Killed 20," *The Star Ledger* (Newark, N.J.), September 8, 1982, p. 9; "Anti-Khomeini Terrorists Stage Attacks to Mark Revolution," ibid., February 7, 1985, p. 1.
28. John B. Wolf, "Supplying Freedom Fighters by Air Is Dangerous," *New York City Tribune*, November 4, 1986, p. 2.

11

THE ANTITERRORIST ANALYST

Maskiroka is a Russian word for a sequence of programs that are intended to disorient an unfriendly intelligence service. These confusion techniques, which consist of a full range of deception operations, have been used to beguile United States intelligence services and to facilitate the deployment of terrorists who are engaged to act as surrogates. These operatives are trained masqueraders, coached to utilize the approaches that are needed to gain the cooperation and confidence of the group they have been tasked to penetrate.

After World War II, operatives working for Soviet intelligence pretended they were Nazi sympathizers. This disguise enabled them to net with pro-Hitler factions. Once the Germans were compromised, the Soviets revealed to them that they were working for the K.G.B.

GROUND TRUTH

These Soviet-controlled machinations and the reliance that American intelligence has placed on the technical means of collecting information have reduced the accuracy and reliability of finished intelligence products (reports). While serving as deputy director of the President's Foreign Intelligence Advisory Board, Robert Butterworth contended that American intelligence operations were overdependent on satellites for information gathering. He said that "many critical elements of the Soviet military machine are impossible to understand from the outside."[1]

A spokesperson for the Reagan administration, who was commenting on the intelligence gap, only emphasized the situation confronting the troops that landed on Grenada when he said, "We had no on-ground intelligence." Agents prepositioned on the island were to collect information for the American amphibious force. Such data, when compared to the information obtained from reconnaissance aircraft and satellites, would be used to establish what individuals in the intelligence community call "ground truth."[2]

TRUTHFUL ANALYSIS

Robert M. Gates, deputy director of Central Intelligence, described another defect in American intelligence in an article published in a recent edition of *Foreign Affairs*. Describing the rivalry between collector and consumer, a conflict responsible for damaging the final intelligence report, Gates contended that ideology clouds analysis:

> Far from kowtowing to policymakers, there is sometimes a strong impulse on the part of intelligence officers to show that a policy or decision is misguided or wrong, to poke an analytical finger in the policy eye. Policymakers know this and understandably resent it.

In this article, Gates said that:

> When Secretary of State Alexander Haig asserted that the Soviets were behind international terrorism, [C.I.A.] intelligence analysts set out not to address the issue in all its aspects, but rather to prove the secretary wrong—to prove simply the Soviets do not orchestrate all international terrorism. But in so doing, they went too far themselves and failed in early drafts to describe extensive and well-documented indirect Soviet support for terrorist groups and their sponsors.[3]

Seeking to "remove the aura of suspicion and mistrust that can hobble our nation's intelligence efforts," President Reagan, on December 4, 1981, issued Executive Order 12333. This policy expanded the information-gathering authority of the C.I.A. and other intelligence organizations, loosening the restrictions imposed on United States intelligence agencies during the administration of President Carter. The order includes a section entitled "Truthful Analysis," the introduction to which reads: "It is not enough, of course, simply to collect information. Thoughtful analysis is vital to sound decision making. The goal of our intelligence analysts can be nothing short of the truth, etc."[4]

COVERT COLLECTION

Guidelines once used to curtail terrorism in the United States have international applications. When serving as director of the F.B.I., William H. Webster cited various covert information-gathering techniques as contributing to the success of his agency's antiterrorist campaign. These methods included the active use of informants, undercover agents, and court-ordered electronic surveillance.[5]

Charles Allen, who managed the C.I.A.'s antiterrorist effort, cited the American air raid on Libya in April 1986 as a deterrent to terrorists. He said that state-supported terrorism, the variety backed by the communist-bloc and its supporters, decreased after the American warplanes bombed Qaddafi's country.[6]

TARGETING OF AMERICAN EMBASSY IN TOGO

Still, surrogates directed by opponents of the United States have continued their unrelenting efforts to inflict damage on American targets. During the summer of 1986, Togo's Interior Minister Kpotiri Lacle said that his country's security forces had thwarted an international terrorist attack on the United States Embassy in Lomé, the capital of the former French colony in West Africa, which is situated on the Gulf of Guinea. Lacle said that two suitcases, which were loaded with explosives, an automatic pistol, and three grenades, were intercepted. These containers had been sent from Libya to its embassy in Cotonu, the capital of neighboring Benin, and then transhipped to Togo. According to Lacle, the grenades were to have been thrown into movie houses in the Togolese capital. Mentioning that the discovery of the explosives was a victory in the battle against international terrorism, he also said that "Togo has always condemned terrorism in all its forms wherever it takes place."

Speaking at an August 1986 meeting of the American Bar Association, Charles Allen mentioned that the sharing of intelligence with allies had increased the C.I.A.'s ability to track terrorist operations, disrupt financial and supply lines, and preempt terrorist attacks. An information exchange among allies is a key ingredient of any antiterrorist campaign. Apparently, antiterrorist data that was furnished to the Togolese security forces enabled them to confiscate the terrorist weaponry.

In addition, Lacle said that Benin had made a positive contribution in enabling nine people to be arrested in his country and that France and the United States had also aided Togo in its inquiries. Although Togo is a small West African country, the ability of the United States and its allies to check terrorism in its capital is proof that American antiterrorist intelligence was being honed as the focus for the crusade against terror.[7]

THE ANTITERRORIST ANALYST

Police intelligence activities, conducted in accordance with constitutional provisions, were among the measures used by American law-enforcement agencies to control domestic terrorism in the last two decades. Terrorist groups operating within the confines of major population centers—New York, Washington, Miami, and San Francisco—have all but evaporated. Some of these organizations, however, have managed to elude authorities for years.

The objective of the antiterrorist analyst is to produce meaningful, objective, and timely reports for dissemination to specified individuals. These assessments must relate to the terrorist group or to activities that the analyst has been assigned to monitor. Analysts should be supervised in a manner that enhances productivity as measured by their ability to generate reports replete with recommendations that are worthy of implementation.

The contemporary antiterrorist analyst must have the skill required to manipulate the keyboard of a personal computer and be able to use the software required to build a data base and a spread-sheet program to uncover the relationships within a clandestine organization. The use of computer-generated tools to target the collection process has proven effective.

Analytical personnel also must be knowledgeable in the use of overt sources: public records, libraries, and the media. Liberal arts courses, in particular, sociology, politics, economics, and history, are an analyst's "internalized data base." These academic subjects help the analyst to mentally integrate the material in a particular area of study.

Newspaper clippings and other public sources of information are also indispensible input into any analytical endeavor involving terrorist matters. Experienced intelligence analysts know that a seasoned reporter functions in a manner markedly similar to their own routine.

Intelligence analysts must read the newspapers, periodicals, and other published materials for the purpose of finding information that relates to their particular area of investigation. Significant articles must then be clipped from the papers *by the analyst* and pasted to index cards, which have been annotated in accordance with an established scheme. The use of clipping services should be avoided. Only the analyst assigned to an antiterrorist investigation is capable of insuring that all essential material is clipped and that any item of interest is not overlooked.

Using simple but proven research tools—a pair of scissors, a pot of glue, and a file of index cards—investigative reporters write articles that simultaneously alarm and inform the intelligence community. An antiterrorist analyst, therefore, should identify all the reporters who seem knowledgeable in this particular area of investigation, verify the details in their stories for accuracy and reliability, and then use these articles to reevaluate the general principles and specific details contained in their study.

Analysts who are associated with antiterrorist operations are often engaged in the seemingly endless culling of file cards for the purpose of extracting bits of information relative to the targets, philosophy, history, organizational structure, membership, foreign connections, and potential of a particular terrorist group.

Target analysis is an integral part of this analytical process. Its purpose is to develop the intelligence required to isolate targets from terrorist attack by: (1) defining the target, (2) identifying the conditions that cause it to be vulnerable, (3) assessing the relationship between the target and the threatening conditions affecting it, and (4) estimating the susceptibility of the target to external influences.

Terrorist operations are primarily multimedia affairs intended to influence the political behavior of a target through the skillful application of armed propaganda: bombings, kidnappings, and assassinations. Formulas that are used to evaluate the impact of mass media, therefore, also can be used to assess the significance of a terrorist action. Although American military personnel and others were killed in the Beirut explosions, the entire civilized world was the primary target.

Information relative to terrorists, when analyzed in accordance with these techniques, should be assembled in a manner that facilitates its rapid exploitation. Computerized analytical frameworks, constructed for this purpose, can serve as useful guides for intelligence analysts seeking to obtain the essential elements of information needed to refine their assessments.

The structure of these analytical frameworks about a terrorist group should contain at least ten primary categories: (1) type and nature of the operation, (2) relationship to a revolutionary process as exhibited by speeches, demonstrations, and armed robberies, (3) organization, (4) ideology, (5) propaganda classifications, (6) tactics, (7) weapons, (8) targets, (9) audience, and (10) media coverage.

Lacking comprehensive intelligence, antiterrorist operatives are apt to flounder about aimlessly, whereas good information could position them where their operations might have an impact. Antiterrorist analysis is destined for oblivion, however, unless those who manage this function recognize the indispensible role of analysts in the processing of collected information.[8]

Not too long ago, the C.I.A. placed an advertisement for personnel in a major newspaper, which read: "We're looking for men and women with special talent. The primary task of the Central Intelligence Agency is to gather information abroad to help protect and guide the international interests of the United States." Without the analytical expertise of John Le Carré's character George Smiley, however, the collected information is meaningless. Yet the C.I.A. recognized perhaps that it would be most difficult to attract applicants for a Smiley-type position whereas it knew that a host of people were anxious to be interviewed for a James-Bond-type career.[9]

Antiterrorist Intelligence and Counterintelligence

A special kind of intelligence system is needed as the nucleus of an antiterrorist campaign, that is, an operation intended to clinically apprehend individuals who violate a country's criminal code by perpetrating acts of a terrorist nature. This system should: (1) be designed to be proactive; (2) be constructed of analytical modules geared to monitor specific terrorist groups; (3) be staffed by disciplined, motivated, and self-directed analysts selected by an assessment process tailored to uncover these values and detect analytical ability; (4) be assigned the mission of producing reports of meaningful value replete with timely, accurate, and cogent information and recommendations; (5) be compatible with electronic filing, word processing, and other automated methods but not dependent on technology to perform its tasks; and (6) be intended to satisfy the tactical and strategic information requirements of operational field units serving as static or mobile response elements.

Although these analytical modules are linked to traditional sources of field information, the collectors assigned to them provide the analyst directing their activities with data gleaned from a variety of field sources; for example, document (depository) searches, informant development, surveillance (physical and electronic), and undercover operations.

Additionally, personnel selected to serve as analysts in the modules must be trained to use tools, techniques, and measurements that are essential to the conduct of antiterrorist intelligence operations. These include target analysis, psychological assessments, propaganda analysis, analytical frameworks, link diagrams, and computer-assisted analysis.

Utilizing the module system of organization, antiterrorist intelligence personnel will be able to: (1) develop a descriptive analysis of terrorist groups operating against a particular target; (2) assess the performance of terrorist and antiterrorist operations; (3) provide integral operational response units with the direction and data needed to conduct antiterrorist operations; (4) identify specific individuals engaged in terrorist and subversive activities; (5) provide integral forensic and special operational units with specific data; (6) provide antiterrorist force commanders with the information needed to develop an appropriate response to reduce the political, sociological, and psychological vulnerability of a particular audience targeted by terrorists; and (7) develop the information needed by a government to counter terrorist propaganda as expressed in actions and words. Thus, antiterrorist intelligence is the process whereby raw information about the who, what, when, why, how, and where of terrorism is transformed into the analytical reports that are needed to plan and execute strikes against terrorists who threaten a country's interests.

Information security is a prerequisite for the successful completion of an antiterrorist operation. All governments should take steps to reduce the leakage of highly sensitive information triggered by legislation that exposes its decision-making process to public scrutiny prior to the conduct of an operation.

The United States must move to reduce the leakage of highly sensitive information caused in part by the continued probing of the American intelligence services. These investigative activities hamper the conduct of overseas liaison activities with human sources of intelligence that are needed to provide ground truth.[10] Ground truth provides information on the motives, intentions, thoughts, and plans of terrorists. Without access to these human sources of intelligence, the analytical assessments needed to focus an antiterrorist operation are incomplete and the comprehensive accomplishment of the task cannot be expected.

The Collection Process

A national intelligence service must engage actively in information-gathering functions to funnel essential elements of information to analysts. Responsible for transforming these raw data into a composite and finished intelligence product, analysts are dependent on the collection process to supply them with the pertinent, accurate, and reliable information that they need to complete a report on a particular subject. Geared to handle specific requests for information, collectors must be capable of identifying any and all specific data elements pertaining to

matters which come to their attention. They should be cautioned, however, to refrain from screening their perceptions and to use their own
background and experience to judge the worth of data: this is the task of
the analyst.

Many members of the United States Congress realize that intelligence gathering is a task vital to the attainment of the national mission.
This activity contains segments designed to detect, assess, deter, and
counter aggression and subversion from domestic and foreign sources.
Some lawmakers are not completely aware of the limitations that legislation, which is intended to restrain the clandestine service's ability to
utilize covert methods to gather information, has placed on the activities
of agents who are officially assigned to field collection activities.[11]

Terrorism involves acts of extraordinary violence of a terroristic or
politically inspired character, and these activities cannot be controlled or
contained by ordinary means.

PRESS CRITICISM OF AMERICAN INTELLIGENCE OPERATIONS

Congressional committees have made recommendations for improving the management of the various American intelligence agencies.
These suggestions are usually contained in a classified annex to a report.
Often the media, utilizing information gleaned from open sources and
citing the paucity of data available to American intelligence agencies
during foreign political transitions, as, for example, in Iran and
Nicaragua, imply that the American clandestine organizations are not
fulfilling their objectives. The shortcomings of American foreign intelligence identified in the press include deficiencies in three critical areas:
organization and management, analysis, and collection.

Liabilities in the area of collection are thought to stem primarily from
the leakage of highly sensitive information caused by the continued
probing of the American intelligence services by the media. These investigative activities hamper the conduct of overseas liaison activities with
sources vital to the flow of information. Additionally, the C.I.A. continues to be accused of relying inordinately on technical methods to
gather information at the expense of human intelligence. Only a spy can
gain access to another person's motives, intentions, and plans.[12]

EARTH–SATELLITE COLLECTION

The C.I.A. regards earth–satellite photography as a central element
in its ongoing program of modern intelligence research and analysis. Its

vehicles travelling in space are able to transmit back to earth the same level of photographic images that the U-2 reconnaissance aircraft snapped in the late 1950s.

Lockheed's "Big Bird," a 12-ton vehicle set to orbit at an elevation about 250 miles above the earth, is equipped with black-and-white, color, and infrared television and still cameras. Capable of making a low-level orbital pass at an altitude of 90 miles, Big Bird is known to have taken pictures of the wing markings of planes situated on an airfield near a key military launch station at Plesetsk in the U.S.S.R.

Another aircraft manufactured by Lockheed and designated as the SR-71 (strategic reconnaissance) is dubbed "Blackbird." This plane, which supplements the U-2, has cameras that can photograph most of the United States in three passes and carries three-dimensional filming equipment that is so precise that a mailbox on a country road can be located with ease.[13]

THE C.I.A.'S PERFORMANCE

The C.I.A. has devised numerous innovations and methods that are related to the processing of information. Press accounts of American intelligence failures, however, are critical of the agency's analytical methods and products. Listed among these shortcomings are:

1. The inability of the C.I.A. to provide a designated person with precise and cleanly focused answers to the policy questions needed to formulate a response to a foreign situation.
2. The publication of scholarly reports that often violate the most important principles for the production of intelligence, readability, and the convincing quality of the reported information.
3. The difficulty experienced by the C.I.A. in assessing the key political, economic, and military issues associated with overseas problems. During the Iranian troubles, agency analysts were criticized by the press for placing too much reliance upon United States Embassy reporting and relegating other available resources to secondary roles.
4. The pressure on analysts to produce "spot news reports."
5. The reluctance of the agency's analysts to challenge preconceptions.
6. The tendency to adjust intelligence estimates for the purpose of dovetailing them with official foreign policy directions.

Additionally, the Freedom of Information Act has created obstacles that impede the collection of valuable information. It is believed that the C.I.A. loses significant information because its foreign sources fear that their identities will be exposed under the measures stipulated by this act.[14]

In recent years, the United States quietly revised its procedures for controlling terrorists as legislators began to realize that the country was not prepared to cope with terrorist incidents. Within its working group on terrorism—an organization containing representatives from 26 agencies—the lines of authority were straightened and a procedure was implemented that facilitated the creation at short notice of groups of experts to deal with a terrorist incident in terms of crisis management.

Regardless of these improvements, the American antiterrorist effort is still weak in these areas:

1. Its antiterrorist military forces do not exhibit the level of training and preparation that is associated with the British, West German, or Israeli units.
2. Its persistent policy is to deal with terrorist incidents on an ad hoc basis, failing to recognize the interrelationships of various events.
3. It lacks a surgical military response to counter a terrorist group.
4. It has not developed a workable set of procedures to enhance understanding and cooperation between military and civilian officials who are responsible for dealing with terrorists.

Any country that is determined to control terrorism must develop and maintain a top-level intelligence network to monitor extremist groups that may be planning bombings, extortions, or kidnappings, which rely on the element of surprise. It is absolutely critical to any response that the surprise aspect be reduced by timely, comprehensive, intelligence assessments that are provided by analysts who are trained to rapidly acquire, analyze, and produce meaningful reports for their managers.

The formation of modules, each consisting of a team of field researchers, investigators, information collectors, and a desk analyst, who work together while concentrating on a specific problem, such as state-directed terrorism or domestic violence in Sri Lanka, is an appropriate design for the antiterrorist component of an intelligence agency.

Strategically, an antiterrorist response would provide:

1. planning units with information pertaining to the known or probable political, sociological, or psychological vulnerabilities of the target audience selected by the terrorist
2. propaganda specialists with information for messages intended to counter the propaganda output of a terrorist organization

3. the coordinators and commanders of an antiterrorist response unit with the data they need to measure the efficiency and effectiveness of past, present, and future operations

Additionally, a government needs antiterrorist intelligence about matters that have an impact on its foreign interests and installations, particularly, information about the people or organizations it hires to perform routine chores within an embassy or other installation. These assessments should provide information regarding:

1. the attitudes of the work force toward domestic and international issues which involve their employer
2. the attitudes of the work force toward their national government, their national leaders, and any people, corporation, or nation closely allied with them
3. detailed biographical information concerning the leaders (informal and formal) of the work forces (unions)
4. the informal communication network at both the clique and systems level

Everett and Rekhu Rogers, authors of *Communication in Organizations*, define clique as "a subsystem whose elements interact with each other relatively more frequently than with other members of the communication system." According to these communication specialists, "most cliques consist of twenty-five members, with some much larger than this."[15]

TARGET ANALYSIS

Target analysis involves the systematic examination and assessment of pertinent data concerning possible target groups, including such aspects as the psychological and ideological predispositions of individuals in the target area. Thus, terrorists regard the multinational corporation, its facilities, employees, and products, as a prime target of their "armed propaganda." They consider this assessment appropriate when they can describe a company's operations as "exploitative of labor and resources in Third World countries" or as allied with governments which allegedly advocate policies resembling South Africa's policy of apartheid, or with any country's reluctance to advance political rights for all of its citizens.

COYUNTURA ASSESSMENT

Terrorists know that their operations have political motives and goals and design them to attract the support of large segments of a targeted population. Before enlisting supporters directly, terrorists try to convince them that their organization is an expression of a "popular struggle." Consequently, terrorists regard armed actions, kidnappings, bombings, and assassinations, as the principal way of manufacturing armed propaganda. Terrorists' attacks are thus undertaken against specific targets whose destruction or abduction becomes propaganda material for the mass communications network.

Obviously, a primary input into the target-selection process used by a terrorist group is a strategic assessment of the political, economic, military, and organizational conditions of both the terrorist movement and the society in which it is enveloped. Labeled by Uruguay's Tupamaros as an assessment of the *coyuntura*, this targeting process recognizes that the choice of every terrorist strategy and tactic is the result of a careful, rational analysis of the present and potential strength of a terrorist organization, as well as of the general conditions and political climate of the society in which it was spawned.[16]

GOALS AND OBJECTIVES

The purpose of an antiterrorist intelligence service should be the identification, reduction, and prevention of the terrorist threat to a particular country or corporation. Its products should be a descriptive analysis of the terrorists and their capabilities. An assessment of the antiterrorist capability and a focus of a nation in which a diplomatic post or a corporate facility is to be sited is another valuable output. Additionally, antiterrorist intelligence should be capable of providing forensic and special-operations units with the data they need to handle any event of a terroristic nature.

Communist disinformation will probably continue to cast most American antiterrorist operations as shams. The Soviets and their clients have so twisted the media that they distribute a line of propaganda that convinces enough people into believing that the "popular masses," with a group of terrorists as their vanguard, are pitted against an oppressive government aided and abetted by the United States. Consequently, a besieged country all too often is confronted with a paradox: the task of maintaining law and order while its military and police forces are vilified in the press. Meanwhile, the terrorists who are engaged in criminal acts against that society are described as patriots.

Often a government may become unwittingly snared by the trap set for it by its opponent when it does not handle terrorists as common criminals. The leaders of terrorist movements know that the propaganda objectives of their campaigns are often enhanced when members of their bands are not afforded due process in accordance with established laws. They also know how to get the media to print and broadcast a series of events erroneously describing terrorists as a political adversary of a government with no claim to legitimacy as evidenced by its misapplication of military force or posture. Even their true identity—a criminal element operating outside the laws promulgated by an elected legislature to maintain order—is masked because it does not lend itself to sensationalism.

Military assistance rendered by the United States to governments that are confronted by state-sponsored terrorism and to those that are considered susceptible to this menace, in particular, countries hosting an American facility which is prone to takeover by a mob unleashed to embarrass the United States, should include elements tailored to emphasize the benefits derived from utilizing established indigenous legal methods to control terrorism.

NOTES

1. Arnold Beichman, "Dark Future for Intelligence?" *The Washington Times*, January 11, 1988, p. 8.
2. "Seized Papers Detail Secret Soviet Arms Deals," *The Star Ledger* (Newark, N.J.), November 1, 1983, p. 9.
3. Robert M. Gates, "The C.I.A. and Foreign Policy," *Foreign Affairs* (Winter, 1987–1988), pp. 215–230.
4. Carolyn Goldinger (ed.), *Historic Documents of 1981* (Washington, D.C.: Congressional Quarterly, 1982), p. 864.
5. Elaine Sciolino, "FBI Hails Gains on Terror," *The New York Times*, August 12, 1986, p. 20.
6. Ibid.
7. "Togolese Thwart Plan to Attack U.S. Embassy," *The New York Times*, August 12, 1986, p. 9.
8. John B. Wolf, "Intelligence Stupidity," *Terrorism, Violence, Insurgency Journal* (Vol. 1, No. 1), pp. 9–12.
9. David Shribman, "Cloak-and-Dagger Business Booming," *The New York Times*, February 18, 1972, p. 12.
10. Lois Kaufman and John B. Wolf, "An Inspection System to Monitor White House Subordinates' Compliance with Presidential Directives," *Presidential Studies Quarterly* (Winter, 1981), pp. 92–98.
11. Philip Taubman, "Gulf War Said to Reveal U.S. Intelligence Lapses," *The New York Times*, September 27, 1980, p. 5.
12. "Casey Asks Panel: Who Said the C.I.A. Lies?", *The New York Times*, May 27, 1983, p. 7.
13. Malcolm W. Browne, "U.S. Increases Reliance on Intelligence Satellites," *The New York Times*, October 18, 1979, p. 2.

14. Philip Taubman, "Major Questions Raised on C.I.A.'s Performance," *The New York Times*, November 3, 1983, p. 21.
15. Everett M. Rogers and Rekhu Agarwala Rogers, *Communication in Organizations* (London: Collier Macmillan, 1976), pp. 127–128.
16. Arturo C. Porzecanski, *Uruguay's Tupamaros: The Urban Guerrilla* (New York: Frederick A. Praeger, 1973), p. 11.

SELECTED BIBLIOGRAPHY

Aron, Raymond. *Clausewitz: Philosopher of War*. Englewood Cliffs, N.J.: Prentice-Hall, 1985.

Baldy, Tom F. *Battle for Ulster: A Study of Internal Security*. Washington, D.C.: National Defense University Press, 1987.

Beckwith, Charles A., and Knox, Donald. *Delta Force*. New York: Harcourt, Brace, Jovanovich, 1983.

Begin, Menachem. *The Revolt*. New York: Nash Publishing, 1977.

Bok, Sissela. *Lying: Moral Choice in Public and Private Life*. New York: Pantheon Books, 1978.

Bok, Sissela. *Secrets: On the Ethics of Concealment and Revelation*. New York: Pantheon Books, 1982.

Bowyer, J. Barton. *Cheating: Deception in War and Magic, Games and Sports, Sex and Religion, Business and Con Games, Politics and Espionage, Art and Science*. New York: St. Martin's Press, 1980.

Clavell, James (ed.). *The Art of War: Sun Tzu*. New York: Delacorte Press, 1983.

Collins, John M. *Green Berets, Seals and Spetsnaz*. Washington, D.C.: Pergamon Brassey's International Defense Publishers, 1987.

Dean, David J. (ed.). *Low-Intensity Conflict and Modern Technology*. Maxwell Air Force Base, Ala.: Air University Press, 1986.

Dulles, Allen. *The Craft of Intelligence*. New York: Harper & Row, 1963.

Godson, Roy (ed.). *Intelligence Requirements for the 1980's: Analysis and Estimates*. New Brunswick, N.J.: Transaction Books, 1980.

Godson, Roy (ed.). *Intelligence Requirements for the 1980's: Clandestine Collection*. New Brunswick, N.J.: Transaction Books, 1981.

Goldinger, Carolyn (ed.). *Historic Documents of 1981*. Washington, D.C.: Congressional Quarterly, 1982.

Griffith, Samuel B. (trans.). *Mao Tse-tung: On Guerrilla Warfare*. New York: Frederick A. Praeger 1965.

Hodges, Donald C. *The Legacy of Che Guevara: A Documentary Study*. London: Thames & Hudson, 1977.

Higgins, Trumbull. *The Perfect Failure: Kennedy, Eisenhower and the C.I.A. at the Bay of Pigs*. New York: W.W. Norton & Company, 1987.

Jonas, George. *Vengeance*. New York: Simon & Schuster, 1984.

Kelley, P.X. *Pentagon Press Conference (April 18, 1987)*. Washington, D.C.: Headquarters, United States Marine Corps, 1987.

Khomeini, Ayatollah Ruhollah. *Islamic Government*. New York: Manor Books, 1979.

Laqueur, Walter. *A World of Secrets: The Uses and Limits of Intelligence*. New York: Basic Books, 1985.

Lasswell, Harold D. *The Analysis of Political Behaviour: An Empirical Approach*. Hamden, Conn.: Archon Books, 1966.

Le Carré, John. *Smiley's People*. New York: Alfred A. Knopf, 1980.

McGraw, Dickinson, and Watson, George. *Political and Social Inquiry*. New York: John Wiley & Sons, 1976.

Meyer, Cord. *Facing Reality: From World Federalism to the CIA*. New York: Harper & Row, 1980.

Mountbatten, Vice-Admiral Lord Louis. *Combined Operations: The Official Story of the Commandos*. New York: Macmillan Company, 1943.

Olivier, Laurence. *On Acting*. New York: Simon & Schuster, 1986.

Osgood, Robert E. *Limited War Revisited*. Boulder, Colo.: Westview Press, 1979.

Parry, Albert. *Terrorism: From Robespierre to Arafat*. New York: Vanguard Press, 1976

Phillips, Robert L. *War and Justice*. Norman: University of Oklahoma Press, 1984

Platt, Washington. *Strategic Intelligence Production*. New York: Frederick A. Praeger, 1957.

Powers, Thomas. *The Man Who Kept the Secrets: Richard Helms and the CIA*. New York: Alfred A. Knopf, 1979.

Public Report of the Vice President's Task Force on Combatting Terrorism. Washington, D.C.: U.S. Government Printing Office, 1986.

Rivers, Gayle. *The Specialist: Revelations of a Counterterrorist*. New York: Stein & Day, 1985.

Sarkesian, Sam C., and Scully, William L. *U.S. Policy and Low Intensity Conflict*. New York: National Strategy Information Center, 1981.

Schmed, Alex P., and deGraaf, Janny. *Violence as Communication: Insurgent Terrorism and the Western News Media*. Beverly Hills, Calif.: Sage Publications, 1982.

Shultz, George. *Current Policy No. 642, The Ethics of Power*. Washington, D.C.: United States Department of State, Bureau of Public Affairs, 1984.

Thompson, Leroy. *U.S. Special Forces; 1941–1987*. Poole, England: Blandford Press, 1987.

Tower, John, Muskie, Edmund, and Snowcroft, Brent. *The Tower Commission Report: The Full Text of the President's Special Review Board*. New York: Bantam Books, 1987.

Treverton, Gregory F. *Covert Action: The Limits of Intervention in the Postwar World*. New York: Basic Books, 1987.

Turner, Stansfield. *Secrecy and Democracy: The C.I.A. in Transition*. New York: Harper & Row, 1980.

United States Senate and House of Representatives. *Public Law 39–399 (H.R. 4151) Omnibus Diplomatic Security and Antiterrorism Act of 1986*. Washington, D.C.: U.S. Government Printing Office, 1986.

Winks, Robin W. *Cloak and Gown: Scholars in the Secret War, 1939–1961*. New York: William Morrow, 1987.

Woodward, Bob. *Veil: The Secret Wars of the C.I.A., 1981–1987*. New York: Simon & Schuster, 1987.

INDEX

Reagan, President Ronald, 15, 18, 56–58
  on the Communist insurgency in the
    Philippines, 145–146
  "go to the source," 183
Rebel Armed Forces (F.A.R.) (Guatemala),
  166
Red Brigades, 24, 78, 158
Remeliin, President Hauro, 148
  assassination, 148
Renette, Luc, 150
Revolutionary Organization of November
  17, 12
Rivera Damas, Archbishop Arturo, 134
Roman Catholic Church, 9
  clerics, 134–136, 137–140
  Congregation for the Doctrine of the
    Faith, 134
  Philippines, 137–140
  Sandinistas, 135
Romania, 24
Rome (Italy), 8, 22
Royal Air Force (R.A.F.), 60–61, 102
Royal Canadian Mounted Police
  (R.C.M.P.), 98
Royal Marines, 113
  capabilities, 113
  equipment, 114
  special boat squadron, 113
Royal Ulster Constabulary, 115
  deployment, 128
  internal affairs units, 115
  training, 115
  See also Police, British

Sadat, Anwar-al, 4–5
Safavi, Ali, 188
Saint Lawrence Island (Alaska), 84
Salvadorean guerrillas, 164
Salvadorean rebels, 103
Sandinistas, 35, 45, 51, 100, 165
  strategy, 168
  surface-to-air missiles, 188
  urban terrorist groups, 164
Sands, Bobby, 122
San Francisco (California), 194
Santeria (saint worship), 93, 95
Saravia, Luis, 163
Satellites, 13, 59–61
  communication security, 181
  technical collection, 191–192, 199

Sebana Seca (Puerto Rico), 36
  ambush, 166
Secret agents, 13
Segunda, Reverend Juan Luis, 135
Sendero Luminoso (Shining Path)
  annihilation squads, 163
  arrests in Lima, 163
  Cuba and the narcotics trade, 162
  leaders, 162
  tactics, 163
Service "A" of the K.G.B., 6
Shah. *See* Pahlavi, Shah Mohammad Rezi
Shultz, George P., 18, 24
  antiterrorism, 183–184, 186
Signals Intelligence (SIGINT), 81
Sikhs, 10, 49–50
Silencer, 28
Silkin, Sam, 124
Sin, Jaime Cardinal, 137–139
  antiterrorism, 140
  See also Roman Catholic Church, clerics
Sinhalese, 151–152
Sison, Jose, 141
Smiley, George, 16
Smith, William French, 64–65
"Smoking gun," 22
Solidarity labor union, 9
Somoza, Anastasio, 51
Sope, Secretary General Barah, 146
Sotheby's Auction House, 48
South Africa, 136, 201
Southern Yemen, 24
Soviet Committee for State Security
  (K.G.B.), 3, 5–8, 10–11, 17, 24, 27, 30,
    33–35, 50
  Central America, 164
  Cuba, 159
  "honey trap," 178
  maskiroka (confusion techniques), 191
  Pacific region, 147, 151
Spain, 135, 137
"Sparrow Teams," 140–141
  killings of Americans, 146
Special Air Services Regiment, 72, 116
  Irish Republican Army (I.R.A.), 118
  plainclothesmen, 129
  See also Sri Lanka; United Kingdom (Brit-
    ish) Army
Special forces. *See* United States Army,
  special forces

Socialist Worker's Party, 62
Spetsnaz (Soviet special designation unit), 17, 83–86
Sri Lanka (Ceylon)
  antiterrorism, 153–154
  attempted coup, 152
  destabilization, 152
  hostage negotiations, 151
  Marxism, 152
  minorities, 150
  police, 151, 154
  political parties, 152
Stakeout squads, 116
Stalker, John, 116
State of Siege (film), 3–4
Stevenson, William, 75
"Stinger" missile, 99, 102–103
Strategic reconnaissance, 199
Sudoplatov, General Paul Anatolevich, 84
Surface-to-air missiles (SAM), 71, 188
  American "Stinger," 99, 102–103
Suriname, 30–31
Surrogate warfare, 17, 22
Svirdlev, Stefan Stefphan, 7
Swan Island, 100
Syria, 24, 27, 33
  in Beirut (Lebanon), 173

Tallahassee (Florida)
  Federal Detention Center, 168
Talmud, 18
Tamils, 151–152
Tattoos, 94
Tehran, 11, 61–62, 73, 76, 78
Thatcher, Prime Minister Margaret, 123
Three Days of the Condor (film), 3
Togo, 193–194
Toronto (Canada), 98
Torres, Reverend Camillo, 135
Trincomollee, Sri Lanka, 151
Trotsky, Leon, 83
Trujillo, Rafael, 100
Tuite, George, 128
Tupamoros, 4, 42
Turkey, 7, 23, 25, 27
Turks, 6
Turner, Stansfield, 76

Uganda, 52, 75
Ulster. *See* Northern Ireland

Ulster Defense Association, 115
Ulster Volunteer Force, 114
undercover operations, 28, 97
Union for the Total Independence of Angola (U.N.I.T.A.), 100
Union of Soviet Socialist Republics (U.S.S.R.), 10, 11–24, 26–27, 32, 34, 49–50, 89
  cooperation with Cuba, 157
  economic strategy in the Americas, 158
  G.R.U. intelligence directorate, 85–86
United Kingdom, 34, 60, 72
United Kingdom (British) Army
  Green Jackets regiment, 107
  Household Cavalry, 123
  information security, 112
  plainclothesmen, 129. *See also* Special Air Services regiment
  tactics, 112
  tours of duty, 129
  troop dispositions, 112
United Nations, 32, 35
United States, 5, 7, 12–13, 17, 24, 32, 51. *See also* Reagan Administration; Reagan, President Ronald
United States Air Force, 73, 77
  bases, 32, 61
  First Air Commando Force, 100
  Puerto Rico Air National Guard, 189
  reconnaissance aircraft, 60
  Special Operations Squadron, 182
United States Army
  bases, 74, 80, 101, 182
  Persian Gulf, 80
  Puerto Rican National Guard, 168
  Rangers, 78
  rapid deployment force, 101. *See also* Delta Unit
  special forces, 17, 57, 61, 78
United States Coast Guard, 90
United States Department of Defense, 19, 24, 55–57, 73
  Belau (Palau) base considerations, 148
  Beirut bombings, 173
  electronic emanations, 182
  Joint Chiefs of Staff, 57, 79–80
United States Department of State, 4, 23–24, 28, 95
  communication security, 181